THEATRE DIRECTIONS

Jonothan Neelands
&
Warwick Dobson

THEATRE DIRECTIONS

Jonothan Neelands

&

Warwick Dobson

Hodder & Stoughton

A MEMBER OF THE HODDER HEADLINE GROUP

Orders: please contact Bookpoint Ltd, 78 Milton Park, Abingdon, Oxon OX14 4TD. Telephone: (44) 01235 827720; Fax: (44) 01235 400454. Lines are open from 9.00–6.00, Monday to Saturday, with a 24 hour message answering service. Email address: orders@bookpoint.co.uk

British Library Cataloguing in Publication Data
A catalogue record for this title is available from The British Library

ISBN 0 340 75861 9

First published 2000
Impression number   10 9 8 7 6 5 4 3 2
Year   2005 2004 2003 2002 2001 2000

Typeset by Multiplex Techniques Ltd, Brook Industrial Park, Mill Brook Road, St. Mary Cray, Kent BR5 3SR.

Printed in Great Britain by Hodder & Stoughton Educational, a division of Hodder Headline Plc, 338 Euston Road, London NW1 3BH by Redwood Books, Trowbridge, Wiltshire.

Dedicated to

**The Dukes Theatre in Education Company
Lancaster, 1975–1995**

Contents

INTRODUCTION

Theatre Directions was originally conceived as a companion volume to our *Drama and Theatre Studies at AS/A Level*. We wanted to gather together a collection of voices writing on theatre, with the aim of opening up some of the important theoretical and practical debates that have arisen during the course of the late nineteenth and twentieth centuries. In the main, the voices chosen represent significant thinkers and practitioners who have, in some important way, either determined the direction in which theatre practice has developed, or shaped the way we have come to think about drama and theatre during the past hundred years.

On reflection, however, our feeling was that the present collection would perhaps be of wider interest. Students who follow AS and A level courses are, of course, embarking on their first serious attempt to make sense of the complex and sometimes contradictory movements and tendencies that have characterised the history of western theatre during the modern period. We therefore intend the book to provide these students with an introduction to the writing of the major theorists and practitioners who figure prominently in our course book, *Drama and Theatre Studies at AS/A Level*. Beyond these AS and A level courses, there are undergraduates on a variety of university courses in Drama, Theatre, Theatre Studies, Theatre Arts, Performing Arts, Performance, Drama in Education, Media Studies and Communications who, we hope, will find the extracts collected here of some interest in their various areas of study. And finally, of course, there are those enthusiastic theatre-goers who may wish to broaden their understandings of the practice and thinking of the past which has contributed to the making of the work they regularly encounter in their visits to the theatre. This is the wider readership that we hope will find the present volume to be of some value.

Our aim throughout has been to track the major currents in twentieth century western theatre; but this has necessitated the inclusion of some important figures who may, at first sight, seem somewhat out of place in a book which has a primary focus on the relatively recent past (Aristotle and Shakespeare, for instance). Aristotle is included here because all of these major contemporary currents can, in some way, be traced back to his *De Poetica*. And, in the case of Shakespeare, in our rush to venerate him as the greatest playwright who ever lived, we often forget that he was, himself, also an actor of some considerable note. His advice to the players in *Hamlet* inaugurates a debate on acting method which continues up until the present day, most recently in a volume of essays by the American playwright, David Mamet.

We have selected extracts by writers who have either advanced our current understandings of theatre or who have been innovators in theatre practice. Naturally, it is impossible to exclude the massive contributions of Stanislavski and Brecht, so the work of these two giants figures prominently in this book. We have also included some less well-known extracts by academics like Arnold Hauser as well as some fascinating analysis by less well-known devisers of theatre and theatre in education practitioners.

The book divides into five sections. In the first, we acknowledge the huge proliferation of drama product that has taken place as a result of the development of new technologies, and the ways in which the changing cultural climate and audience expectation has influenced and altered the dramatic means of expression. The second part begins with Aristotle, and seeks to indicate how the major twentieth century theatrical currents are all traceable to the drama of fifth century Athens. In section three we have included extracts that capture something of the flavour of the ongoing debate about contemporary approaches to acting. Section four examines the impact of the director on twentieth century practice and finally section five offers a number of descriptions of the devising process.

The linking text provides a thread which holds the different contributions together so that it is possible to read the book from beginning to end and gain some sense of the major developments in modern theatre practice; alternatively, of course, it is a volume for dipping in and out of. Whichever approach is chosen, we are sure that the extracts will provide plenty of stimulus for critical thinking and lively debate.

Part One: The Changing Face of Drama

In everyday conversation, the words theatre and drama are almost inter-changeable; many people assume that they refer to essentially the same activity – the live staging of a play, enacted by one or more performers in a building set aside for that specific purpose. But, historically, those who study theatre have maintained a distinction between the words. **The term 'drama' is usually reserved for the body of written works we call dramatic literature** *(to distinguish it from other branches of literature, like poetry and fiction).* **The word 'theatre'**, *apart from being the name of the building in which the enactment takes place,* **usually refers to the actual performance of a piece of dramatic literature.**

Until recently, this was a useful distinction. But, during the twentieth century, developments in technology (in particular, cinema, radio, television and video) mean that the term drama is now used much more extensively, and refers to much more than the texts which are performed in the theatre building.

1: The Field of Drama

Drama, there can be no doubt about it, has become immensely important in our time. More human beings than ever before see more drama than ever before and are more directly influenced, conditioned, programmed by drama than ever before. Drama has become one of the principal vehicles of information, one of the prevailing methods of 'thinking' about life and its situations.

Our time has witnessed a veritable explosion of drama through the photographic and electronic mass media. Where, previously, stage drama, live theatre, was the only method for the communication of dramatic performance, today dramatic performance can reach its audiences in a multitude of ways: through the cinema, television, videotape, radio, cassette-recordings. Consequently, not only has the *audience* for drama increased by truly astronomical progression as compared to previous ages, the actual *quantity* of dramatic performances produced has gone up in equal proportion.

Hence the immensely increased importance of drama in the life and culture of our time: never before has drama been so pervasive in the lives of the large masses of people...

What is drama and where are the boundaries of its field?...

The boundaries of the term will always be fluid, the different related fields will always tend to overlap. Nevertheless the concept has a centre that is common to all its multifarious overlapping manifestations. How can we delimit it? We use the terms 'drama' and 'dramatic' in a multitude of contexts: a football match, a race, a riot, an assassination are 'dramatic' because they contain the elements of heightened intensity of incident and emotion that are one of the essential ingredients of drama. What distinguishes them from drama in its proper sense is that they are 'real' rather than fictional. So the element of the fictional is an essential element of drama? Only up to a point, for there is also 'documentary drama', based on 'real' events. The essential element here is that the documentary drama 're-enacts' past events, that is: puts them before an audience as though they were happening before them at that very moment.

This brings out one of the essential aspects of drama: the aspect of 'acting'. Drama simulates, enacts or re-enacts events that have, or may be imagined to have, happened in the 'real' or in an imagined world. What these different types of representation have in common is that they are all 'mimetic action'.

A dramatic text is a blueprint for such mimetic action, it is not yet itself, in the full sense, drama. A dramatic text, unperformed, is literature. It can be read as a story. This is the area where the fields of narrative fiction, epic poetry, and drama overlap. The element which distinguishes drama from these types of fiction is, precisely, that of 'performance', *enactment*. Dickens giving readings from his novels, in some sense acted them out, and thus transformed them into drama. Clearly his vocal characterisation of his fruity and highly individualised characters amounted to 'acting'. And as to the purely narrative, descriptive, dialogue-free portions of the text: Dickens, in reading these, in a highly emotional and subtly differentiated voice that painted the mood and the scenery, was still an actor: he acted the role of the character 'Charles Dickens', the compulsive story-teller... Such narrations, acted out in character, have always been an important ingredient of drama. The messengers of Greek tragedy, after all, were also merely *narrating* events, describing them as a novelist would, though 'in character'...

Dramatic reading of narrative texts has revived in our time on radio and in cassette recordings. And probably under the influence of such dramatic readings on radio the acted performance of narrative material on the stage has become popular and widespread: the American forms of 'story-theatre' fall under this heading, so do the numerous solo performances by star-actors of the works of writers of narrative, diaries or letters. Emlyn Williams re-enacted Dickens reading from his novels... What this demonstrates is the essential difference between the narrative and the dramatic mode: the narrative, when read is perceived as lying in the *past*, the dramatic... creates an eternal *present*: in this case a narrator present in the room, telling his story here and now becomes – re-enacts himself as – a character...

And, if we approach the fluid boundary between narrative fiction and drama from the opposite direction: there is Brecht's 'epic theatre' which endeavours to import the detachment, the critical, 'historical' viewpoint of the epic poem and the novel into dramatic performance, so that the audience should be enabled to see the action with the detachment, the distanced analytical eye and critical mind of the reader of a novel, or historical narrative, as though it was *not* happening 'here and now' but 'there and then'.

If the boundaries between fiction and 'mimesis' are fluid, they are equally so at the other end of the spectrum, that of non-fictional 'action' or 'events': Renaissance *triomfi*; elaborate Corpus Christi processions... involving huge puppets parading through the streets (and revived by Peter Schumann's Bread and Puppet theatre); carnival processions and parades with floats depicting scenes and characters; masked balls in which individuals are costumed...; the circus... evoking the excitement of intense emotions are all very closely akin to that of drama more rigidly defined. Pageantry of all kinds involves the highly dramatic element of *spectacle*: the military parade or religious procession is something to be looked at in awe and wonder – gorgeous uniforms, spectacular vestments share with drama 'proper' the element of costume and spectacular groupings of characters; religious processions and *triomfi* also used 'floats' which can be regarded as mobile stages on which 'tableaux' of mythological or religious characters were displayed (as do contemporary carnival processions or the London 'Lord Mayor's parade'). Masked balls are often held in halls that have been turned into elaborate stage sets and the participants are not only costumed as 'characters' they also tend to want to improvise dialogue and actions appropriate to their dress – in other words turn themselves into 'actors'. Circus artists (such as bare-back riders, jugglers, trapeze artists, acrobats, tight-rope walkers) do not appear as 'fictional' characters, yet their glittering costumes make them figures of fantasy; nor must one forget that the display of physical skills and physical beauty is an important part of dramatic performance itself – great actors often excel by their beauty and physical prowess as well as by other qualities...

Contemporary avant-garde performance art, environmental theatre, 'happenings' and similar experimental works derive in many ways from these traditions of pageantry: here too often the performers remain themselves, or do not attempt to turn themselves into fictional characters, yet the 'images' they create, or the way in which they transform the audience into participants of improvised dialogue are clearly well within the boundaries of the 'dramatic'. One need only mention practitioners like the 'Living Theatre' of the sixties and seventies, Robert Wilson, Ariane Mnouchkine... in this context.

And then, at yet another boundary of the field of drama, there are the highly ritualised spectacular ceremonials involving kings and queens and other political figure-heads, like the 'Trooping of the Colour' in Britain... the inauguration of the President of the United States.

Closely akin to the vast field of drama and sharing and overlapping its boundaries there is the equally immense field of religious ritual (historically so closely related to the origins of drama itself) which frequently not only involves spectacular 'action' but also includes a strong 'mimetic' element, as the re-enactment of Christ's archetypal handling of bread and wine, in a variety of more or less symbolic forms, in the Eucharist. If from these boundaries of the concept, we return to its central core, we can perhaps sum it up as consisting of: mimetic action, in the sense of the re-enactment of 'real' or fictional events, involving the actions and interaction of human beings, real or simulated (e.g. puppets or cartoon characters) before an audience as though they were happening at that very moment.

The audience is an essential ingredient here. Even a rehearsal has an audience: the director or, indeed, the actors themselves, who are observing the evolution and effectiveness of their own performance, in order to shape or improve it further.

The artist who performs the mimetic action, the actor, thus stands at the very centre of the art of drama. The art form truly specific to drama is the art of acting. But drama also can and does use all the other arts: painting, sculpture and architecture to represent the environment, music to provide mood, rhythm – and indeed to represent the practice of music (people shown singing or dancing within the context of the world that is being represented) and of course 'literature' in the widest sense, for its verbal element. In drawing on the other arts and fusing them into a new whole, drama thus is the most hybrid (if we look at it in a purist spirit) or the most complete synthesis of all the arts: what Richard Wagner called the Gesamtkunstwerk – the 'total work of art'....

What, then, are the boundaries of the field of drama?

A filmed version of a stage play, whether by Pinter or Shakespeare, clearly is still drama. But is a film based on an original screenplay drama? Or a situation comedy on television? Or the circus? Is a musical play drama? And if so, is opera drama? Or ballet? Or the puppet theatre? I, for one, am convinced that all of these different forms of 'art' or 'entertainment' *are* essentially drama, or at least contain an important ingredient of 'the dramatic'.

Drama is unique among the representational arts in that it represents 'reality' by using real human beings and often also real objects, to create its fictional universe... But these real elements can be combined with any imaginable means to create illusion. The square in Verona (on which a real young man, representing the fictional Romeo, dressed in 'real' clothes uses a 'real' sword to fight with another 'real' young man, representing the fictional Tybalt), might be represented by a painted backdrop. Yet again, if we think of a filmed version of *Romeo and Juliet*, that square in Verona might be represented by patterns of light thrown onto a screen which forms a photographic image of a real piazza in Verona...

For if the outline of the central essentials of the concept of drama that I have attempted is correct a filmed version of Romeo and Juliet is still drama...

Taken from: *The Field of Drama*, by Esslin, M., London and New York: Methuen, 1987, pages 13–29.

Hand in hand with the general expansion in the field of drama goes the development of new dramatic forms. We can see an illustration of this inter-dependence if we take the relatively new medium of cinema as an example. The narrative structure of the Hollywood movie is substantially based on the form of the nineteenth century 'well-made play'; but the technical possibilities of the cinematic medium allow for significant developments in the existing dramatic form. Although the

Hollywood film absorbs certain conventions from the 'well-made play' (for example: strong opening exposition, battles of wits, reversals of fortune, rapid denouements), the use of the camera to cross-cut from scene to scene and the development of continuity editing makes it possible for the narrative to progress much more smoothly and seamlessly.

Developments in dramatic form do not only occur as a result of technological progress. More fundamental shifts in the broader cultural climate can bring about major changes in artistic practices. One of the major functions of the artist is to register these cultural shifts and reflect them in her/his work. This is how innovation occurs in an art form; the artist seeks new means of expression that can adequately capture a sense of the changing social, aesthetic and cultural climate. Innovation is the life-blood of art; and, in order for any art form to maintain a vitality and vigour, it needs practitioners who are constantly seeking to capture and communicate the complex and changing spirit of the times. This quest often requires the development of new forms and conventions.

2: The Conventions of Drama and Structures of Feeling

... the idea of convention is basic to any understanding of drama as a form.

The ordinary dictionary senses provide a useful starting-point. Thus, *convention* is the act of coming together; an assembly; union; coalition, specially of representatives for some definite purpose; an agreement previous to a definitive treaty; a custom. *Conventional*, similarly, is: settled by stipulation or by tacit consent; as sanctioned and currently accepted by tacit agreement; agreeable to accepted standards; agreeable to contract. As we go through these senses... we see an ambiguity which is important both because it indicates a possible source of confusion, which requires discussion, and because it indicates an important point of entry for an analysis of the place of conventions in drama.

The possible source of confusion is the fact that convention covers both *tacit consent* and *accepted standards*, and it is easy to see that the latter has often been understood as a set of formal rules. Thus it is common in adverse comment to say that a work is just *conventional; a familiar routine; old stuff; the mixture as before.* We use the word in the same way in adverse comment on people and actions that we find dull, or narrow, or old-fashioned, or unoriginal, or unreceptive to new ideas… The development of *conventional* as an adverse term in criticism… is the result of the controversy that was part of the Romantic Movement, in which emphasis fell heavily on the right of the artist to disregard, where he saw fit, the rules that had been laid down by others for the practice of his art. This was an original emphasis, from which we have all gained. But it is then unfortunate that *convention* and *conventional* should have been so heavily compromised. For an artist only leaves one convention to follow or create another; that is the whole basis of his communication. Yet when *conventional* carries the implications of old-fashioned, or narrow… it is difficult to use the word at all without being misunderstood. Yet it is possible to think of the ambiguity as the means of an important insight; and it is this that must now be discussed.

Convention, as we have seen, covers *tacit agreement* as well as *accepted standards*. In the actual practice of drama, the convention, in any particular case, is simply the terms upon which author, performance and audience agree to meet, so that the performance may be carried on. *Agree to meet*, of course, is by no means always a formal or definite process; much more usually, in any art, the consent is largely customary, and often indeed it is virtually unconscious.

This can be seen most readily in the conventions of our own period. In a naturalist play, for example, the convention is that the speech and action should as closely as possible appear to be those of everyday life; but few who watch such a play realize that this is a convention: to the majority it is merely "what a play is like", "the sort of thing a play tries to do". Yet it is, in fact, a very remarkable convention that actors should represent people behaving naturally, and usually privately, before a large audience, while all the time maintaining the illusion that, as characters, these persons are unaware of the audience's presence. The most desperate private confession, or the most dangerous conspiracy, can be played out on the stage, in full view and hearing of a thousand people; yet it will not occur to either actors or audience that this is in any way strange, because all, by the tacit consent of custom, have accepted this procedure as a convention.

Not long ago, and perhaps still in some places, it was, however, thought very strange if a character spoke in soliloquy, whether this was thought of as "thinking aloud" or "directly addressing the audience". The complaint would be that this is "artificial", or "not true to life", or even "undramatic"; yet it is surely as natural, and as "true to life", when one is on a stage before a thousand people, to address them, as to pretend to carry on as if they were not there. As for the soliloquy being "undramatic", this is the kind of conditional statement, elevated into a "law", which continually confuses dramatic criticism, since it is well known that the soliloquy, in many periods, has been a normally accepted part of dramatic method...

Since the use of conventions... is inherent in the process of drama, it is at first surprising that when the basic convention, that of acted performance, has been accepted, there should be any difficulty in particular instances. Yet it is obvious that such difficulties are acute and recurrent. We will agree that the person on the stage is a spirit, and that, quite unaware of our intent presence, he is talking privately to his widow, in the year 1827; but if the widow attempts to address us in an aside, we can become uneasy. We will agree that a murderer may hide behind a door (where we can still see him), and that he may look down, with an expression of agony, at his hands (which we at once agree are stained with innocent blood); but if he should come forward to the front of the stage, and in twenty lines of verse, or in recitative or song, or in dance, express (if more fully and more intensely) the same emotion, we at once, or many of us, feel uneasy, and are likely to say afterwards that it was "unreal". We may even conclude... that the play was highbrow, or surrealist, or pretentious.... And while we may be able to reject this kind of simplification, we shall not be able, merely by taking thought, to create an alternative convention...

... for while it is true that... the basis for change and development in convention always potentially exists, it is only academically true that a dramatist may use any convention that suits his material and intention. A convention, in the simplest sense, is only a method, a technical piece of machinery, which facilitates the performance. But methods change, and techniques change, and while, say, a chorus of dancers, or a cloak of invisibility, or a sung soliloquy, are known dramatic methods, they cannot be satisfactorily used unless, at the time of a performance, they are more than methods; unless, in fact, they are conventions. Dramatists, actors and audience must be able to agree that the particular method to be employed is acceptable; and, in the nature of the case, an important part of the agreement must usually *precede* the performance, so that what is to be done may be accepted without damaging friction.

Ultimately, however, we judge a convention, not by its abstract useful-ness, and not by referring it to some ultimate criterion of probability, but rather by what it manages, in an actual work of art, to get done. If in fact it were not historically true that certain works have been able, by their own strength, to modify old conventions and to introduce new ones, we should have had no change at all...

Yet the history of art is not one of continual evolution into higher and better forms; there is debasement as well as refinement, and a novelty, even a transformation may be bad as well as good. It would be absurd to imagine that our own contemporary segment from the great arc of dra-matic possibility is, because the latest, necessarily the best. Yet, because of the nature of convention, because of the dependence of any dramatic method upon this particular type of agreement, it is not possible, in any age, to go very far from the segment which is that age's living tradition, or to begin from anywhere but within or on its borders.

Thus we have the necessity of tradition – convention as tacit consent – and at times the equal necessity of experiment, from the development of new modes of feeling, and from the perception of new or rediscov-ered technical means – convention as dramatic method. It is to the interplay of these two senses of convention that we must now turn.

If we think of a dramatic convention as a technical means in an acted performance, it is clear that there is no absolute reason why any means should not be employed, and judged by its dramatic result. But we have seen that, in practice, this absolute freedom of choice is not available: a dramatist must win the consent of his audience to any particular means that he wishes to employ, and while he may often be able to do this in the course of a work itself, by the power of the effect which the method makes possible, he cannot entirely rely on this, for even if the audience is sympathetic, too great a consciousness of the novelty or strangeness of the means may as effectively hamper the full communication of a play as would open hostility. It seems probable, when we look back into the history of drama, that the effective changes took place when there was already a latent willingness to accept them, at least among certain groups in society, from whom the artist drew his support. But while it is possible to see this in retrospect, it could never have been easy, and it is not easy now, to see such a situation, with sufficient clarity, in the flux of present experience. It is here that we find our-selves considering the very difficult relations between conventions and structures of feeling.

All serious thinking about art must begin from the recognition of two apparently contradictory facts: that an important work is always, in an irreducible sense, individual; and yet that there are authentic communities of works of art, in kinds, periods and styles. In everyday discussion, we succeed in maintaining both ideas at the same time, without real consideration of the relations between them. We see a particular play, and say, often genuinely, that in this speech, this character, this action, a particular dramatist makes himself known; it is for this specific achievement that we value his work. But then, sometimes in the next breath, we look at the speech, the character or the action and say: this is characteristic of a particular kind of drama, in a particular period. Each kind of observation is important; each helps us, every day, to understand drama better. But the difficulty raised by their apparent contradiction – here pointing to a single hand, there to a group or period – must in the end be faced. For the contradiction cannot be resolved by saying that we are in each case pointing at a different kind of fact. It is true that in some works it is possible to separate out different elements, and to say: here the dramatist is simply following the conventions of his genre or period, but here he is contributing something entirely his own. Yet in many important works it is not possible to do this: the individual genius and the particular conventions through which it is expressed are or seem inseparable. In pointing to what a particular man has done, in a particular style, we are often in the position of learning what that style is, what it is capable of doing. The individual dramatist has done this, yet what he has done is part of what we then know about a general period or style.

It is to explore this essential relationship that I use the term 'structure of feeling'. What I am seeking to describe is the continuity of experience from a particular work, through its particular form, to its recognition as a general form, and then the relation of this general form to a period. We can look at this continuity, first, in the most general way. All that is lived and made, by a given community in a given period, is, we now commonly believe, essentially related, although in practice, and in detail, this is not always easy to see. In the study of a period, we may be able to reconstruct, with more or less accuracy, the material life, the general social organization, and, to a large extent, the dominant ideas. It is often difficult to decide which, if any, of these aspects, in the whole complex, is determining; their separation is, in a way, arbitrary, and an important institution like the drama will, in all probability, take its colour in varying degrees from them all. But while we may, in the study of a past period, separate out particular aspects of life, and treat them as if they were self-contained, it is obvious that this is only how they may be studied, not how they were experienced. We examine each element as a precipitate, but in the living experience of the time every element was in solution, an inseparable part of a complex whole. And it seems to be true, from the nature of art, that it is from such a totality that the artist draws; it is in art, primarily, that the effect of a whole lived experience is expressed and embodied. To relate a work of art to any part of that whole may, in varying degrees, be useful; but it is a common experience, in analysis, to realize that when one has measured the work against the separable parts, there yet remains some element for which there is no external counterpart. It is this, in the first instance, that I mean by the structure of feeling. It is as firm and definite as "structure" suggests, yet it is based in the deepest and often least tangible elements of our experience. It is a way of responding to a particular world which in practice is not felt as one way among others – a conscious "way" – but is, in experience, the only way possible. Its means, its elements, are not propositions or techniques; they are embodied, related feelings. In the same sense, it is accessible to others – not by formal argument or by professional skills, on their own, but by direct experience – a form and a meaning, a feeling and a rhythm – in the work of art, the play as a whole.

We can often see this structure in the drama of the past. But then it follows, from the whole emphasis of the term, that it is precisely the structure of feeling which is most difficult to distinguish while it is still being lived. Just because it has then not passed, or wholly passed, into distinguishable formations and beliefs and institutions, it is known primarily as a deep *personal* feeling; indeed it often seems, to a particular writer, unique, almost incommunicable and lonely. We can see this most clearly in the art and thought of past periods, when, while it was being made, its creators seemed often, to themselves and others, isolated, cut off, difficult to understand. Yet again and again, when the structure of feeling has been absorbed, it is the connections, the correspondences, even the period similarities, which spring most readily to the eye. What was then a living structure, not yet known to be shared, is now a recorded structure, which can be examined and identified and even generalized. In one's own lifetime, before this has happened, it is probable that those to whom the new structure is most accessible, in whom indeed it is most clearly forming, will know their experience primarily as their own: as what cuts them off from other men, though what they are actually cut off from is the set of received formations and conventions and institutions which no longer express or satisfy their own most essential life. When such a man speaks, in his work, often against what is felt to be the grain of the time, it is surprising to him and to others that there can be recognition of what had seemed this most difficult, inaccessible, unshared life. Established formations will criticize or reject him, but to an increasing number of people he will seem to be speaking for them, for their own deepest sense of life, just because he was speaking for himself. A new structure of feeling is then becoming articulate. It is even possible, though very difficult even by comparison with the analysis of past structures, to begin to see this contemporary structure directly, rather than only in the power of particular works. Many such expositions are too early, too superficial or too rigid, but it remains true that discovery of actual contemporary structures of feeling (usually masked by their immediate and better recognized predecessors) is the most important kind of attention to the art and society of one's own time.

The artist's importance, in relation to the structure of feeling, has to do above all with the fact that it is a *structure*: not an unformed flux of new responses, interests and perceptions, but a formation of these into a new way of seeing ourselves and our world. Such a formation is the purpose of all authentic contemporary activity, and its successes occur in fields other than art. But the artist, by the character of his work, is directly involved with just this process, from the beginning. He can only work at all as such formations become available, usually as a personal discovery and then a scatter of personal discoveries and then the manner of work of a generation. What this means, in practice, is the making of new conventions, new forms.

It is in this respect, finally, that I see the usefulness of "structure of feeling" as a critical term. For it directs our attention, in practical ways, to a kind of analysis which is at once concerned with particular forms and the elements of general forms. We can begin, quite locally, in what is still called practical criticism, with direct analysis: to discover the structure of feeling of a particular play. This structure, always, is an experience, to which we can directly respond. But it is also an experience communicated in a particular form, through particular conventions. There is indeed always a critical relation between the form and the experience: an identity, a tension, at times, in effect, a disintegration. It is not at all a question of applying an external form, and its rules, to a particular play; it is how the experience and its means of communication relate, by a primarily internal criterion. The first study of a structure of feeling is then always local, particular, unique.

But what is being drawn on, in the means of communication, is already wider than the particular work: in a language, in methods, in conventions. As we collect our experience of particular plays, we see the structure of feeling at once extending and changing: important elements in common, as experience and as method, between particular plays and dramatists; important elements changing, as the experience and the conventions change together, or as the experience is found to be in tension with existing conventions, and either succeeds or fails in altering them. Slowly, what emerges is much wider than particular work: it is a problem of form, but also, crucially, a problem of experience, for many dramatists, and in effect for a period and for successive periods. In any real analysis, the relationships are usually very difficult to sustain; but there is the possibility... of substantial connections between the most particular and the most general forms. What the analysis often shows is a change in dramatic method, but the point of my argument, through the relation of conventions and structures of feeling, is that we can look at dramatic method with a clear technical definition, and yet know, in detail, that what is being defined is more than technique: is indeed the practical way of describing those changes in experience – the responses and their communication; the "subjects" and the "forms" – which make the drama in itself and as a history important.

Taken from: *Drama from Ibsen to Brecht* by Williams, R., London: Hogarth, 1968, pages 12–20.

Part Two: The Origins of Drama and Developments in Modern Theatre Practice

In the last section, we saw how new conventions develop in order to express changing structures of feeling. As these innovations come to be accepted, they gradually become the established means by which artists express and communicate their intentions. In the classical Greek theatre of the fifth century BC, the innovations of playwrights like Aeschylus and Sophocles became the accepted methods of writing tragedy. Aristotle, an Athenian philosopher of the fourth century BC, analysed the tragic plays of these great playwrights and formulated a theory of tragedy which remains influential right up until the present day.

3: Poetics

Imitation is natural to man from childhood, one of his advantages over the lower animals being this, that he is the most imitative creature in the world, and learns at first by imitation. And it is also natural for all to delight in works of imitation...

Poetry... broke up into two kinds according to the differences of character in the individual poets; for the graver among them would represent noble actions, and those of noble personages; and the meaner sort the actions of the ignoble...

Homer... was in the serious style the poet of poets, standing alone not only through the literary excellence, but also through the dramatic character of his imitations, so too he was the first to outline for us the general forms of Comedy by producing... a dramatic picture of the Ridiculous; his *Margites* in fact stands in the same relation to our comedies as the *Iliad* and *Odyssey* to our tragedies...

Tragedy... certainly began in improvisations – as did also Comedy... And its advance after that was little by little, through their improving on whatever they had before them at each stage. It was in fact only after a long series of changes that the movement of Tragedy stopped on its attaining to its natural form. (1) The number of actors was first increased to two by Aeschylus, who curtailed the business of the Chorus, and made the dialogue, or spoken portion, take the leading part in the play. (2) A third actor and scenery were due to Sophocles.

(3) Tragedy acquired also its magnitude. Discarding short stories and a ludicrous diction... it assumed, though only at a late point in its progress, a tone of dignity; and its metre changed then from trochaic to iambic. The reason for their original use of the trochaic tetrameter was that their poetry was... more connected with dancing than it now is. As soon, however, as a spoken part came in, nature herself found the appropriate metre. The iambic, we know, is the most speakable of metres, as is shown by the fact that we very often fall into it in conversation, whereas we rarely talk hexameters, and only when we depart from the speaking tone of voice. (4) Another change was a plurality of episodes or acts...

Comedy... is an imitation of men worse than the average; worse, however, not as regards any and every sort of fault, but only as regards one particular kind, the Ridiculous, which is a species of the Ugly. The Ridiculous may be defined as a mistake or deformity not productive of pain or harm to others; the mask, for instance, that excites laughter, is something ugly and distorted without causing pain...

Let us now proceed to the discussion of Tragedy... A tragedy... is the imitation of an action that is serious and also, as having magnitude, complete in itself... with incidents arousing pity and fear, wherewith to accomplish its catharsis of such emotions.... There are six parts... of every tragedy... viz. A Fable or Plot, Characters, Diction, Thought, Spectacle and Melody...

The most important of the six is the combination of the incidents of the story. Tragedy is essentially an imitation not of persons but of action and life, of happiness and misery. All human happiness or misery takes the form of action... Character gives us qualities, but it is in our actions – what we do – that we are happy or the reverse. In a play accordingly they do not act in order to portray the Characters; they include the Characters for the sake of the action. So that it is the action in it, ie its Fable or Plot, that is the end and purpose of the tragedy; and the end is everywhere the chief thing. Besides this, a tragedy is impossible without action... The first essential, the life and soul, so to speak, of Tragedy is the Plot; and that the Characters come second. ...Third comes the element of Thought, ie the power of saying whatever can be said, or what is appropriate to the occasion... One must not confuse it with Character. Character in a play is that which reveals the moral purpose of the agents, ie the sort of thing they seek or avoid... Thought, on the other hand, is shown in all they say when proving or disproving some particular point, or enunciating some universal proposition. Fourth among the... elements is the Diction of the personages... the expression of their thoughts in words. ...As for the two remaining parts, the Melody is the greatest of the pleasurable accessories of Tragedy. The Spectacle, though an attraction, is the least artistic of all the parts, and has least to do with the art of poetry.

Having thus distinguished the parts, let us now consider the proper construction of the Fable or Plot, as that is at once the first and the most important thing in Tragedy. We have laid it down that a Tragedy is an imitation of an action that is complete in itself, as a whole of some magnitude... Now a whole is that which has beginning, middle and end. A beginning is that which is not itself necessarily after anything else, and which has naturally something else after it; an end is that which is naturally after something itself, either as its necessary or usual consequent, and with nothing else after it; and a middle, that which is by nature after one thing and has also another after it. A well-constructed Plot, therefore, cannot either begin or end at any point one likes; beginning and end in it must be of the forms just described... To be beautiful, a living creature, and every whole made up of parts, must not only present a certain order in its arrangement of parts, but also be of a certain definite magnitude. Beauty is a matter of size and order... Just in the same way, then, as a beautiful whole made up of parts, or a beautiful living creature, must be of some size, but a size to be taken in by the eye, so a story or Plot must be of some length, but of a length to be taken in by the memory. As for the limit of its length... as a rough general formula, 'a length which allows of the hero passing by a series of probable or necessary stages from misfortune to happiness, or from happiness to misfortune', may suffice as a limit for the magnitude of the story.

The Unity of a Plot does not consist, as some suppose, in its having one man as its subject. An infinity of things befall that one man, some of which it is impossible to reduce to unity; and in like manner there are many actions of one man which cannot be taken to form one action... The truth is that, just as in the other imitative arts, one imitation is always of one thing, so in poetry the story, as an imitation of an action, must represent one action, a complete whole, with its several incidents so closely connected that the transposal or withdrawal of any one of them will disjoin and dislocate the whole. For that which makes no perceptible difference by its presence or absence is no real part of the whole.

From what we have said it will be seen that the poet's function is to describe, not the thing that has happened, but a kind of thing that might happen, ie what is possible as being probable or necessary... In Tragedy... what convinces is the possible...

Tragedy... is an imitation not only of a complete action, but also of incidents arousing pity or fear. Such incidents have the very greatest effect on the mind when they occur unexpectedly and at the same time in consequence of one another; there is more of the marvellous in them then than if they happened of themselves or by mere chance...

Plots are either simple or complex, since the actions they represent are naturally of this twofold description. The action, proceeding in the way defined, as one continuous whole, I call simple, when the change in the hero's fortunes takes place without Peripety or Discovery; and complex, when it involves one or the other, or both. These should each of them arise out of the Plot itself, so as to be the consequence, necessary or probable, of the antecedents...

A Peripety is the change of the kind described from one state of things within the play to its opposite... in the probable or necessary sequence of events; as it is for instance in *Oedipus*: here the opposite state of things is produced by the Messenger, who, coming to gladden Oedipus and to remove his fears as to his mother, reveals the secret of his birth... A Discovery is, as the very word implies, a change from ignorance to knowledge, and thus to either love or hate, in the personages marked for good or evil fortune. The finest form of Discovery is one attended by Peripeties, like that which goes with the Discovery in *Oedipus*... This, with a Peripety will arouse either pity or fear – actions of that nature being what Tragedy is assumed to represent; and it will also serve to bring about the happy or unhappy ending...

Two parts of the Plot then, Peripety and Discovery, are on matters of this sort. A third part is Suffering; which we may define as an action of a destructive or painful nature, such as murders on the stage, tortures, woundings, and the like...

The next points after what we have said above will be these: (1) What is the poet to aim at, and what is he to avoid, in constructing his Plots? and (2) What are the conditions on which the tragic effect depends?

We assume that, for the finest form of Tragedy, the Plot must be not simple but complex; and further, that it must imitate actions arousing fear and pity, since that is the distinctive function of this kind of imitation.

It follows, therefore, that there are three forms of Plot to be avoided. (1) A good man must not be seen passing from happiness to misery, or (2) a bad man from misery to happiness. The first situation is not fear-inspiring or piteous, but simply odious to us. The second is the most untragic that can be; it has no one of the requisites of Tragedy; it does not appeal either to the human feeling in us, or to our pity, or to our fears. Nor, on the other hand, should (3) an extremely bad man be seen falling from happiness to misery. Such a story may arouse the human feeling in us, but it will not move us to either pity or fear; pity is occasioned by undeserving misfortune, and fear by that of one like ourselves; so that there will be nothing either piteous or fear-inspiring in the situation. There remains, then, the intermediate kind of personage, a man not pre-eminently virtuous and just, whose misfortune, however, is brought upon him not by vice and depravity but by some error of judgement... The perfect Plot, accordingly, must have a single, and not (as some tell us) a double issue; the change in the hero's fortunes must be not from misery to happiness, but on the contrary from happiness to misery; and the cause of it must lie not in any depravity, but in some great error on his part; the man himself being either such as we have described, or better, not worse, than that...

The tragic fear and pity may be aroused by the Spectacle; but they may also be aroused by the very structure and incidents of the play – which is the better way... The Plot in fact should be so framed that, even without seeing the things take place, he who simply hears the account of them shall be filled with a horror and pity at the incidents; which is just the effect that the mere recital of the story of *Oedipus* would have on one. To produce this same effect by means of the Spectacle is less artistic, and requires extraneous aid. Those, however, who make use of the Spectacle to put before us that which is merely monstrous and not productive of fear, are wholly out of touch with Tragedy...

The tragic pleasure is that of pity and fear, and the poet has to produce it by a work of Imitation; it is clear, therefore, that the causes should be included in the incidents of his story. Let us see, then, what kinds of incident strike one as horrible, or rather as piteous. In a deed of this description the parties must necessarily either be friends, or enemies, or indifferent to one another. Now when enemy does it on enemy, there is nothing to move us to pity either in his doing or in his meditating the deed, except so far as the actual pain of the sufferer is concerned; and the same is true when the parties are indifferent to one another. Whenever the tragic deed, however, is done within the family – when murder or the like is done or meditated by brother on brother, by son on father, by mother on son, or son on mother – these are the situations the poet should seek after…

On the construction of the Plot, and the kind of Plot required for Tragedy, enough has now been said.

In the Characters there are four points to aim at. First and foremost, that they shall be good. There will be an element of character in the play, if… what a personage says or does reveals a certain moral purpose; and a good element of character, if the purpose so revealed is good. Such goodness is possible in every type of personage… The second point is to make them appropriate. The Character before us may be, say, manly; but it is not appropriate in a female Character to be manly… The third is to make them like the reality, which is not the same as their being good or appropriate, in our sense of the term. The fourth is to make them consistent and the same throughout; even if inconsistency be part of the man before one for imitation as presenting that form of character, he should still be consistently inconsistent… The right thing, however, is in the Characters just as in the incidents of the play to endeavour always after the necessary or the probable; so that whenever such-and-such a personage says and does such-and-such a thing, it shall be the necessary and probable outcome of his character; and whenever this incident follows on that, it shall either be the necessary or probable consequence of it. From this one sees… that the Denouement also should arise out of the plot itself, and not depend on a stage-artifice… The artifice must be reserved for matters outside the play – for past events beyond human knowledge, or events yet to come, which require to be foretold or announced; since it is the privilege of the Gods to know everything. There should be nothing improbable among the actual incidents… But to return to the Characters. As Tragedy is an imitation of personages better than the ordinary man, we in our way should follow the example of good portrait-painters, who reproduce the distinctive features of a man, and at the same time, without losing the likeness, make him handsomer than he is. The poet in like manner, in portraying men quick or slow to anger, or with similar infirmities of character, must know how to represent them as such, and at the same time as good men…

At the time when he is constructing his Plots, and engaged on the Diction in which they are worked out, the poet should remember (1) to put the actual scenes as far as possible before his eyes. In this way, seeing everything with the vividness of an eye-witness as it were, he will devise what is appropriate, and be least likely to overlook incongruities... (2) As far as may be, too, the poet should even act his story with the very gestures of his personages. Given the same natural qualifications, he who feels the emotions to be described will be the most convincing; distress and anger, for instance, are portrayed most truthfully by one who is feeling them at the moment... (3) His story, again, whether already made or of his own making, he should first simplify and reduce to a universal form, before proceeding to lengthen it out by the insertion of episodes...

(4) There is a further point to be borne in mind. Every tragedy is in part Complication and in part Denouement; the incidents before the opening scene, and often certain also of those within the play, forming the Complication; and the rest the Denouement. By Complication I mean all from the beginning of the story to the point just before the change in the hero's fortunes; by Denouement, all from the beginning of the change to the end... (5) There are four distinct species of Tragedy... first, the complex Tragedy, which is all Peripety and Discovery; second the Tragedy of suffering; ...third, the Tragedy of Character.... The fourth constituent is that of 'Spectacle'... The poet's aim, then, should be to combine every element of interest, if possible, or else the more important and the major part of them... (6) One should also remember... and not write a tragedy on an epic body of incident... by attempting to dramatize, for instance, the entire story of the *Iliad*... (7) The Chorus too should be regarded as one of the actors; it should be an integral part of the whole, and take a share in the action...

The Plot and Characters having been discussed, it remains to consider the Diction and Thought... The Thought of the personages is shown in everything to be effected by their language – in every effort to prove or disprove, to arouse emotion (pity, fear, anger, and the like), or to maximize or minimize things. It is clear, also, that their mental procedure must be on the same lines in their actions likewise, whenever they wish them to arouse pity or horror, or to have a look of importance or probability. The only difference is that with the act the impression has to be made without explanation; whereas with the spoken word it has to be produced by the speaker, and result from his language...

As regards the Diction, one subject for inquiry under this head is the turns given to the language when spoken; eg the difference between command and prayer, simple statement and threat, question and answer, and so forth...

Taken from: Aristotle's *De Poetica*, in *The Works of Aristotle, Volume XI*, edited by W.D. Ross, Oxford: Oxford University Press, 1971, pages 1448–1456.

The principles set out in Aristotle's Poetics *continued to inform dramaturgy well into the early years of the eighteenth century. The early Elizabethan writers of tragedy in England owed a considerable debt to the Greek philosopher; but in the hands of Shakespeare and the Jacobeans, tragedy began to break away from the strict rules set out in the* Poetics. *In France though, the neo-classic writers, like Racine and Corneille, followed Aristotle's precepts slavishly; and it was not until the Romantic revolution of the late-eighteenth and early-nineteenth centuries that Aristotle's influence began to wane. Although the romantic dramas of writers like Victor Hugo supplanted the neo-classic tragedies on the stage in France, Aristotle's concept of 'imitation' (or, mimesis) subsequently formed the basis of nineteenth century realism and naturalism.*

4: Naturalism on the Stage

… we must now endeavour to define the present position of dramatic literature. But before entering upon it I will rapidly recall… the great evolutions of the stage in France.

… tragedy and comedy were born, under the influence of the classical renaissance. Great geniuses consecrated this movement – Corneille, Moliere, Racine. They were the product of the age in which they lived. The tragedy and comedy of that time, with their unalterable rules, their etiquette of the court, their grand and noble air, their philosophical dissertations and oratorical eloquence are the exact reproduction of contemporaneous society. And this identity, this close affinity of the dramatic formula and the social surroundings, is so strong that for two centuries the formula remains almost the same… The ancient society is then profoundly disturbed; the excitement which agitates it even touches the stage. There is a need for greater action, there is a sullen revolt against the rules, a vague return to nature. Even at this period Diderot and Mercier laid down squarely the basis of the naturalistic theatre; unfortunately, neither one nor the other produced a masterpiece, and this is necessary to establish a new formula. Besides, the classical style was so solidly planted in the soil of the ancient monarchy that it was not carried away entirely by the tempest of the Revolution. It persisted for some time longer, weakened, degenerated, gliding into insipidity and imbecility. Then the romantic insurrection, which had been hatching for years, burst forth. The romantic drama killed the expiring tragedy... Romantic drama became the antithesis of the tragedy; it opposed passion to duty, action to words, colouring to psychological analysis, the Middle Ages to antiquity. It was this sparkling contrast which assured its triumph. Tragedy must disappear, its knell has sounded... The romantic drama, however, was not to have as long a reign as tragedy. After performing its revolutionary task it died out, suddenly, leaving the place clear for reconstruction... As a result of this inevitable crisis in romanticism, the traditions of naturalism reappear, the ideas of Diderot and Mercier come more and more to the surface... The naturalistic formula will be to our century what the classical formula has been to past centuries.

Now we have arrived at our own period. Here I find a considerable activity, an extraordinary outlay of talent. It is an immense workroom in which each one works with feverish energy. All is confusion as yet, there is a great deal of lost labour, very few blows strike out direct and strong; still the spectacle is none the less marvellous. One thing is certain that each labourer is working toward the definite triumph of naturalism. They are, in spite of everything, borne along by the current of the time; they go of necessity where it goes. As none in the theatre has been of large enough calibre to establish the formula at a stroke by the sheer force of his genius, it would almost seem as if they had divided the task, each one giving in turn, and with reference to a definite point, the necessary shove onward...

No one contests the point that all the different forms of literary expression hold together and advance at the same time. When they have been stirred up, when the ball is once set rolling, there is a general push toward the same goal. The romantic insurrection is a striking example of this unity of movement under a definite influence. I have shown that the force of the current of the age is toward naturalism. Today this force is making itself felt more and more; it is rushing on us, and everything must obey it. The novel and the stage are carried away by it. Only it has happened that the evolution has been much more rapid in the novel; it triumphs there while it is just beginning to put in an appearance on the stage. This was bound to be. The theatre has always been the stronghold of convention for a multiplicity of reasons... The naturalistic formula, however complete and defined in the novel, is very far from being so on the stage, and I conclude from that that it will be completed, that it will assume sooner or later there its scientific rigour, or else the stage will become flat, and more and more inferior...

I am waiting for someone... to put a man of flesh and bones on the stage, taken from reality, scientifically analysed, without one lie. I am waiting for them to rid us of fictitious characters, of conventional symbols of virtue and vice, which possess no value as human data. I am waiting for the surroundings to determine the characters, and for the characters to act according to the logic of facts, combined with the logic of their own temperament. I am waiting until there is no more jugglery of any kind, no more strokes of a magical wand, changing in one minute persons and things. I am waiting for the time to come when they will tell us no more incredible stories, when they will no longer spoil the effects of just observations by romantic incidents, the result being to destroy even the good parts of a play. I am waiting for them to abandon the cut and dried rules, the worked-out formulas, the tears and cheap laughs. I am waiting until a dramatic work free from declamations, big words and grand sentiments has the high morality of truth, teaches the terrible lesson that belongs to all sincere inquiry. I am waiting, finally, until the evolution accomplished in the novel takes place on the stage; until they return to the source of science and modern arts, to the study of nature, to the anatomy of man, to the painting of life, in an exact reproduction, more original and powerful than anyone so far has dared to place upon the boards.

This is what I am waiting for... Some people are very much irritated with me... They shrug their shoulders and reply to me that I shall wait forever. Their decisive argument is that you must not expect these things on the stage. The stage is not the novel...

Now we are at the very pith of the quarrel. I am trying to uproot the very conditions of existence on the stage. What I ask is impossible, which amounts to saying that fictions are necessary on the stage; a play must have some romantic corners, it must turn in equilibrium around certain situations, which must unravel themselves at the proper time... An act must be played in three hours, no matter what its length is; then the characters are endowed with a particular value, which necessitates setting up fictions. I will not put forth all the arguments. I arrive at the intervention of the public, which is really considerable; the public wishes this, the public will not have that; it will not tolerate too much truth; it exacts four attractive puppets to one real character taken from life. In a word, the stage is the domain of conventionality; everything is conventional, from the decorations to the footlights which illuminate the actors, even down to the characters, who are led by a string. Truth can only enter by little doses adroitly distributed. They even go so far as to swear that the theatre will cease to exist the day it ceases to be an amusing lie, destined to console the spectators in the evening for the sad realities of the day...

It is evident that each kind of literature has its own conditions of existence. A novel, which one reads alone in his room... is not a play which is acted before two thousand spectators. The novelist has time and space before him; all sorts of liberties are permitted him; he can use one hundred pages, if it pleases him, to analyse at his leisure a certain character; he can describe his surroundings as much as he pleases; he can cut his story short, can retrace his steps, changing places twenty times – in one word, he is absolute master of his matter. The dramatic author, on the contrary, is enclosed in a rigid frame; he must heed all sorts of necessities. He moves only in the midst of obstacles. Then, above all, there is the question of the isolated reader and the spectators taken *en masse*; the solitary reader tolerates everything, goes where he is led, even when he is disgusted; while the spectators, taken *en masse*, are seized with prudishness, with frights, with sensibilities of which the author must take notice under pain of a certain fall. All this is true, and it is precisely for this reason that the stage is the last citadel of conventionality... If the naturalistic movement had not encountered on the boards, a difficult ground, filled with obstacles, it would already have taken root there with the intensity and the success which have attended the novel. The stage, under its conditions of existence, must be the last, the most laborious, and the most bitterly disputed conquest of the spirit of truth.

I will remark here that the evolution of each century is of necessity incarnated in a particular form of literature. Thus the seventeenth century evidently incarnated itself in the dramatic formula. Our theatre then threw forth an incomparable glitter, to the detriment of lyrical poetry and the novel. The reason was that the stage then exactly responded to the spirit of the period. It abstracted man from nature, studied him with the philosophical tool of the time; it has the swing of a pompous rhetoric, the polite manners of a society which had reached perfect maturity. It is the fruit of the ground; its formula is written from that point where the then civilisation flowed with the greatest ease and perfection... The spirit of the nineteenth century, with its return to nature, with its need of exact inquiry, quitted the stage, where too much conventionality hampered it, in order to stamp itself indelibly on the novel, whose field is limitless. And thus it is that scientifically the novel has become the form, *par excellence*, of our age, the first path in which naturalism was to triumph...

Let us admit for one moment that criticism has some show of reason when it asserts that naturalism is impossible on the stage. Here is what they assert. Conventionality is inevitable on the stage; there must always be lying there... What do you wish us to do with the stage, we other seekers after truth, anatomists, analysts, searchers of life, compilers of human data, if you prove to us that there we cannot make use of our tools and our methods? Really! The theatre lives only on conventionalities; it must lie; it refuses our experimental literature! Oh, well, then, the century will put the stage on one side, it will abandon it to the hands of the public amusers, while it will perform elsewhere its great and glorious work. You yourself pronounce the verdict and kill the stage. It is very evident that the naturalistic evolution will extend itself more and more, as it possesses the intelligence of the age. While the novelists are always digging further forward, producing newer and more exact data, the stage will flounder deeper every day in the midst of its romantic fictions, its worn-out plots, and its skilfulness of handicraft. The situation will be the more sad because the public will certainly acquire a taste for reality in reading novels. The movement is making itself forcibly felt even now. There will come a time when the public will shrug its shoulders and demand an innovation. Either the theatre will be naturalistic or it will not be at all; such is the formal conclusion...

I have perfect faith in the future of our stage. I will not admit that the critics are right in saying that naturalism is impossible on the stage, and I am going to explain under what conditions the movement will without question be brought about.

It is not true that the stage must remain stationary; it is not true that its actual conventionalities are the fundamental conditions of its existence.

Everything marches, I repeat; everything marches forward. The authors of today will be over-ridden; they cannot have the presumption to settle dramatic literature forever. What they have lisped forth others will cry from the house top; but the stage will not be shaken to its foundations on that account; it will enter, on the contrary, on a wider, straighter path. People have always denied the march forward; they have denied to the newcomers the power and the right to accomplish what has not been performed by their elders. The social and literary evolutions have an irresistible force; they traverse with a slight bound the enormous obstacles which were reputed impassable. The theatre may well be what it is today; tomorrow it will be what it should be. And when the event takes place all the world will think it perfectly natural.

At this point I enter into mere probabilities, and I no longer pretend to the same scientific rigour. So long as I have reasoned on facts I have demonstrated the truth of my position. At present I am content to foretell. The evolution will take place, that is certain. But will it pass to the left? Will it pass to the right? I do not know. One can reason. And that is all.

In the first place, it is certain that the conditions existing on the stage will always be different. The novel, thanks to its freedom, will remain perhaps the tool, *par excellence*, of the century, while the stage will but follow it and complete the action. The wonderful power of the stage must not be forgotten, and its immediate effect on the spectators. There is no better instrument for propagating anything. If the novel, then, is read by the fireside in several instances with a patience tolerating the longest details, the naturalistic drama should proclaim before all else that it has no connection with this isolated reader, but with a crowd who cry out for clearness and consciousness. I do not see that the naturalistic formula is antagonistic to this conciseness and this clearness. It is simply a question of changing the composition and the body of the work. The novel analyses at great length and with a minuteness of detail which overlooks nothing; the stage can analyse as briefly as it wishes by actions and words. A word, a cry, in Balzac's works is often sufficient to present the entire character. This cry belongs essentially to the stage. As to the acts, they are consistent with analysis in action, which is the most striking form of action one can make. When we have got rid of a child's play of a plot, the infantile game of tying up complicated threads in order to have the pleasure of untying them again; when a play shall be nothing more than a real and logical story – we shall then enter into perfect analysis; we shall analyse necessarily the double influence of characters over facts, of facts over characters. This is what has led me to say so often that the naturalistic formula carries us back to the source of our national stage, the classical formula. We find this continuous analysis of character, which I consider so necessary, in Corneille's tragedies and Moliere's comedies; plot takes a secondary place, the work is a long dissertation in dialogue on man. Only instead of an abstract man I would make a natural man, put him in his proper surroundings, and analyse all the physical and social causes which make him what he is. In a word, the classical formula is to me a good one, on condition that the scientific method is employed in the study of actual society. In the same way that the chemist studies minerals and their properties.

As to the long descriptions of the novelist, they cannot be put upon the stage; that is evident. The naturalistic novelists describe a great deal... because it is part of their formula to be circumstantial, and to complete the character by means of his surroundings. Man is no longer an intellectual abstraction for them, as he was looked upon in the seventeenth century; he is a thinking beast, who forms part of nature, and who is subject to the multiplicity of influences of the soil on which he grows and where he lives. This is why a climate, a country, a horizon, a room, are often of decisive importance. The novelist no longer separates his characters from the air which he breathes; he does not describe him in order to exercise his rhetorical powers... he simply notes the material conditions in which he finds his characters at each hour, and in which the facts are produced, in order to be absolutely thorough in order that his inquiry may belong to the world's great whole and reproduce the reality in its entirety. But it is not necessary to carry descriptions to the stage; they are found there naturally. Are not the stage settings a continual description which can be made much more exact and startling than the descriptions in a novel... After the scenery, so surprisingly true, that we have recently seen in our theatres, no one can deny the possibility of producing on the stage the reality of surroundings. It now remains for dramatic authors to utilise this reality, they furnishing the characters and the facts, the scene painters, under their directions, furnishing the descriptions, as exact as shall be necessary. It but remains for a dramatic author to make use of his surroundings as the novelists do, since the latter know how to introduce them and make them real.

I will add that the theatre, being a material reproduction of life, external surroundings have always been a necessity there. In the seventeenth century, however, as nature was not taken into consideration, as man was looked upon only as a purely intellectual being, the scenery was vague... Today the naturalistic movement has brought about a more and more perfect exactness in the stage settings...

I now come to the language. They pretend to say that there is a special style for the stage. They want it to be a style altogether different from the ordinary style of speaking, more sonorous, more nervous, written in a higher key... I would rather see more elasticity, greater naturalness... What I want to hear on the stage is the language as it is spoken every day; if we cannot produce on the stage a conversation with its repetitions, its length and its useless words, at least the movement and the tone of the conversation could be kept; the particular turn of mind of each talker, the reality, in a word, reproduced to the necessary extent... The best style on the stage is that which best sets forth the spoken conversation, which puts the proper word in the right place, giving it its just value. The naturalistic novelists have already written excellent models of dialogue, reduced to strictly useful words.

There now remains but the question of sentimental characters. I do not disguise the fact that it is of prime importance. The public remain cold and irresponsive when their passion for an ideal character... is not satisfied. A play which presents to them but living characters taken from real life looks black and austere to them, when it does not exasperate them. It is on this point that the battle of naturalism rages most fiercely. We must learn to be patient. At the present moment, a secret change is taking place in the public feeling; people are coming little by little, urged onward by the spirit of the century, to admit the bold reproduction of real life, and are even beginning to acquire a taste for it. When they can no longer stand certain falsehoods we shall very nearly have gained our point. Already the novelists' work is preparing the soil in accustoming them to the idea. An hour will strike when it will be sufficient for a master to reveal himself on the stage to find a public ready to become enthusiastic in favour of the truth. It will be a question of tact and strength. They will see then that the highest and most useful lessons will be taught by depicting what is, and not by oft-dinned generalities, nor by airs of bravado, which are chanted merely to tickle our ears.

The two formulas are before us: the naturalistic formula, which makes the stage a study and a picture of real life; and the conventional formula, which makes it purely an amusement for the mind, an intellectual speculation, an art of adjustment and symmetry regulated after a certain code. In fact, it all depends on the idea one has of literature, and of dramatic literature in particular. If we admit that literature is but an inquiry about men and things entered into by original minds, we are naturalists; if we pretend that literature is a framework superimposed upon the truth, that a writer must make use of observation merely to exhibit his power of invention and arrangement, we are idealists and proclaim the necessity of conventionality...

We shall yet have life on the stage as we already have it in the novel. This pretended logic of actual plays, this equality and symmetry obtained by processes of reasoning, which come from ancient metaphysics, will fall before the natural logic of facts and beings such as reality presents to us. Instead of a stage of fabrication we shall have a stage of observation. How will the evolution be brought about? Tomorrow will tell us. I have tried to foresee, but I leave to genius the realisation. I have already given my conclusion: Our stage will be naturalistic, or it will cease to exist...

I am but the most earnest soldier of truth. If I am mistaken, my judgements are there in print; and fifty years from now I shall be judged, in my turn; I may perhaps be accused of injustice, blindness, and useless violence. I accept the verdict of the future.

Taken from: 'Naturalism on the Stage' by Emile Zola in *The Experimental Novel and Other Essays*, translated by B.M. Sherman, New York: Haskell House, 1964, pages 129–157.

Zola's reflections on the crisis in French theatre and his predictions about the inevitability of naturalism were published in 1881. Henrik Ibsen's early social problem plays (A Doll's House *and* Ghosts) *had already scandalised audiences in Norway and in London; and six years later another Scandinavian playwright, August Strindberg, published (in his Preface to* Miss Julie) *a scathing attack on the moribund theatrical climate across Europe. Strindberg picks up many of Zola's concerns and amplifies them in an even more forthright manner. But, whereas Zola offers a general analysis of the literary conditions of his time, Strindberg sets out, in much more specific terms, exactly what he was trying to achieve in his own naturalistic plays.*

5: Author's Preface to *Miss Julie*

Theatre, like religion, is dying out... Supporting this assertion is the serious theatre crisis now prevailing throughout Europe, especially in those bastions of culture that produced the greatest thinkers of the age, England and Germany, where the art of drama, like most of the other fine arts, is dead.

In other countries people have believed it possible to create a new drama, by filling old forms with new contents. For a number of reasons, however, this has failed: in part because there has not been sufficient time to popularise the new ideas, so that the public does not understand the basic questions; in part because partisan politics has stirred up emotions, making dispassionate enjoyment impossible – how can people be objective when their innermost beliefs are offended or when they are subjected in the confines of a theatre to the public pressure of an applauding or hissing audience?; and in part because new forms have not been found for the new contents, so that the new wine has burst the old bottles.

In the following play (ie *Miss Julie*), instead of trying to do anything new – which is impossible – I have simply modernised the form in accordance with demands I think contemporary audiences make upon this art. Toward this end, I have chosen, or let myself be moved by, a theme that can be said to lie outside partisan politics since the problem of social climbing or falling, of higher or lower, better or worse, man or woman, are, have been, and will be of lasting interest. When I took this theme from a true story I heard told some years ago, which made a strong impression on me, I found it appropriate for tragedy, for it still seems tragic to see someone favoured by fortune go under, much more to see a family die out. Perhaps the time will come when we will be so advanced, so enlightened, that we can witness with indifference what now seems the coarse, cynical, heartless dramas life has to offer, when we have closed down those lower, unreliable mechanisms of thought called feelings, because better developed organs of judgement will have found them superfluous and harmful. The fact that the heroine arouses compassion is because we are too weak to resist the fear that the same fate could overtake us. A hypersensitive spectator may not be satisfied with compassion alone, while a man with faith in the future may demand some positive proposals to remedy the evil, in other words, a programme of some kind. But for one thing there is no absolute evil. The fall of one family can mean a chance for another family to rise, and the alternation of rising and falling fortunes is one of life's greatest delights since happiness lies only in comparison. And to the man who wants a programme to remedy the unpleasant fact that the bird of prey eats the dove and the louse eats the bird of prey I ask: why should it be remedied? Life is not so idiotically mathematical that only the great eat the small; it is just as common for a bee to kill a lion or at least drive it mad.

If my tragedy depresses many people, it is their own fault. When we become as strong as the first French revolutionaries, it will afford nothing but pleasure and relief to witness the thinning out in royal parks of over-age, decaying trees that have long stood in the way of others equally entitled to their time in the sun, the kind of relief we feel when we see someone incurably ill die!

Recently, my tragedy *The Father* was criticised for being too sad, as if one should expect cheerful tragedies. People clamour pretentiously for the "joy of life", and theatre managers call for farces, as if the joy of life lay in being silly and depicting people as if they were all afflicted with St Vitus's dance of imbecility. I find the joy of life in its cruel and powerful struggles, and my enjoyment comes from being able to know something, being able to learn something. That is why I have chosen an unusual case, but one from which we can learn much – in a word an exception, but an important exception which proves the rule – though this will probably offend those who love the conventional and predictable. What will next shock simple minds is that I have not motivated the action in a simple way, nor is there a single point of view. Every event in life – and this is a rather new discovery! – is ordinarily the result of a whole series of more or less deep-lying motives. The spectator usually, however, singles out the one that is either easiest for him to understand or is most advantageous to him personally. Take the case of a suicide. "Financial problems," says a businessman. "Unrequited love," says a woman. "Physical illness," says an invalid. "Dashed hopes," says a shipwrecked man. It might be that all or none of these were motives and that the deceased concealed the real motive by advancing a totally different one that would bring the most credit to his memory!

I have motivated Miss Julie's tragic fate by a great number of circumstances: her mother's primary instincts, her father raising her incorrectly, her own nature, and the influence of her fiancé on her weak and degenerate brain. Also, more particularly: the festive atmosphere of midsummer night, her father's absence, her monthly indisposition, her preoccupation with animals, the provocative effect of the dancing, the magical midsummer twilight, the powerfully aphrodisiac influence of flowers, and, finally, the chance that drives the couple together into a room alone – plus the boldness of the aroused man.

My treatment of the subject has thus been neither one-sidedly physiological nor exclusively psychological. I have not put the entire blame on what she inherited from her mother, nor on her monthly indisposition, nor on immorality. I have not even preached morality – this I left to the cook in the absence of a minister.

This multiplicity of motives, it pleases me to assert, is in keeping with the times. And if others have done it before me, then it pleases me that I have not been alone in my "paradoxes", as all discoveries are called.

As for characterisation, I have made my people rather "characterless" for the following reasons:

The word *character* has come to mean many things over the course of time. Originally it must have meant the dominant trait in the soul-complex and was confused with temperament. Later it became the middle-class expression for the automaton, one whose disposition was fixed once and for all or had adapted himself to a particular role in life. In a word, someone who had stopped growing was called a character. In contrast, the person who continued to develop, the skilful navigator on the river of life, sailing not with sheets belayed, but veering before the wind to luff again, was called characterless – in a derogatory sense, of course – because he was so difficult to understand, classify, and keep track of. This bourgeois concept of the immobility of the soul was transferred to the stage, which the bourgeoisie has always dominated. There a character became a man who was ready-made; whenever he appeared, he was drunk or comical or sad. The only thing necessary to characterise him was to give him a physical defect – a clubfoot, a wooden leg, a red nose – or have him repeat an expression such as "that was splendid"... I do not believe in simple, theatrical characters. And an author's summary judgements of people – this one is stupid, that one brutal, this one jealous, that one stingy – should be challenged by naturalists, who know how rich the soul-complex is and realise that "vice" has a reverse side closely resembling virtue.

As modern characters living in an age of transition more compulsively hysterical than the one that preceded it at least, I have depicted my people as more vacillating and disintegrating than their predecessors, a mixture of the old and the new...

My souls (characters) are conglomerates of past and present cultural phases, bits from books and newspapers, scraps of humanity, pieces torn from fine clothes and become rags, patched together as is the human soul...

As for my dialogue, I have broken with tradition somewhat by not making my characters catechists who ask stupid questions in order to elicit clever replies. I have avoided the symmetrical, mathematical, constructed dialogue of French drama and let characters' minds function irregularly, as they do in a real-life conversation, where no topic of discussion is exhausted entirely and one mind by chance finds a cog in another mind in which to engage. Consequently, the dialogue also wanders, presenting material in the opening scenes that is later taken up, reworked, repeated, expanded, and developed, like the theme in a musical composition.

The plot is serviceable enough, and since it really concerns only two people, I have concentrated on them, including only one minor character, the cook, and having the father's unhappy spirit hover over and behind the action. I have done this because I believe that people of today are most interested in the psychological process. Our inquisitive souls are not satisfied just to see something happen; we want to know how it happened. We want to see the strings, the machinery, examine the double-bottomed box, feel for the seam in the magic ring, look at the cards to see how they are marked.

As for the technical aspects of composition, I have experimented with eliminating act divisions. The reason is that I believe our dwindling capacity for accepting illusion is possibly further disturbed by intermissions, during which the spectator has time to reflect and thereby to escape the suggestive influence of the author-hypnotist. My play will probably run an hour and a half, and since people can listen to a lecture, a sermon, or conference discussion for just as long or longer, I imagine that a ninety-minute theatre piece will not be too tiring... My hope for the future is to so educate audiences that they can sit through a one-act play that lasts an entire evening...

As for the scenery, I have borrowed from impressionist painting the device of making a setting appear cut off and asymmetrical, thus strengthening the illusion. When we see only part of a room and a portion of the furniture, we are left to conjecture, that is to say, our imagination goes to work and complements what is seen. I have also profited by doing away with those tiresome exits through doors because scenery doors, made of canvas, wobble at the slightest touch; they cannot even allow a father to express his anger after a bad dinner by going out and slamming the door behind him "so that the whole house shakes". (In the theatre it wobbles). I have also confined the action to one setting, both to allow the characters more time to interact with their environment and to break with the tradition of expensive scenery. With only one setting we should be able to demand that it be realistic, but nothing is more difficult to get a room on stage to look like a room, however easily the scene painter can produce flaming volcanoes and waterfalls. Even if the walls must be of canvas, it is surely time to stop painting shelves and kitchen utensils on them. We have so many other stage conventions in which we are asked to believe, we should not have to strain ourselves trying to believe in painted pots and pans...

Another perhaps necessary innovation is the removal of footlights. The purpose of this lighting from below is said to be to make the actors' faces fatter, but I ask: why must all actors have fat faces? Does not this lighting obliterate many subtleties in the lower part of the face, especially the jaws, distort the shape of the nose, and cast shadows up over the eyes? Even if this were not so, one thing is certain: actors find it so painful for their eyes that they are unable to use them with full expressiveness. Footlights strike the retina in places usually protected... and so we seldom see anything but a crude rolling of the eyes, either to the side or up toward the balconies, exposing the whites. Perhaps this also accounts for the tedious habit, especially common among actresses, of blinking eyelashes. And when anyone on stage wants to speak with his eyes, he must resort to staring straight out, thus breaking the wall of the curtain line and coming into direct contact with the audience. Justly or unjustly, this practice is called "greeting your friends".

Would not sufficiently strong side lighting... provide the actor with a new advantage: the strengthening of mime effects through the most expressive asset in his face – the play of his eyes?

I have no illusions about getting the actor to play for the audience rather than with it, although this would be desirable. I cannot hope to see an actor play with his back to the audience throughout an entire important scene, though I wish very much that crucial scenes were staged, not next to the prompter's box, like duets intended to evoke applause, but in places more appropriate to the action. In other words, I call for no revolution, just small modifications, for to really transform the stage into a room where the fourth wall is removed, and consequently a portion of the furniture faces away from the audience, would probably, for the present, produce a disturbing effect.

When it comes to makeup, I dare not hope to be listened to by the ladies, who would rather be beautiful than believable. But the actor might consider, whether it is really to his advantage when putting on makeup to fix an abstract character, like a mask, on his face. Picture an actor who has put the sharp, charcoal lines of anger on an old man between his eyes and then, with that incensed look, has to smile in response to someone else's line. What a terrible grimace there would be as a result! And how would the false forehead attached to the wig, bald as a billiard ball, wrinkle when the old man got angry?

In a modern psychological drama, where the subtlest movements of the soul must be revealed more through the face than through gesture and sound, it would probably be best to experiment with strong side lighting on a small stage, and with actors wearing no makeup, or at least a minimum of it.

If, in addition, we could avoid having the orchestra visible, its lights disturbing, and the musicians' faces turned towards the audience; if the seating in the auditorium were raised so that eye level for the spectators was higher than the hollow of the actor's knee; if we could get rid of stage boxes (behind bull's-eye openings), with their grinning late arrivals from dinners and supper parties; if we could have complete darkness during performances; and, finally, and most importantly, a *small* stage and a *small* auditorium, then perhaps we might see a new drama arise, or at the very least a theatre that was once again a place of entertainment for educated people. While waiting for this theatre, we will just have to go on writing, preparing the repertoire that will one day be needed.

Here is an attempt! If it fails, there is surely time enough for another!

Taken from: the 'Author's Preface' to *Miss Julie* in *Strindberg: Five Plays*, translated by H.G. Carlson, Berkeley & Los Angeles, California: University of California Press, 1983, pages 63–75.

The great nineteenth century naturalist playwrights (Ibsen and Strindberg amongst them) eventually moved to explore and experiment with more symbolic modes of expression. The symbolist poets also came to prominence during the last two decades of the nineteenth century, and it was not long before the symbolist movement began to make an impact on European theatre.

We can see from Strindberg's comments on scenery and setting that the naturalists were much preoccupied with the accurate reproduction of interiors: furniture; doors that could be opened and closed without making the whole set shake; kitchen utensils. But, as a character in Maeterlinck's 1984 play, L'Interieur, says as he contemplates a young girl's suicide by drowning, "You can't look into the soul as you can into a room". With these words, Maeterlinck's character expresses the symbolists preoccupation with a different kind of interior: the inner life of the human spirit, the soul.

This concern to discover ways in which the soul, and the inner life of the human being, could be presented on stage had already exercised the mind of the great composer of operas, Richard Wagner. In his influential book, The Art-Work of the Future *(1849), Wagner argues that art was the vital expression of **instinctive** life. His goal was the creation of the* gesamkunstwerk *(total art-work) which would bring together music, poetry and the visual arts into a single, harmonious whole. He conceived of a kind of dialogue, half-way between speech and song, which recalled the choral tone of Greek tragedy. In his next book,* Opera and Drama *(1851), Wagner began to turn his thoughts to* *myth as the creation of the instinctive imagination. Thus, the choral and mythic elements associated with the classical Greek drama re-emerge as part of Wagner's early manifestation of symbolist theatre.*

For Wagner, musical drama was the theatre of the future. He dreamed of bringing together the genius of Shakespeare with the genius of Beethoven, resulting in a supreme work of art.

6: The Ideas of Richard Wagner

... Wagner demanded, in the combination of the arts, two main factors: poetry, carried to its utmost limits in drama; and music carried to its utmost limits as the interpreter and deepener of dramatic action... His ideas about music and about drama are almost equally significant and fundamental. We shall be more likely to realise their full meaning if we take them not, as he generally insisted on taking them, together, but, as far as we can, separately; and we will begin, as he began, with the foundation of his scheme, with drama.

Drama, 'the one, indivisible, supreme creation of the mind of man', was... celebrated by the Greeks as a religious festival. Now, as in ancient Greece, the theatre is the chronicle and epitome of the age; but with what a difference! With us, in the most serious European countries, religion is forbidden to be dealt with on the stage... What has killed art in the modern world is commercialism. 'The rulership of public taste in art', says Wagner in *Opera and Drama*, 'has passed over to the person... who orders the art-work for his money, and insists on ever novel variations of his one beloved theme, but at no price a new theme itself; and this ruler and order-giver is the Philistine'. 'I simply take in view', he says in 1878, in his article on 'The Public and Popularity', 'our public art-conditions of the day when I assert that it is impossible for anything to be truly good if it is to be reckoned in advance for presentation to the public, and if this intended presentation rules the author in his sketch and composition of an art-work'. Thus the playwright has to endure 'the sufferings of all the other artists turned into one', because what he creates can only become a work of art by 'entering into open life', that is, by being seen on the stage. 'If the theatre is at all to answer to its high and natural mission it must be completely freed from the necessity of industrial speculation'. For the playwright, therefore, a public is a necessary part of his stock-in-trade. The Greeks had it, supremely; Shakespeare, Moliere had it; but, though Wagner himself

has violently conquered it for music, for drama it still remained uncon-
quered.

Wagner points out the significant fact that from Aeschylus to Moliere,
through Lope de Vega and Shakespeare, the great dramatic poet has
always been himself an actor, or has written for a given company of
actors. He points out how in Paris, where alone the stage has a measure
of natural life, every genre has its theatre, and every play is written for a
definite theatre. Here, then, is the very foundation of the dramatic art,
which is only realised by the complete interdependence of poet and
actor, the poet 'forgetting himself' as he creates his poetry in terms of
living men and women, and the actor divesting himself of self in carrying out the intentions of the poet. Wagner defines the Shakespearian
drama as 'a fixed mimetic improvisation of the highest poetic value'
and he shows how, in order to rise to drama, poetry must stoop to the
stage; it must cease to be an absolute thing, pure poetry, and must
accept aid from life itself, from the actor who realises it according to its
intention. The form of a Shakespearian play would be as unintelligible
to us as that of a Greek play without our knowledge of the stage necessities which shaped both the one and the other. Neither, though both
contain poetry which is supreme as poetry, took its form from poetry;
neither is intelligible as poetic form. The actor's art is like 'the life-dew
in which the poetic aim was to be steeped, to enable it, as in a magic
transformation, to appear as the mirror of life'.

In the Greek play the chorus appeared in the... midst of the audience,
while the personages, masked and heightened, were seen in a ghostly
illusion of grandeur on the stage. Shakespeare's... actors, who acted in
the midst of the audience, had to be absolutely natural if they were not
to be wholly ridiculous. We expect, from his time, no less of nature
from the actor, a power of illusion which must be absolute.

Man interprets or is the ape of nature; the actor is the ape of, and interprets man. He is 'Nature's intermediate link through which that
absolutely realistic mother of all being incites the ideal within us'. And
now Wagner takes his further step from drama into music, which he
justifies, in one place, by representing the mirrored image of life, which
is the play, 'dipped in the magic spring of music, which frees it from all
the realism of matter', and in another place, by the affirmation: 'What
to Shakespeare was practically impossible, namely, to be the actor of all
his parts, the tone-composer achieves with complete certainty, for out
of each executant musician he speaks to us directly'... He imagines the
playwright resenting the intrusion of music, and he asks him in return

of what value can be 'those thoughts and situations to which the lightest and most restrained accompaniment of music should seem importunate and burdensome?'. Could there be a more essential test of drama, or a test more easily applied by a moment's thought? Think of any given play, and imagine a musical accompaniment of the closest or loosest kind. I can hear a music as of Mozart coming up like an atmosphere about Congreve's *Way of the World*, as easily as I can hear Beethoven's *Coriolan* overture leading in Shakespeare's *Coriolanus*. Tolstoy's *Power of Darkness* is itself already a kind of awful tragic music; but would all of Ibsen go quite well to a musical setting?... And remember, rightly or wrongly, Maeterlinck's *Pelleas et Melisande* has only succeeded on the stage since it has been completed by the musical interpretation of Debussy.

The root of all evil in modern art, and especially in the art of drama, Wagner finds to be the fact that 'modern art is a mere product of culture, and not sprung from life itself'. The drama written as literature, at a distance from the theatre, and with only a vague consciousness of the actor, can be no other than a lifeless thing, not answering to any need. The only modern German dramatic work in which there is any vitality, Goethe's *Faust*, springs from the puppet-stage of the people; but German actors are incapable of giving it, for the verse must be spoken with absolute naturalness, and the actor has lost the secret of speaking verse naturally. Thus the actor must be trained; must be taught above all to speak. 'Only actors can teach each other to speak; and they would find their best help in sternly refusing to play bad pieces, that is, pieces which hinder them from entering that ecstasy which alone can ennoble their art.' Wagner is never tired of proclaiming his debt to Wilhelmine Schroder-Devrient, who first inspired in him, he tells us, the desire to write music worthy of her singing. Was her voice so wonderful? 'No', answers Wagner; 'she had no "voice" at all; but she knew how to use her breath so beautifully, and to let a true womanly soul stream forth in such wonderful sounds, that we never thought of either voice or singing... All my knowledge of mimetic art', he goes on to say, 'I owe to this great woman; and through that teaching I can point to truthfulness as the foundation of that art'.

Wagner's best service to drama, in his theories as in his practice, is the insistence with which he has demonstrated the necessary basis of the play in the theatre. 'The thorough "stage-piece"', he says, 'in the modernest of senses, would assuredly have to form the basis, and the only sound one, of all future dramatic efforts'. And not merely does he see that the play must be based upon the theatre, but that the particular play must be conditioned by the particular theatre. No one has seen more clearly the necessity of 'tempering the artistic ends to be realised' to the actual 'means of execution' which are at the artist's disposal. 'Even the scantiest means are equal to realising an artistic aim, provided it rules itself for expression through these means.' Thus there is not one among his many plans of theatre reform which has not some actual building in view, whether the Vienna Opera-house there visibly before him, or that *Buhnenfestspielhaus* which he saw no less clearly in his mind before the first stone of the foundation had been set in the earth at Bayreuth. And whenever he speaks of the theatre it is as a kind of religious service and with a kind of religious awe, which, in one of his essays, burst out into a flame of warning exultation. 'If we enter a theatre', he says gravely, 'with any power of insight, we look straight into a daemonic abyss of possibilities, the lowest as well as the highest... Here in the theatre the whole man, with his highest and lowest passions, is placed in terrifying nakedness before himself, and by himself is driven to quivering joy, to surging sorrow, to hell and heaven...'.

Taken from: 'The Ideas of Richard Wagner' by Arthur Symons in *The Theory of the Modern Stage*, edited by Eric Bentley, Harmondsworth: Penguin, 1990, pages 309–314.

Wagner's thinking about the theatre of the future inspired the philosopher, Friedrich Nietzsche, to enquire into the origins of Greek tragedy. In Nietzsche's view, all of Western Europe's significant theatrical achievements can be traced back to the classical Greek drama of the fifth century BC. He therefore sought the origins of tragedy in the ritual celebrations of Dionysus, the central figure in a mystical, orgiastic cult. Dionysius represents the emotional and irrational side of the human being. In Apollo, on the other hand, the thinking, rational side of the human personality is to be found. According to Nietzsche, in the book he dedicated to Wagner, great drama results from the conflict between Dionysus and Apollo; advancing Wagner's thinking, he argued that music was Dionysiac while drama was Apollonian.

7: The Birth of Tragedy

... Only the Greeks can teach us what such a sudden miraculous birth of tragedy means to the heart and soul of a nation...

Tragedy absorbs the highest orgiastic music and in so doing consummates music. But then it puts beside it the tragic myth and the tragic hero. Like a mighty titan, the tragic hero shoulders the whole Dionysiac world and removes the burden from us. At the same time, tragic myth, through the figure of the hero, delivers us from our avid thirst for earthly satisfaction and reminds us of another existence and a higher delight. For this delight the hero readies himself, not through his victories but through his undoing. Tragedy interposes a noble parable, *myth*, between the universality of its music and the Dionysiac disposition of the spectator and in so doing creates the illusion that music is but a supreme instrument for bringing to life the plastic world of myth. By virtue of this noble deception it is now able to move its limbs freely in dithyrambic dance and to yield without reserve to an orgiastic abandon, an indulgence which, without this deception it could not permit itself. Myth shields us from music while at the same time giving music its maximum freedom. In exchange, music endows the tragic myth with a convincing metaphysical significance, which the unsupported word and image could never achieve, and, moreover, assures the spectator of a supreme delight – though the way passes through annihilation and negation, so that he is made to feel that the very womb of things speaks audibly to him.

Since, in the last passage, I have tentatively set forth a difficult notion, which may not be immediately clear to many, I would now invite my friends to consider a particular instance that is within our common experience and which may support my general thesis... 'How can anyone experience the third act of *Tristan and Isolde*, apart from either word or image, simply as the movement of a mighty symphony, without exhausting himself in the overstretching of his soul's pinions?' How is it possible for a man who has listened to the very heartbeat of the world-will and felt the unruly lust for life rush into all the veins of the world, now as a thundering torrent and now as a delicately foaming brook – how is it possible for him to remain unshattered? How can he bear, shut in the paltry glass bell of his individuality, to hear the echoes of innumerable cries of weal and woe sounding out of the 'vast spaces of cosmic night', and not wish, amidst these pipings of metaphysical pastoral, to flee incontinent to his primordial home? And yet the reception of such a work does not shatter the recipient, the creation of it the creator. What are we to make of this contradiction?

It is at this point that the tragic myth and the tragic hero interpose between our highest musical excitement and the music, giving us a parable of those cosmic facts of which music alone can speak directly. And yet, if we reacted wholly as Dionysiac beings, the parable would fail entirely of effect, and not for a single moment would it distract our attention from the reverberations of the *universalia ante rem*. But now the Apollonian power, bent upon reconstituting the nearly shattered individual, asserts itself, proffering the balm of a delightful illusion. Suddenly we see only Tristan, lying motionless and torpid, and hear him ask, 'Why does that familiar strain waken me?'. And what before had seemed a hollow sigh echoing from the womb of things now says to us simply, 'Waste and empty the sea'. And where, before, we had felt ourselves about to expire in a violent paroxysm of feeling, held by a most tenuous bond to this our life, we now see only the hero, mortally wounded yet not dying, and hear his despairing cry: 'Too long, even in death, and be unable to die for longing!'… No matter how deeply pity moves us, that pity saves us from the radical 'pity of things', even as the parable of myth saves us from the direct intuition of the cosmic idea, as idea and word save us from the undammed pouring forth of the unconscious will. It is through the workings of that marvellous Apollonian illusion that even the realm of sound takes plastic shape before us, as though it were only a question of the destinies of Tristan and Isolde, molded in the finest, most expressive material.

Thus the Apollonian spirit rescues us from the Dionysiac universality and makes us attend, delightfully, to individual forms. It focuses our pity on these forms and so satisfies our instinct for beauty, which longs for great and noble embodiments. It parades the images of life before us and incites us to seize their ideational essence. Through the massive impact of image, concept, ethical doctrine, and sympathy, the Apollonian spirit wrests man from his Dionysiac self-destruction and deceives him as to the universality of the Dionysiac event. It pretends that he sees only the particular image, eg Tristan and Isolde, and that the music serves only to make him see it more intensely. What could possibly be immune from the salutary Apollonian charm, if it able to create in us the illusion that Dionysus may be an aid to Apollo and further enhance his effects? that music is at bottom a vehicle for Apollonian representations? In the pre-established harmony obtaining between the consummate drama and its music, that drama reaches an acme of visual power unobtainable to the drama of words merely. As we watch the rhythmically moving characters of the stage merge with the independently moving lines of melody into a single curving line of motion, we experience the most delicate harmony of sound and visual movement. The relationships of things thus become directly available to the senses, and we realise that in these relationships the essence of a character and of a melodic line are simultaneously made manifest. And as music forces us to see more, and more inwardly than usual, and spreads before us like a delicate tissue the curtain of the scene, our spiritualised vision beholds the world of the stage at once infinitely expanded and illuminated from within. What analogue could the verbal poet possibly furnish – he who tries to bring about that inward expansion of the visible stage world, its inner illumination, by much more indirect and imperfect means, namely word and concept? But, once musical tragedy has appropriated the word, it can at the same time present the birthplace and subsoil of the word and illuminate the genesis of the word from within. And yet it must be emphatically stated that the process I have described is only a marvellous illusion, by whose effects we are delivered from the Dionysiac extravagance and onrush. For, at bottom, music and drama stand in the opposite relation: music is the true idea of the cosmos, drama but a reflection of that idea. The identity between the melodic line and the dramatic character, between relations of harmony and character, obtains in an opposite sense from what we experience when we witness a musical tragedy. However concretely we move, enliven and illuminate the characters from within, they will always remain mere appearance, from which there is no gateway leading to the true heart of reality. But music addresses us from that centre; and though countless appearances were to file past that same music, they would never exhaust its nature but remain external replicas only. Nothing is gained for the understanding of either music or drama by resorting to that popular and utterly false pair of opposites, body and soul...

If our analysis has shown that the Apollonian element in tragedy has utterly triumphed over the Dionysiac quintessence of music, bending the latter to its own purposes – which are to define the drama completely – still an important reservation must be made. At the point that matters most the Apollonian illusion has been broken through and destroyed. This drama which deploys before us, having all its movements and characters illuminated from within by the aid of music – as though we witnessed the coming and going of the shuttle as it weaves the tissue – this drama achieves a total effect quite beyond the scope of any Apollonian artifice. In the final effect of tragedy the Dionysiac element triumphs once again: its closing sounds are such as were never heard in the Apollonian realm. The Apollonian illusion reveals its identity as the veil thrown over the Dionysiac meanings for the duration of the play, and yet the illusion is so potent that at its close the

Apollonian drama is projected into a sphere where it begins to speak with Dionysiac wisdom, thereby denying itself and its Apollonian concreteness. The difficult relations between the two elements in tragedy may be symbolised by a fraternal union between the two deities: Dionysus speaks the language of Apollo, but Apollo, finally, the language of Dionysus; thereby the highest goal of tragedy and of art in general is reached.

Taken from: *The Birth of Tragedy* by Friedrich Nietzsche, translated by Francis Golffing, New York: Anchor Books, 1956, pages 126–131.

Despite the enthusiastic endorsement of Nietzsche, Wagner's ideas were never fully realised in practice, although they continued to be influential within the symbolist movement. Essentially, symbolism exerted its most significant impact on poetry, but many of the French symbolist poets were fascinated by the possibilities that theatre and performance offered. Charles Baudelaire, an important forerunner of symbolism, was familiar with melodrama and he carried out a number of theatrical experiments which mixed together modern poetry and popular theatre forms; poetry in performance became an important feature of literary life in the Paris of the 1880s and 1890s. But, the first manifesto of theatrical symbolism was produced by Gustave Kahn in 1889. Wagner's influence is readily discernible.

8: The First Manifesto of the Theatrical Symbolism

Kahn's main idea for the new theatre is a synthesis of poetry and various theatrical genres. To make the argument, he reaches into the past to point to theatrical traditions that he sees as relevant for the symbolists. Greek tragedies, plays by Corneille and Shakespeare, and Goethe's *Faust* are for him examples of when poetry was an integral part of theatre. But Kahn does not argue for the adaptation of past poetic modes. For him the new symbolist drama must be based on the same principles as the new poetry. And since he advocated the poetic concept of verbal orchestration, it meant the application of the principles of music to drama and theatre. Kahn also made interesting staging suggestions for this new poetic drama, some of which found its way into theatrical productions: the elimination of crowd scenes (to be played with three actors at most with few or no speeches, functioning almost as a set...); (stylised and declamatory) acting; and the dependence of gesture on (speech).

Besides poetic drama, Kahn proposed four other theatrical genres: character comedy in an undefined setting, modern and clownish pantomime, circus comedy and visual spectacle. The visual spectacle, a series of short and expressive images, was supposed to be a form of text-less theatre. In these 'poems of form and colour', language would be unnecessary, since it would only hinder the evocation of mystery. A more elaborate form of this visual spectacle could be based on an existing text, such as De Quincey's *Confessions of an Opium Eater.* Kahn did not intend to stage these texts, but rather from these texts to inspire a visual evocation which would be of a completely different character than one based on language. The modern and clownish pantomime was based on the acrobatic pantomimes popular from around the 1870s until the end of the century... These pantomimes incorporated into a dramatic structure, usually melodrama or farce, a series of circus techniques (acrobatics, juggling, clowning) and spectacular scenic trickwork. All of the rescue scenes, escapes and chases were done by acrobats which heightened their effectiveness. Kahn intended to keep the basic format of these pantomimes but wanted their texts to be written by poets.

Taken from: *Symbolist Theatre: The Formation of an Avant-Garde* by Frantisek Deak, Baltimore and London: John Hopkins University Press, 1993, pages 29–30.

Villiers de l'Isle-Adam, a little-known French playwright, wrote six plays which ranged from old-fashioned romantic dramas to the kind of plays which Gustave Kahn was advocating in his manifesto. His play, Axel, was enormously popular, probably because it reflected his interest in the occult and mysticism. The play dramatises the poet's sense of disconnection and alienation from society, and compares it with the solitary, contemplative life of the mystic. In this way, the artist is seen to be a special kind of person who is able to perceive secrets and mysteries that are denied to the rest of us.

The symbolist poet, Stéphane Mallarmé, saw himself very much in these terms: a solitary figure in the Parisian literary world, hopelessly at odds with the society around him. Mallarmé imagined that his own presence as a writer could be eliminated from his works, so all that would remain would be the text that was produced. Each Tuesday, Mallarmé would invite a select few acquaintances to his home where he would read his poetry and speak about his ideas. The element of performance at these gatherings testifies to Mallarmé's interest in theatre. He conceived a performance of one of his works, called The

Book. *For many, this performance provided a model for symbolist theatre; and, from Mallarmé's manuscript, a hypothetical perform-ance of* The Book *can be constructed.*

9: Mallarmé's *The Book*: The Ideal Symbolist Theatre

The performance would take place in Mallarmé's apartment. The set consists of a lacquered library against the wall, facing the audience, and a single electrical lamp under which he would read/perform the text. The beginning of the performance is announced by the sound of a bell. Slightly bent, Mallarmé the performer/operator enters through the space between the chairs. He greets the audience on the right and glances to the other side. He approaches the lacquered library, which has a set of six pigeon holes on a diagonal. Each hole contains five easily visible sheets. He takes one sheet from each pigeon hole, flips through them and begins to read and comment on them. He shows some sheets physically to the audience... After he goes through all the sheets, which would take him about forty-five minutes, Mallarmé pretends to finish the performance and brusquely leaves, taking with him sheets of 'The Book'. But after a fifteen minute intermission he returns, again announced by the sound of a bell. He goes directly to the lacquered library and redistributes the sheets in a different order, then in another forty-five minute performance another series of confronta-tions between various texts takes place.

Mallarmé's performance is planned in such detail that one can speak of a complete *mise en scene*. As a performer, he would complete certain tasks: choose the sheets, shuffle them, and then confront the possibili-ties that the juxtaposed sheets provided. This suggests an aspect of improvisation on the part of the performer. Since the performance of 'The Book' was intended for an elite audience to show the inner work-ings of the structure (of Mallarmé's text), theatre then is the supreme genre that reveals the final reality... The performer/operator would demonstrate in the performance the inner workings of the structure. As the two sheets of 'The Book' confronted each other, the performer/operator would act as a link between them and the meaning they imply.

Now, when the function of the performer/operator is described, we can identify it as acting. Mallarmé is an actor because he... transforms himself into the impersonal performer/operator. Acting... is defined, first of all, by the act of self-transformation; the transformation of the ambiguous personality into the formalised work of art. Mallarmé's impersonal performance style is radical and admittedly on the boundaries of acting, reading and oratory, but since it involves both self-transformation and public presence, it can be defined as acting.

Taken from: *Symbolist Theatre: The Formation of an Avant-Garde* by Frantisek Deak, Baltimore and London: John Hopkins University Press, 1993, pages 89–90.

By insisting that the writer (and any intentions s/he might have) is disconnected from the writing, Mallarmé is suggesting that the structure of the text in performance is what carries some concealed, mystical meaning; and that the role of the performer/operator is simply to bring together the pages from The Book *so that this meaning can be revealed to a select few.*

It is obvious that this kind of private performance before a carefully selected, invited audience can have no great appeal beyond the confines of the walls of a literary salon. But some extremely influential theatre practitioners attempted to realise a symbolist theatre that would have much broader audience appeal. Vsevolod Myerhold mounted a symbolist production of Ibsen's Hedda Gabler *in 1906.*

10: Meyerhold's Symbolist *Hedda Gabler*

The theatre has chosen to use a single backdrop as a setting... The costumes, instead of being naturalistically authentic, are intended to harmonise as colour-masses with the background and present a synthesis of the style of the period and society in question, the subjective view of the designer, and the... simplified representation of the character's inner nature. For instance, ... the costume of Tesman corresponds to no definite fashion; although it is somewhat reminiscent of the 1820s, one is reminded equally of the present day. But in giving Tesman a loose jacket with sloping shoulders, an exaggeratedly wide tie and broad trousers tapering sharply towards the bottoms, the designer... has sought to express the essence of 'Tesmanism', and this has been stressed by the director in the way that Tesman is made to move and in the position he occupies in the general composition. To harmonise with the colours of (the) painted back-cloth, (the costume designer) has dressed Tesman in dull grey. The walls... are all light blue; the tapestry that covers an entire wall and the open-work screens on either side of the stage are painted in pale gold autumnal tints. The colours of the costumes harmonise against themselves and with the background: green (Hedda), brown (Lovborg), pale pink (Thea), dark grey (Brack). The table in the centre, the pouffes and the long narrow divan standing against the wall under the tapestry are all covered in light blue fabric flecked with gold to give it the appearance of brocade. A huge armchair stage-left is covered entirely in white fur, the same fur being used to cover part of the divan; a white grand piano projects from behind the screen stage-right and has the same blue and gold fabric hanging from it…

The stage comprises a broad, shallow, strip, 10 metres wide and 4 metres deep, higher than the usual stage level and as close as possible to the footlights. The lighting is from the footlights and overhead battens…

What is the significance of this setting which gives the impression of a vast, cold blue, receding expanse but which actually looks like nothing whatsoever? Why are both sides (where there should be doors – or nothing, if the room is to continue offstage) hung with gold net cur-tains where the actors make their exits and their entrances? Is life really like this? Is this what Ibsen wrote?

Life is not like this, and this is not what Ibsen wrote. *Hedda Gabler* on the stage of the Dramatic Theatre is *stylized*. Its aim is to reveal Ibsen's play to the spectator by employing unfamiliar new means of scenic presentation, to create an impression of (but only an *impression*) of a vast, cold blue, receding expanse. Hedda is visualised in cool blue tones against a golden autumnal background. Instead of autumn being depicted outside the window where the blue sky is seen, it is suggested by the pale golden tints of the tapestry, the upholstery and the curtains. The theatre is attempting to give primitive, purified expression to what it senses behind Ibsen's play: a cold, regal, autumnal Hedda.

Precisely the same aims are adopted in the actual production of the play, in the work of the director with the actors. Rejecting authenticity, the customary 'lifelikeness', the theatre seeks to submit the spectator to its own inspiration by adopting a barely mobile, stylised method of pro-duction with a minimum of mime and gesture, with the emotions concealed and manifested externally only by a brief lighting of the eyes or a flickering smile.

The wide stage, its width emphasised by its shallowness, is particularly suited to widely spaced groupings and the director takes full advantage of this by making two characters converse from opposite sides of the stage (the opening of the scene between Hedda and Lovborg in Act

Three), by seating Hedda and Lovborg wide apart on the divan in Act Two. Sometimes... there may seem to be little justification in this, but it arises from the director's attempt to create an overall impression of cold majesty. The huge armchair covered in white fur is meant as a kind of throne for Hedda; she plays the majority of her scenes either on it or near it. The spectator is intended to associate Hedda with her throne and carry away this combined impression in his memory.

Brack is associated with (a) pedestal bearing (a) large vase. He sits by it with one leg crossed over the other and clasps his hands round his knee, keeping his eyes fixed on Hedda throughout their keen sparkling battle of wits. He reminds one of a faun. Admittedly, Brack moves about the stage and occupies other positions (as do Hedda and the other characters) but it is the pose of a faun by the pedestal that one associates with him – just as one associates the throne with Hedda...

The first scene between Lovborg and Hedda... takes place at the table. Throughout the entire scene they sit side by side, tense and motionless, looking straight ahead. Their soft, disquieting words fall rhythmically from lips which seem dry and cold. Before them stand two glasses and a flame burns beneath the punch bowl (Ibsen stipulates Norwegian 'cold punch'). Not once throughout the entire long scene do they alter the direction of their gaze or their pose. Only on the line 'Then you too have a thirst for life!' does Lovborg make a violent motion towards Hedda, and at this point the scene comes to an abrupt conclusion.

Realistically speaking, it is inconceivable that Hedda and Lovborg should play the scene in this manner, that any two real people should ever converse like this. The spectator hears the lines as though they were being addressed directly at him; before him the whole time he sees the faces of Hedda and Lovborg, observes the slightest change of expression; behind the monotonous dialogue he senses the concealed inner dialogue of presentiments and emotions that are incapable of expression in mere words. The spectator may forget the actual words exchanged by Hedda and Lovborg, but he cannot possibly forget the overall impression that the scene creates.

Taken from: *Meyerhold: A Revolution in Theatre* by Edward Braun, London: Methuen, 1995, pages 52–55.

From this description it is possible to imagine how difficult it would be to watch this production, with minimal movement and lines spoken in a monotone. The public reaction to Meyerhold's production was predictably cold and even those critics who found something to admire were forced to admit that it was somewhat at odds with what Ibsen intended. Meyerhold's attempt to realise a symbolist theatre was quickly abandoned.

The most concerted attempt to formulate a truly symbolist theatre is to be found in the theatrical experiments of Edward Gordon Craig, and particularly in his book, On the Art of the Theatre.

11: Craig and Symbolism

Symbolism is really quite proper; it is sane, orderly, and it is universally employed. It cannot be called theatrical if by theatrical we mean something flashy, yet it is the very essence of the Theatre if we are to include its art among the fine arts.

Symbolism is nothing to be afraid of – it is delicacy itself; it is understood as easily by the ploughman or sailor as by kings and other men in high places. Some there are who are afraid of symbolism, but it is difficult to discover why, and these persons sometimes grow very indignant and insinuate that the reason why they dislike symbolism is because there is something unhealthy or harmful about it. "We live in a realistic age", is the excuse they put forward. But they cannot explain how it is that they make use of symbols to tell us this, nor how it is that all their lives they have made use of this same thing that they find so incomprehensible.

For not only is Symbolism at the roots of all art, it is at the root of all life, it is only by means of symbols that life becomes possible for us; we employ them all the time.

The letters of the alphabet are symbols… The numerals are symbols, and chemistry and mathematics employ them. All the coins of the world are symbols and businessmen rely upon them. The crown and the sceptre of the kings and the tiara of the popes are symbols. The works of poets and painters, of architects and sculptors, are full of symbolism; Chinese, Egyptian, Greek, Roman, and the modern artists since the time of Constantine have understood and valued the symbol. Music only became intelligible through the employment of symbols and is symbolic in its essence. All forms of salutation and leave-taking are symbolic and employ symbols, and the last act of affection rendered to the dead is to erect a symbol over them.

I think there is no one who should quarrel with Symbolism – nor fear it.

Taken from: *On the Art of the Theatre* by Edward Gordon Craig, London: Heinemann, 1968, pages 293–294.

Craig saw this work as a manifesto for the art of the future and proposed that the theatre needed a new kind of theatre artist. This artist would need to be a visionary, capable of bringing together all of the diverse elements of theatre into one harmonious whole. Craig offers his ideas in the form of a dialogue between an expert (the stage director, ie the 'the artist of the theatre') and a playgoer.

12: Craig on the Artist of the Theatre

STAGE DIRECTOR

... Tell me, do you know what is the Art of the Theatre?

PLAYGOER

To me it seems that Acting is the Art of the Theatre.

STAGE DIRECTOR

Is a part, then, equal to the whole?

PLAYGOER

No, of course not. Do you, then, mean that the play is the Art of the Theatre?

STAGE DIRECTOR

A play is a work of literature, is it not? Tell me, then, how one art can possibly be another?

PLAYGOER

Well, then, if you tell me that the Art of the Theatre is neither the acting nor the play, then I must come to the conclusion that it is the scenery and the dancing. Yet I cannot think you will tell me this is so.

STAGE DIRECTOR

No: the Art of the Theatre is neither acting nor the play, it is not scene or dance, but it consists of all the elements of which these things are composed: action, which is the very spirit of acting; words, which are the body of the play; line and colour, which are the very heart of the scene; rhythm, which is the very essence of dance.

PLAYGOER

Action, words, line, colour, rhythm? And which of these is all-important to the art?

STAGE DIRECTOR

One is no more important than the other, no more than one colour is more important to a painter than another, or one note more important than another to a musician. In one respect, perhaps, action is the most valuable part. Action bears the same relation to the Art of the Theatre as drawing does to painting, and melody does to music. The Art of the Theatre has sprung from action – movement – dance.

PLAYGOER

I always was led to suppose that it had sprung from speech, and that the poet was the father of the theatre.

STAGE DIRECTOR

This is the common belief, but consider it for a moment. The poet's imagination finds voice in words, beautifully chosen; he then either recites or sings these words to us, and all is done. That poetry, sung or recited, is for our ears, and, through them, for our imagination. It will not help the matter if the poet shall add gesture to his recitation or to his song; in fact, it will spoil all.

PLAYGOER

Yes, that is clear to me. I quite understand that the addition of gesture to a perfect lyric poem can but produce an inharmonious result. But would you apply the same argument to dramatic poetry?

STAGE DIRECTOR

Certainly I would. Remember I speak of a dramatic poem, not of a drama. The two things are separate things. A dramatic poem is to be read. A drama is not to be read, but to be seen upon the stage. Therefore gesture is a necessity to a drama, and it is useless to a dramatic poem. It is absurd to talk of these two things, gesture and poetry, as having any-thing to do with one another. And now, just as you must not confound the dramatic poem with the drama, neither must you confound the dramatic poet with the dramatist. The first writes for the reader, or listener, the second writes for the audience of a theatre. Do you know who was the father of the dramatist?

PLAYGOER

No, I do not know, but I suppose he was the dramatic poet.

STAGE DIRECTOR

You are wrong. The father of the dramatist was the dancer. And now tell me from what material the dramatist made his first piece?

PLAYGOER

I suppose he used words in the same way as the lyric poet.

STAGE DIRECTOR

Again you are wrong, and that is what every one else supposes who has not learnt the nature of dramatic art. No; the dramatist made his first piece by using action, words, line, colour, and rhythm, and making his appeal to our eyes and ears by a dexterous use of these five factors.

PLAYGOER

And what is the difference between the work of the first dramatists and that of the modern dramatists?

STAGE DIRECTOR

The first dramatists were children of the theatre. The modern dramatists are not. The first dramatist understood what the modern dramatist does not yet understand. He knew that when he and his fellows appeared in front of them the audience would be more eager to *see* what he would *do* than to *hear* what he might *say*. He knew that the eye is more swiftly and powerfully appealed to than any other sense; that it is without question the keenest sense of the body of man. The first thing which he encountered on appearing before them was many pairs of eyes, eager and hungry. Even the men and women sitting so far from him that they would not always be able to hear what he might say, seemed quite close to him by reason of the piercing keenness of their questioning eyes. To these, and all, he spoke either in poetry or prose, but always in action: in poetic action which is dance, or in prose action which is gesture.

PLAYGOER

I am very interested, go on, go on.

STAGE DIRECTOR

No – rather let us pull up and examine our ground... People will still flock to see, not to hear, plays... Audiences have not altered. They are there with their thousand pairs of eyes, just the same as of old. And this is all the more extraordinary because the playwrights and the plays have altered. No longer is the play a balance of actions, words, dance and scene, but it is either all words or all scene. Shakespeare's plays, for instance, are a very different thing to the less modern miracle and mystery plays, which were made entirely for the theatre... the Masques – the Pageants – these were light and beautiful examples of the Art of the Theatre... The theatre must not forever rely upon having a play to perform, but must in time perform pieces of its own art...

Taken from: *On the Art of the Theatre* by Edward Gordon Craig, London: Heinemann, 1968, pages 137–144.

There is no denying the significance of symbolism as a major movement in European poetry, but none of the attempts to transfer the principles of symbolism to the theatre (including Craig's own) were entirely successful. And so the question presents itself: why bother studying symbolism as a theatrical movement at all?

*Although it could never be argued that symbolism constituted a major theatrical movement in its own right, it did give rise to a number of other artistic movements which had a major impact on western theatre. One of the most important of these was **expressionism**, which blossomed in Germany between 1910 and 1920 (and, later, in the USA in the work of Eugene O'Neill); and, in France in 1927, Antonin Artaud formed the* Alfred Jarry Theatre *(with Roger Vitrac and Robert Aron) with the declared aim of realising a **surrealist** theatre. This was a short-lived venture and the quest for a surrealist theatre was quickly abandoned; but, out of the ashes of the* Alfred Jarry Theatre, *Artaud went on to develop his thinking in a series of essays which were published under the title of* The Theatre and Its Double. *Artaud argued that if theatre is the double of life, then life is the double of theatre; it is not the responsibility of art to passively mirror the world. For Artaud, as it had been for Wagner and Craig before him, art constitutes a higher form of reality, with real life only existing as an imperfect copy of what art expresses symbolically. In 1935, Artaud set out to realise the theoretical ideas set out in his essays. He set up his* Theatre of Cruelty.

13: Artaud's *Theatre of Cruelty* : First Manifesto

We cannot continue to prostitute the idea of a theatre whose only value lies in its agonising magic relationship to reality and danger. Put in this way, the problem of theatre must arouse universal attention, it being understood that theatre, through its physical aspect and because it requires *spatial expression* (the only real one in fact) allows the sum total of the magic means in the arts and words to be organically active... From the foregoing it becomes apparent that theatre will never recover its own specific powers of action until it has also recovered its own language.

That is, instead of harking back to texts regarded as sacred and definitive, we must first break theatre's subjugation to the text and rediscover the idea of a kind of unique language somewhere in between gesture and thought.

We can only define this language as expressive, dynamic, spatial potential in contrast with expressive spoken dialogue potential. Theatre can still derive possibilities for extension from speech outside words, the development in space of its dissociatory, vibratory action on the sensibility. We must take inflection into account here, the particular way a word is pronounced, as well as the visual language of things (audible, sound-language aside), also movement, attitudes and gestures, providing their meanings are extended, their features connected even as far as those signs, making a kind of alphabet out of those signs. Having become conscious of this spatial language, theatre owes it to itself to organise these shouts, sounds, lights and onomatopoeic language, creating true hieroglyphs out of characters and objects, making use of their symbolism and interconnections in relation to every organ and on all levels.

Therefore we must create word, gesture and expressive metaphysics, in order to rescue theatre from its human, psychological prostration. But all this is of no use unless a kind of real metaphysical temptation, invoking certain unusual notions, lies behind such an effort, for the latter by their very nature cannot be restricted or even formally depicted. These ideas on Creation, Growth and Chaos are all of a cosmic order, giving us an initial idea of a field now completely alien to theatre. They can create a kind of thrilling equation between Man, Society, Nature and Objects...

Here we ought to mention the purely physical side of this language, that is to say all the ways and means it has of acting on our sensibility.

It would be futile to say it calls on music, dancing, mime or mimicry. Obviously it uses moves, harmonies, rhythms, but only up to the point where they can co-operate in a kind of pivotal expression without favouring any particular art. However this does not mean that it omits ordinary facts and emotions, but it uses them as a springboard in the same way as HUMOUR as DESTRUCTION can serve to reconcile laughter with our reasoning habits.

But this tangible, objective theatre language captivates and bewitches our senses by using a truly Oriental concept of expression. It runs through our sensibility. Abandoning our Western ideas of speech, it turns words into incantation. It expands the voice. It uses vocal vibrations and qualities, wildly trampling them underfoot. It pile-drives sounds. It aims to exalt, to benumb, to bewitch, to arrest our sensibility. It liberates a new lyricism of gestures which because it is distilled and spatially amplified, ends by surpassing the lyricism of words. Finally it breaks away from language's intellectual subjugation by conveying the sense of a new, deeper intellectualism hidden under these gestures and signs and raised to the dignity of special exorcisms.

For all this magnetism, all this poetry, all these immediately bewitching means would be to no avail if they did not put the mind bodily on the track of something, if true theatre could not give us the sense of a creation where we are in possession of only one of its facets, while its completion exists on other levels.

And it makes no difference whether these other levels are really conquered by the mind, that is to say by our intellect, for this curtails them, a pointless and meaningless act. What matters is that our sensibility is put into a deeper, subtler state of perception by assured means, the very object of magic and ritual, of which theatre is only a reflection.

Technique

The problem is to turn theatre into a function in the proper sense of the word, something as exactly localised as the circulation of our blood through our veins, or the apparently chaotic evolution of dream images in the mind, by an effective mix, truly enslaving our attention.

Theatre will never be itself again, that is to say, will never be able to form truly illusive means, unless it provides the audience with truthful distillations of dreams where its taste for crime, its erotic obsessions, its savageness, its fantasies, its utopian sense of life and objects, even its cannibalism, do not gush out on an illusory, make-believe, but on an inner level.

In other words, theatre ought to pursue a re-examination not only of all aspects of an inner world, that is to say man viewed metaphysically, by every means at its disposal. We believe that only in this way will we be able to talk about imagination's rights in the theatre once more. Neither Humour, Poetry, or Imagination mean anything unless they re-examine man organically through anarchic destruction, his ideas on reality and his poetic position in reality, generating stupendous flights of forms constituting the whole show.

But to view theatre as a second-hand psychological or moral operation and to believe dreams themselves only serve as a substitute is to restrict both dreams' and theatre's deep poetic range. If theatre is as bloody and as inhuman as dreams, the reason for this is that it perpetuates the metaphysical notions in some Fables in a present-day, tangible manner, whose atrocity and energy are enough to prove their origins and intentions in fundamental first principles rather than to reveal and unforgettably tie down the idea of continual conflict within us, where life is continually lacerated, where everything in creation rises up and attacks our condition as created beings.

This being so, we can see that by its proximity to the first principles poetically infusing it with energy, this naked theatre language, a non-virtual but real language using man's nervous magnetism, must allow us to transgress the ordinary limits of art and words, actively, that is to say magically to produce a kind of total creation *in real terms*, where man must reassume his position between dreams and events.

Subjects

We do not mean to bore the audience to death with transcendental cosmic preoccupations. Audiences are not interested whether there are profound clues to the show's thought and action, since in general this does not concern them. But these must still be there and that concerns us.

*

The Show: Every show will contain physical, objective elements perceptible to all. Shouts, groans, apparitions, surprise, dramatic moments of all kinds, the magic beauty of the costumes modelled on certain ritualistic patterns, brilliant lighting, vocal, incantational beauty, attractive harmonies, rare musical notes, object colours, the physical rhythm of the moves whose build and fall will be wedded to the beat of moves familiar to all, the tangible appearance of new, surprising objects, masks, puppets many feet high, abrupt lighting changes, the physical action of lighting stimulating heat and cold, and so on.

Staging: This archetypal theatre language will be formed around staging not simply viewed as one degree of refraction of the script on stage, but as the starting point for theatrical creation. And the old duality between author and producer will disappear, to be replaced by a kind of single Creator using and handling this language, responsible both for the play and the action.

Stage Language: We do not intend to do away with dialogue, but to give words something of the significance they have in dreams.

Moreover we must find new ways of recording this language, whether these ways are similar to musical notation or to some kind of code.

As to ordinary objects, or even the human body, raised to the dignity of signs, we can obviously take our inspiration from hieroglyphic characters not only to transcribe these signs legibly so they can be reproduced at will, but to compose exact symbols on stage that are immediately legible.

Then again, this coding and musical notation will be valuable as a means of vocal transcription.

Since the basis of this language is to initiate a special use of inflexions, these must take up a kind of balanced harmony, a subsidiary exaggeration of speech able to be reproduced at will.

Similarly the thousand and one facial expressions caught in the form of masks, can be listed and labelled so they may directly and symbolically participate in this tangible stage language, independently of their particular psychological use.

Furthermore, these symbolic gestures, masks, postures, individual or group moves, whose countless meanings constitute an important part of the tangible stage language of evocative gestures, emotive arbitrary postures, the wild pounding of rhythms and sound, will be multiplied, added to by a kind of mirroring of the gestures and postures, consisting of an accumulation of all the impulsive gestures, all the abortive postures, all the lapses in the mind and of the tongue in which speech's incapabilities are revealed, and on occasion we will not fail to turn to this stupendous existing wealth of expression.

Besides, there is a tangible idea of music where sound enters like a character, where harmonies are cut in two and become lost precisely as words break in.

Connections, levels, are established between one means of expression and another; even lighting can have a predetermined intellectual meaning.

Musical Instruments: These will be used as objects, as part of the set.

Moreover they need to act deeply and directly on our sensibility through the senses, and from the point of view of sound they invite research into utterly unusual sound properties and vibrations which present-day musical instruments do not possess, urging us to use ancient or foreign instruments or to invent new ones. Apart from music, research is also needed into instruments and appliances based on special refining and new alloys which can reach a new scale in the octave and produce an unbearably piercing sound or noise.

Lights – Lighting: The lighting equipment currently in use in the theatre is no longer adequate. The particular action of light on the mind comes into play, we must discover oscillating lighting effects, new ways of diffusing lighting in waves, sheet lighting like a flight of fire-arrows. The colour scale of the equipment currently in use must be revised from start to finish. Fineness, density and opacity factors must be reintroduced into lighting so as to produce special tonal properties, sensations of heat, cold, anger, fear and so on.

Costume: As to costume, without believing there can be any uniform stage costume that would be the same for all plays, modern dress will be avoided as much as possible not because of a fetishistic superstition for the past, but because it is perfectly obvious certain age-old costumes of ritual intent, although they were once fashionable, retain a revealing beauty and appearance because of their closeness to the traditions which gave rise to them.

The Stage – The Auditorium: We intend to do away with stage and auditorium, replacing them by a kind of single, undivided locale without any partitions of any kind and this will become the very scene of the action. Direct contact will be established between the audience and the show, between actors and audience, from the very fact that the audience is seated in the centre of the action, is encircled and furrowed by it. This encirclement comes from the shape of the house itself.

Abandoning the architecture of present-day theatres, we will rent some kind of barn or hanger rebuilt along lines culminating in the architecture of some churches, holy places, or certain Tibetan temples.

This building will have special interior height and depth dimensions. The auditorium will be enclosed with four walls stripped of any ornament, with the audience seated below, in the middle, on swivelling chairs allowing them to follow the show taking place around them. In effect, the lack of a stage in the normal sense of the word will permit the action to extend itself to the four corners of the auditorium. Special places will be set aside for the actors and action in the four cardinal points of the hall. Scenes will be acted in front of washed walls designed to absorb light. In addition, overhead galleries run right around the circumference of the room as in some Primitive paintings. These galleries will enable actors to pursue one another from one corner of the hall to the other as needed, and the action can extend in all directions at all perspective levels of height and depth. A shout could be transmitted by word of mouth from one end to the other with a succession of amplifications and inflexions. The action will unfold, extending its trajectory from floor to floor, from place to place, with sudden outbursts flaring up in different spots like conflagrations. And the show's truly illusive nature will not be empty words any more than the action's direct, immediate hold on the spectators. For the action, diffused over a vast area, will require the lighting for one scene and the varied lighting for a performance to hold the audience as well as the characters – and physical lighting methods, the thunder and wind whose repercussions will be experienced by the spectators, will correspond with several actions at once, several phases in one action with the characters clinging together like swarms, will endure all the onslaughts of the situations and the external assaults of weather and storms.

However, a central site will be retained which, without acting as a stage properly speaking, enables the body of the action to be concentrated and brought to a climax whenever necessary.

Objects – Masks – Props: Puppets, huge masks, objects of strange proportions appear by the same right as verbal imagery, stressing the physical aspect of all imagery and expression – with the corollary that all objects requiring a stereotyped physical representation will be discarded or disguised.

Décor: No décor. Hieroglyphic characters, ritual costume, thirty foot high effigies of King Lear's beard in the storm, musical instruments as tall as men, objects of unknown form and purpose are enough to fulfil this function.

Topicality: But, you may say, theatre so removed from life, facts or present-day activities... news and events, yes! Anxieties, whatever is profound about them, the prerogative of the few, no! In the *Zohar*, the story of the Rabbi Simeon is as inflammatory as fire, as topical as fire.

Works: We will not act written plays but will attempt to stage productions straight from subjects, facts or known words. The type and lay-out of the auditorium itself governs the show as no theme, however vast, is precluded to us.

Show: We must revive the concept of an integral show. The problem is to express it, spatially nourish and furnish it like tap-holes drilled into a flat wall of rock, suddenly generating geysers and bouquets of stone.

The Actor: The actor is both a prime factor, since the show's success depends on the effectiveness of his acting, as well as a kind of neutral, pliant factor since he is rigorously denied any individual initiative. Besides, this is a field where there are no exact rules. And there is a wide margin dividing a man from an instrument, between an actor required to give nothing more than a certain number of sobs and one who has to deliver a speech using his own powers of persuasion.

Interpretation: The show will be coded from start to finish, like a language. Thus no moves will be wasted, all obeying a rhythm, every character being typified to the limit, each gesture, feature and costume to appear as so many shafts of light.

Cinema: Through poetry, theatre contrasts pictures of the unformulated with the crude visualisation of what exists. Besides, from an action viewpoint, one cannot compare a cinema image, however poetic it may be, since it is restricted by the film, with a theatre image which obeys all life's requirements.

Cruelty: There can be no spectacle without an element of cruelty as the basis of every show. In our present degenerative state, metaphysics must be made to enter the mind through the body.

The Audience: First, this theatre must exist.

Programme: Disregarding the text, we intend to stage:

1. An adaptation of a Shakespearian work, absolutely consistent with our present confused state of mind, whether this be an apocryphal Shakespeare play such as *Arden of Feversham* or another play from the period.
2. A very free poetic play by Leon-Paul Fargue.
3. An excerpt from *The Zohar*, the story of Rabbi Simeon which has the ever-present force and virulence of a conflagration.
4. The story of Bluebeard, reconstructed from historical records, containing a new concept of cruelty and eroticism.
5. The Fall of Jerusalem, according to the Bible and the Scriptures. On the one hand a blood red colour flowing from it, that feeling of running wild and mental panic visible even in daylight. On the other hand, the prophet's metaphysical quarrels, with the dreadful intellectual agitation they cause, their reaction rebounding bodily on the King, the Temple, the Masses and Events.
6. One of the Marquis de Sade's tales, its eroticism transposed, allegorically represented and cloaked in the sense of a violent

externalisation of cruelty, masking the remainder.

7.   One or more Romantic melodramas where the unbelievable will be an active, tangible, poetic factor.

8.   Buchner's *Woyzeck* in a spirit of reaction against our principles, and as an example of what can be drawn from an exact text in terms of the stage.

9.   Elizabethan theatre works stripped of the lines, retaining only their period machinery, situations, character and plot.

Taken from: 'The Theatre of Cruelty: First Manifesto' in *The Theatre and Its Double* by Antonin Artaud, New York: Grove, 1958, pages 68–78.

We have already noted how naturalism has its origins in Aristotle's concept of imitation, or mimesis, which dates back to fifth century BC Athens and we have just seen how profoundly Greek tragedy influenced the symbolist movement in the theatre. Many theatre historians have written about the important social function served by the classical Greek drama in the political and social life of the Athenian city-state; so we now turn to an examination of drama's social function.

14: Classical Drama and Democracy

Tragedy is the characteristic creation of Athenian democracy; in no form of art are the inner conflicts of its social structure so directly and clearly to be seen as in this. The externals of its presentation to the masses were democratic, but its content, the heroic sagas with their tragic-heroic outlook on life, was aristocratic. From the first, it is addressed to a more numerous and varied audience than those distin-guished companies at whose tables the heroic… epics were recited. On the other hand, it unquestionably propagates the standards of the great-hearted individual… It owed its origin to the separation of the choir-leader from the choir, which turned collective performance of songs into dramatic dialogue – and this separation by itself marks a trend towards individualism; but, on the other hand, tragedy depends for its effect upon the existence of a sense of community in the audi-ence and upon its appreciation by large masses who are on the same level – it can only really succeed as a mass experience. But even the audience of Greek tragedy is to some extent a selected one; at best it consists of all the free citizens and is not much more democratic in its composition than are the classes which govern the city-state. And the spirit in which the official theatre is managed is far less popular even than the make-up of its public, for the masses that form the audience do not have any decisive influence upon the choice of plays or the distribution of the prizes. The former is naturally in the hands of the rich citizens who have to pay the cost of the performances as a 'special contribution'; the latter is in the hands of judges, who are nothing more than executive officials of the council and whose judgement is determined primarily by political considerations. The free entrance and the payment of allowances for time spent at the theatre (advantages which are customarily praised as the last word in democracy) are just the very factors which completely prevented the masses from having any influence on the fate of the theatre. Only a theatre whose very existence depends upon the shillings paid for entry will really be a 'people's theatre'. The notion, popularised by classicist and romanticist critics alike, of the Attic theatre as the perfect example of a national theatre, and of its audiences as realising the ideal of a whole people united in support of art, is a falsification of historical truth. The festival theatre of Athenian democracy was certainly no 'people's theatre' – the German classical and romantic theorists could only represent it as such, because they conceived the theatre to be an educational institution. The true 'people's theatre' of ancient times was the mime, which received no subvention from the state, in consequence did not have to take instructions from above, and so worked out its artistic principles simply and solely from its own immediate experience with the audiences. It offered its public not artistically constructed dramas of tragi-heroic manners and nobles or even sublime personages, but short, sketchy, naturalistic scenes with subjects and persons drawn from the most trivial, everyday life. Here at last we have to do with an art which has been created not merely for the people but also in a sense by the people. Mimers may have been professional actors, but they remained popular and had nothing to do with the educated elite, at least until the mime came into fashion. They came from the people, shared their taste and drew upon their common sense. They wanted neither to educate nor instruct, but to entertain their audience. This unpretentious, naturalistic, popular theatre was the product of a much longer and more continuous development, and had to its credit a much richer and more varied output than the official classical theatre; unfortunately, this output has been almost completely lost to us. Had these plays been preserved, we should certainly take quite a different view of Greek literature and probably of the whole of Greek culture from that taken now. The mime is not merely much older than tragedy; it is probably prehistoric in origin and directly connected with the symbolic-magical dances, vegetation rites, hunting magic, and the cult of the dead. Tragedy originates in the dithyramb, an undramatic art form, and to all appearances it got its dramatic form – involving the transformation of the performers into fictitious personages and the transposition of the epic past into the present – from the mime. In tragedy, the dramatic element certainly always remained subordinate to the lyrical and didactic element; the fact that the chorus was able to survive shows that tragedy was not exclusively concerned to get dramatic effect and so was intended to serve other ends than mere entertainment.

In its festival theatre, the city-state possessed its most valuable instrument of propaganda, and certainly would not think of letting a poet do what he liked with it. The tragedians are in fact state-bursars and state-purveyors – the state pays them for the plays that are performed, but naturally does not allow pieces to be performed that would run counter to its policy or the interests of the governing classes. The tragedies are frankly tendentious and do not pretend to be otherwise. They treat questions of current politics and centre around problems that all have a direct or indirect connection with the burning questions of the day... The punishment of Phrynicus, alleged to have been due to his choosing the recent capture of Miletus as the subject of a play, was no doubt due to the fact that his treatment of this subject did not conform to official views, not to his having confounded politics with art. Nothing could have been less in line with contemporary conceptions of art than that the theatre should be divorced from all relations to life and politics. Greek tragedy was in the strictest sense 'political drama'; the finale of *Eumenides*, with its fervent prayers for the prosperity of the Attic state, betrays the main purpose of the piece. This political control of the theatre brought back to currency the old view that the poet is guardian of a higher truth and an educator who leads his people up to a higher plane of humanity. Through the performance of tragedies on the state-ordained festivals and the circumstances that tragedy came to be looked upon as the authoritative interpretation of the national myths, the poet once more attains to a position almost equivalent to that of the priestly seer of prehistoric times.

Taken from: *The Social History of Art, Vol I: From Prehistoric Times to the Middle Ages* by Arnold Hauser, London: Routledge & Kegan Paul, 1962, pages 75–78.

According to Hauser then, Greek tragedy functioned as a form of state propaganda, with the rich citizens and officials of the city-state keeping strict control of the plays which were allowed to be performed at the festivals. Historically, the political nature of theatre has often been submerged. This is often the case when theatre operates, as in the case of Greek tragedy, in the interests of governments and officialdom. Existing side by side with the 'official' theatres, we usually find a popular people's theatre, like the Greek mime, which operates oppositionally – representing and expressing the interests of the masses against those of their rulers. In the early part of the twentieth century, Bertold Brecht formulated his own openly political, oppositional, epic theatre.

15: Theatre for Pleasure or Theatre for Instruction
The epic theatre

Many people imagine that the term 'epic theatre' is self-contradictory, as the epic and dramatic ways of narrating a story are held, following Aristotle, to be basically distinct. The difference between the two forms was never thought simply to lie in the fact that the one is performed by living beings while the other operates via the written word; epic works such as those of Homer and the medieval singers were at the same time theatrical performances, while dramas like Goethe's *Faust* and Byron's *Manfred* are agreed to have been more effective as books. Thus even by Aristotle's definition the difference between the dramatic and epic forms was attributed to their different methods of construction, whose laws were dealt with by two different branches of aesthetics. The method of construction depended on the different way of presenting the work to the public, sometimes via the stage, sometimes through a book; and independently of that there was the 'dramatic element' in epic works and the 'epic element' in dramatic. The bourgeois novel in the last century developed much that was 'dramatic', by which was meant the strong centralisation of the story, a momentum that drew the separate parts into a common relationship. A particular passion of utterance, a certain emphasis on the clash of forces are hallmarks of the 'dramatic'. The epic writer Doblin provided an excellent criterion when he said that with an epic work, as opposed to a dramatic, one can as it were take a pair of scissors and cut it into individual pieces, which remain fully capable of life.

This is no place to explain how the opposition of epic and dramatic lost its rigidity after having long been held to be irreconcilable. Let us just point out that the technical advances alone were enough to permit the stage to incorporate an element of narrative in its dramatic productions. The possibility of projections, the greater adaptability of the stage due to mechanisation, the film, all completed the theatre's equipment, and did so at a point where the most important transactions between people could no longer be shown simply by personifying the motive forces or subjecting the characters to invisible metaphysical powers.

To make these transactions intelligible the environment in which the people lived had to be brought to bear in a big and 'significant' way.

This environment had of course been shown in the existing drama, but only as seen from the central figure's point of view, and not as an independent element. It was defined by the hero's reactions to it. It was seen as a storm can be seen where one sees the ships on a sheet of water unfolding their sails, and the sails filling out. In the epic theatre it was to appear standing on its own.

The stage began to tell a story. The narrator was no longer missing, along with the fourth wall. Not only did the background adopt an attitude to the events on stage – by big screens recalling other simultaneous events elsewhere, by projecting documents which confirmed or contradicted what the characters said, by concrete and intelligible figures to accompany abstract conversations, by figures and sentences to support mimed transactions whose sense was unclear – but the actors too refrained from going over wholly into their role, remaining detached from the character they were playing and clearly inviting criticism of him.

The spectator was no longer in any way allowed to submit to an experience uncritically (and without practical consequences) by means of simple empathy with the characters in a play. The production took the subject-matter and the incidents shown and put them through a process of defamiliarisation: the defamiliarisation that is necessary to all understanding. When something seems 'the most obvious thing in the world' it means that any attempt to understand the world has been given up.

What is 'natural' must have the force of what is startling. This is the only way to expose the laws of cause and effect. People's activity must simultaneously be so and be capable of being different.

It was all a great change.

The dramatic theatre's spectator says: Yes, I have felt like that too – Just like me – It's only natural – It'll never change – The sufferings of this man appal me, because they are inescapable – That's great art; it all seems the most obvious thing in the world – I weep when they weep, I laugh when they laugh.

The epic theatre's spectator says: I'd never have thought it – That's not the way – That's extraordinary, hardly believable – It's got to stop – The sufferings of this man appal me, because they are unnecessary – That's great art: nothing obvious in it – I laugh when they weep, I weep when they laugh.

The instructive theatre

The stage began to be instructive.

Oil, inflation, war, social struggles, the family, religion, wheat, the meat market, all became subjects for theatrical representation. Choruses enlightened the spectator about facts unknown to him. Films showed a montage of events from all over the world. Projections added statistical material. And as the 'background' came to the front of the stage so people's activity was subjected to criticism. Right and wrong courses of action were shown. People were shown who knew what they were doing, and others who did not. The theatre became an affair for philosophers, but only for such philosophers as wished not just to explain the world but also to change it. So we had philosophy, and we had instruction. And where was the amusement in all that? Were they sending us back to school, teaching us to read and write? Were we supposed to pass exams, work for diplomas?

Generally there is felt to be a very sharp distinction between learning and amusing oneself. The first may be useful, but only the second is pleasant. So we have to defend the epic theatre against the suspicion that it is a highly disagreeable, humourless, indeed strenuous affair.

Well: all that can be said is that the contrast between learning and amusing oneself is not laid down by divine rule; it is not one that has always been and must continue to be.

Undoubtedly there is much that is tedious about the kind of learning familiar to us from school, from our professional training, etc. But it must be remembered under what conditions and to what end that takes place.

It is really a commercial transaction. Knowledge is just a commodity. It is acquired in order to be resold. All those who have grown out of going to school have to do their learning virtually in secret, for anyone who admits that he still has something to learn devalues himself as a man whose knowledge is inadequate. Moreover the usefulness of learning is very much limited by factors outside the learner's control. There is unemployment, for instance, against which no knowledge can protect one. There is the division of labour, which makes generalised knowledge unnecessary and impossible. Learning is often among the concerns of those whom no amount of concern will get any forwarder. There is not much knowledge that leads to power, but plenty of knowledge to which only power can lead.

Learning has a very different function for different social strata. There are strata who cannot imagine any improvement in conditions: they find the conditions good enough for them. Whatever happens to oil they will benefit from it. And: they feel the years beginning to tell. There can't be all that many years more. What is the point of learning a lot now? They have said their final word: a grunt. But there are also strata 'waiting their turn' who are discontented with conditions, have a vast interest in the practical side of learning, want at all costs to find out where they stand, and know that they are lost without learning; these are the best and keenest learners. Similar differences apply to countries and peoples. Thus the pleasure of learning depends on all sorts of things; but none the less there is such a thing as pleasurable learning, cheerful and militant learning.

If there was not such amusement to be had from learning the theatre's whole structure would unfit it for teaching.

Theatre remains theatre even when it is instructive theatre, and in so far as it is good theatre it will amuse.

Theatre and knowledge

But what has knowledge got to do with art? We know that knowledge can be amusing, but not everything that is amusing belongs to the theatre.

I have often been told, when pointing out the invaluable services that modern knowledge and science, if properly applied, can perform for art and specifically for theatre, that art and knowledge are two estimable but wholly distinct fields of human activity. This is a fearful truism, of course, and it as well to agree quickly that, like most truisms, it is perfectly true. Art and science work in quite different ways: agreed. But, bad as it may sound, I have to admit that I cannot get along as an artist without the use of one or two sciences… and… that I look askance at all sorts of people who I know do not operate on the level of scientific understanding… In my view the great and complicated things that go on in the world cannot be adequately recognised by people who do not use every possible aid to understanding.

Let us suppose that great passions or great events have to be shown which influence the fate of nations. The lust for power is nowadays held to be such a passion. Given that a poet 'feels' this lust and wants to have someone strive for power, how is he to show the exceedingly complicated machinery within which the struggle for power nowadays takes place? If his hero is a politician, how do politics work? If he is a businessman, how does business work? And yet there are writers who find business and politics nothing like so passionately interesting as the individual's lust for power. How are they to acquire the necessary knowledge? They are scarcely likely to learn enough by going round and keeping their eyes open, though even then it is more than they would get by just rolling their eyes in an exalted frenzy. The foundation of a paper like the *Volkischer Beobachter* or a business like Standard Oil is a pretty complicated affair, and such things cannot be conveyed just like that. One important field for the playwright is psychology. It is taken for granted that a poet, if not an ordinary man, must be able without further instruction to discover the motives that lead a man to commit murder; he must be able to give a picture of a murderer's mental state 'from within himself'. It is taken for granted that one only has to look inside oneself in such a case; and then there's always one's imagination... There are various reasons why I can no longer surrender to this agreeable hope of getting a result quite so simply. I can no longer find in myself all those motives which the press or scientific reports show to have been observed in people. Like the average judge when pronouncing sentence, I cannot without further ado conjure up an adequate picture of a murderer's mental state. Modern psychology, from psychoanalysis to behaviourism, acquaints me with facts that lead me to judge the case quite differently, especially if I bear in mind the findings of sociology and do not overlook economics and history. You will say: but that's getting complicated. I have to answer that it *is* complicated. Even if you let yourself be convinced, and agree with me that a large slice of literature is exceedingly primitive, you may still ask with profound concern: won't an evening in such a theatre be a most alarming affair? The answer to that is: no.

Whatever knowledge is embodied in a piece of poetic writing has to be wholly transmuted into poetry. Its utilisation fulfils the very pleasure that the poetic element provokes. If it does not at the same time fulfil that which is fulfilled by the scientific element, none the less in an age of great discoveries and inventions one must have a certain inclination to penetrate deeper into things – a desire to make the world controllable – if one is to be sure of enjoying its poetry.

Is the epic theatre some kind of 'moral institution'?

According to Friedrich Schiller the theatre is supposed to be a moral institution. In making this demand it hardly occurred to Schiller that by moralising from the stage he might drive the audience out of the theatre. Audiences had no objection to moralising in his day. It was only later that Friedrich Nietzsche attacked him for blowing a moral trumpet. To Nietzsche any concern with morality was a depressing affair; to Schiller it seemed thoroughly enjoyable. He knew of nothing that could give greater amusement and satisfaction than the propagation of ideas. The bourgeoisie was setting about forming the ideas of the nation.

Putting one's house in order, patting oneself on the back, submitting one's account, is something highly agreeable. But describing the collapse of one's house, having pains in the back, paying one's account, is indeed a depressing affair, and that was how Friedrich Nietzsche saw things a century later. He was poorly disposed towards morality, and thus towards the previous Friedrich too.

The epic theatre was likewise often objected to as moralising too much. Yet in the epic theatre moral arguments only took second place. Its aim was less to moralise than observe. That is to say it observed, and then the thick end of the wedge followed: the story's moral. Of course we cannot pretend that we started our observations out of a pure passion for observing and without any more practical motive, only to be completely staggered by their results. Undoubtedly there were some painful discrepancies in our environment, circumstances that were barely tolerable and this not merely on account of moral considerations. It is not only moral considerations that make hunger, cold and oppression hard to bear. Similarly the object of our inquiries was not just to arouse moral objections to such circumstances (even though they could easily be felt – though not by all the audience alike; such objections were seldom for instance felt by those who profited by the circumstances in question) but to discover means for their elimination. We were not in fact speaking in the name of morality, but in that of the victims. These truly are two distinct matters, for the victims are often told that they ought to be contented with their lot, for moral reasons. Moralists of this sort see man as existing for morality, not morality for man. At least it should be possible to gather from the above to what degree and in what sense the epic theatre is a moral institution.

Can epic theatre be played anywhere?

Stylistically speaking, there is nothing all that new about the epic theatre. Its expository character and its emphasis on virtuosity bring it close to the old Asiatic theatre. Didactic tendencies are to be found in the medieval mystery plays and the classical Spanish theatre, and also in the theatre of the Jesuits.

These theatrical forms corresponded to particular trends of their time, and vanished with them. Similarly the modern epic theatre is linked with certain trends. It cannot by any means be practised universally. Most of the great nations today are not disposed to use the theatre for ventilating their problems. London, Paris, Tokyo and Rome maintain their theatres for quite different purposes. Up to now favourable circumstances for an epic and didactic theatre have only been found in a few places and for a short period of time. In Berlin Fascism put a very definite stop to the development of such a theatre.

It demands not only a certain technological level but a powerful movement in society which is interested to see the vital questions freely aired with a view to their solution, and can defend this interest against every contrary trend.

The epic theatre is the broadest and most far-reaching attempt at large-scale modern theatre, and it has all those immense difficulties to overcome that always confront the vital forces in the sphere of politics, philosophy, science and art.

Taken from: 'Theatre for Pleasure or Theatre for Instruction' by Bertolt Brecht in *Brecht on Theatre*, **edited by John Willett, London: Eyre Methuen, 1964, pages 70–76.**

On a number of occasions during this section, we have come across the idea of theatre as a mirror reflecting life. However, from the preceding extract, it will be apparent that the mirror metaphor is inadequate when we come to consider Brecht's epic theatre; the following short extract offers a more appropriate conception.

16: The Mirror and the Dynamo

Brecht's mature aesthetic... presents us... with the problem of the relationship between Art and Nature, known in aesthetics as the Aristotelian question of mimesis...From the very beginning of *Poetics*... Aristotle defines most poetry... as mimesis...

The changing fortunes in the use and abuse of mimesis... would... explain why Brecht persisted in calling his dramaturgy 'non-Aristotelian'...

By the nineteenth century, bourgeois aesthetics had wholly forgotten the traditional implications of mimesis – reacting with a sterile denial of any relation between art and nature. In most of the nineteenth and in the early twentieth century, it rested on the twin axioms of *individualism* – conceiving the world from the individual as the ultimate reality, and *illusionism* – taking for granted that an artistic representation in some mystic way directly reproduces or 'gives' man and his world. Against this, Brecht took up the position of productive *critique*, showing the world as changeable... conceiving the world as a process... keeping in mind the possibility and necessity of change. Art is not a *mirror* which reflects the truth existing outside the artist; art is not a static presentation of a given Nature in order to gain the audience's empathy: Brecht sees art as a *dynamo*, an artistic and scenic vision which penetrates Nature's possibilities, which finds out the laws of its... processes, and makes it possible for critical understanding to intervene into them... Art... is experimental, testing its own presuppositions – in theatre, by feedback from the effect in practice of its text and performance. Seeing the world as sets of changing possibilities, it is a reflection *on*, not *of* nature - including human nature as it is developing within history...

The 'mirroring' attitude corresponds to the alienated reality which was characteristic of the nineteenth century, but which lives tenaciously (among other places) on all the Broadways and *boulevards* of the world. The 'dynamic' attitude corresponds to the twentieth-century tendencies toward de-alienation, although some of its champions may also be found in a long tradition: since, say, Epicurus and Lucretius, and including, notably, isolated oppositional figures in the nineteenth century such as Marx, Buchner and Rimbaud – all of them, logically enough, Brecht's favourites...

Taken from: 'The Mirror and the Dynamo' by Darko Suvin in *Tulane Drama Review,* *No 37,* **1968, pages 58–61.**

The overall social function of Brechtian theatre is perhaps best summed up in the words of Edward Bond's poem.

17: On Leaving the Theatre

Do not leave the theatre satisfied
Do not be reconciled

Have you been entertained?
Laughter that's not also an idea
Is cruel

Have you been touched?
Sympathy that's not also action
Corrodes

To make the play the writer used god's scissors
Whose was the pattern?
The actors rehearsed with care
Have they moulded you to their shape?
Has the lighting man blinded you?
The designer dressed your ego?

You cannot live on our wax fruit
Leave the theatre hungry
For change

Taken from: *Theatre Poems and Songs* by Edward Bond, London: Eyre Methuen, 1978, page 5.

Part Three: Acting

18: Hamlet's Advice to the Players

Speak the speech, I pray you, as I pronounced it to you – trippingly on the tongue; but if you mouth it, as many of your players do, I had as lief the town-crier had spoke my lines, Nor do not saw the air too much with your hand, thus, but use all gently; for in the very torrent, tempest, and as I may say the whirlwind of your passion, you must acquire and beget a temperance that may give it smoothness. O, it offends me to the soul to hear a robustious, periwig-pated fellow tear a passion to tatters, to very rags, to split the ears of the groundlings, who for the most part are capable of nothing but inexplicable dumb shows and noise. I would have such a fellow whipped for o'e'doing Termagant. It out-Herods Herod. Pray you avoid it...

Be not too tame, neither; but let your own discretion be your tutor. Suit the action to the word, the word to the action, with this special obser-vance: that you o'erstep not the modesty of nature. For anything so overdone is from the purpose of playing, whose end, both at the first and now, was and is to hold as 'twere the mirror up to nature, to show virtue her own feature, scorn her own image, and the very age and body of the time his form and pressure. Now this overdone, or come tardy off, though it make the unskilful laugh, cannot but make the judicious grieve; the censure of the which one must in your allowance o'erweigh a whole theatre of others. O, there be players that I have seen play, and heard others praise, and that highly, not to speak it profanely, that neither having the accent of Christians nor the gait of Christian, pagan, nor no man, have so strutted and bellowed that I have thought some of nature's journeymen had made men, and not made them well, they imitated humanity so abominably...

And let those that play your clowns speak no more than is set down for them; for there be of them that will themselves laugh to set on some quantity of barren spectators to laugh too, though in the mean time some necessary question of the play be then to be considered. That's villainous, and shows a most pitiful ambition in the fool that uses it.

Taken from: *Hamlet* by William Shakespeare, Act III, scene ii, lines 1–45.

These words of advice, spoken by Hamlet to the Player King, are generally thought to provide us with important clues about the performance style favoured by Shakespeare and his company, The King's Men. The key line in Hamlet's speech is: 'O'erstep not the modesty of nature'. We can, I think, take this as a plea for a 'natural' style of acting.

Each successive generation of actors believes, of course, that it has developed a style more natural than the one that went before. Sarah Siddons, the great actress of the late-eighteenth/early-nineteenth centuries, was universally praised for her natural ease with which she conveyed emotion. According to Thomas Campbell, in his Life of Mrs Siddons, *she was always 'guiltless of ever overstepping the modesty of nature to produce stage-effect'.*

But, by modern standards, the acting of someone as recent as Henry Irving (at the end of the nineteenth century) would seem to us to be highly exaggerated and declamatory. With the coming of the realist plays of Ibsen, Strindberg and Chekhov, a much more 'natural', true-to-life approach was required. It was left to Konstantin Stanislavski to formulate the principles of the acting style which was to become the norm for realist acting during the twentieth century. Stanislavski's approach is set out in three books: An Actor Prepares; Building a Character; *and* Creating a Role. *In the first of these, he uses the example of Tommaso Salvini, an actor much admired by Stanislavski, to examine the* **art** *of acting.*

19: When Acting is an Art

Salvini said: "The great actor should be full of feeling, and especially he should feel the thing he is portraying. He must feel an emotion not only once or twice while he is studying his part, but to a greater or lesser degree every time he plays it…" Unfortunately this is not within our control. Our subconscious is inaccessible to our consciousness. We cannot enter into that realm. If for any reason we do penetrate into it, then the subconscious becomes conscious and dies.

The result is a predicament; we are supposed to create under inspiration; only our subconscious gives us inspiration; yet we apparently can use this subconscious only through our consciousness which kills it.

Fortunately there is a way out. We find the solution in an oblique instead of a direct approach. In the soul of a human being there are certain elements which are subject to consciousness and will. These accessible parts are capable in turn of acting on psychic processes that are involuntary.

To be sure, this calls for an extremely complicated creative work. It is carried on in part under the control of our consciousness, but a much more significant proportion is subconscious and involuntary.

To rouse your subconscious to creative work there is a special technique. We must leave all that is in the fullest sense subconscious to nature, and address ourselves to what is within our reach. When the subconscious, when intuition, enters into our work we must know how not to interfere.

One cannot always create subconsciously and with inspiration. No such genius exists in the world. Therefore our art teaches us first of all to create consciously and rightly, because that will best prepare the way for the blossoming of the subconscious, which is inspiration. The more you have of conscious creative moments in your role the more chance you will have of a flow of inspiration.

"You may play well or you may play badly; the important thing is that you should play truly," wrote Shchepkin...

To play truly means to be right, logical, coherent, to think, strive, feel and act in unison with your role.

If you take all these internal processes, and adapt them to the spiritual and physical life of the person you are representing, we call that living the part. This is of supreme significance in creative work. Aside from the fact that it opens up avenues for inspiration, living the part helps the artist to carry out one of his main objectives. His job is not to present merely the external life of the character. He must fit his own human qualities to the life of this other person, and pour into it all of his own soul. The fundamental aim of our art is the creation of this inner life of a human spirit, and its expression in an artistic form.

That is why we begin by thinking about the inner side of a role, and how to create its spiritual life through the help of the internal process of living the part. You must live it by actually experiencing feelings that are analogous to it, each and every time you repeat the process of creating it...

Our subconscious power cannot function without... our conscious technique. It is only when an actor feels that his inner and outer life on the stage is flowing naturally and normally, in the circumstances that surround him, that the deeper sources of his subconscious gently open, and from them come feelings we cannot always analyse. For a shorter or longer space of time they take possession of us whenever some inner instinct bids them. Since we do not understand this governing power, and cannot study it, we actors call it simply nature.

But if you break the laws of normal organic life, and cease to function rightly, then this highly sensitive subconscious becomes alarmed, and withdraws. To avoid this, plan your role consciously at first, then play it truthfully. At this point realism and even naturalism in the inner preparation of a part is essential, because it causes your subconscious to work and induces outbursts of inspiration...

Our aim is not only to create the life of the human spirit, but also to 'express it in a beautiful, artistic form'. An actor is under the obligation to live his part inwardly, and then to give his experience an external embodiment...

Taken from: *An Actor Prepares* by Konstantin Stanislavski, translated by Elizabeth Hapgood, London: Geoffrey Bles, 1948, pages 13–15.

An Actor Prepares *takes the form of a working textbook in which a fictional director, Tortsov (who is really Stanislavski), is teaching a group of students who are just setting out on their actor-training. The enthusiastic student who keeps a record of Tortsov's training programme represents the younger Stanislavski who, years before, had been working out the methods which came to form the heart of his system.*

20: The Functions of *If*

...(Tortsov) told me Maria had just inherited a fortune! That she had taken this apartment, and is celebrating her good luck by a housewarming, to which she has invited all her fellow students... But the apartment is very chilly... Can some wood for an open fire be found?

Some sticks might be borrowed from a neighbour. A little fire is started, but it smokes badly, and must be put out. Meanwhile it has grown late. Another fire is started, but the wood is green, and will not burn. In another minute the guests will be here.

'Now,' he continued, 'let me see what you would do if my supposed facts were true.'

When it was all over, the Director said: 'Today I can say that you acted with a motive. You have learned that *all action in the theatre must have an inner justification, be logical, coherent and real*. Second: *if* acts as a lever to lift us out of the world of actuality into the realm of imagination.'

Today the Director proceeded to enumerate the various functions of *if*.

'The word has a peculiar quality, a kind of power which you sensed, and which produced in you an instantaneous, inner stimulus'...

'With this special quality of *if*,' explained the Director, 'nobody obliges you to believe or not believe anything. Everything is clear, honest and above-board. You are given a question, and you are expected to answer it sincerely and definitely.

'Consequently, the secret of the effect of *if* lies first of all in the fact that it does not use... force, or make the artist do anything. On the contrary, it reassures him through its honesty, and encourages him to have confidence in a supposed situation. That is why... the stimulus was produced so naturally.

'This brings me to another quality. *It arouses an inner and real activity*, and does this by natural means...

'This important characteristic of *if* brings it close to one of the fundamentals of our school of acting – *activity in creativeness and art*.'

*

'...Analogous feelings... draw you close to the character.

'To achieve this kinship between the actor and the person he is portraying add some concrete detail which will fill out the play, giving it point and absorbing action. The circumstances which are predicted on *if* are taken from sources near to your own feelings, and they have a powerful influence on the inner life of an actor. Once you have established this contact between your life and your part, you will find that inner... stimulus. Add a whole series of contingencies based on your own experience in life, and you will see how easy it will be for you sincerely to believe in the possibility of what you are called upon to do on the stage.

'Work out an entire role in this fashion, and you will create a whole new life.

'The feelings aroused will express themselves in the acts of this imaginary person had he been placed in the circumstances made by the play.

'Are they conscious or unconscious?' I asked.

'Make the test yourself. Go over every detail in the process and decide what is conscious, in its origin. You will never unravel the puzzle, because you will not even remember some of the most important moments in it. These will arise, in whole or in part, of their own accord, and will pass by unnoticed, all in the realm of the subconscious.

'...Ask an actor, after some great performance, how he felt while on the stage, and what he did there. He will not be able to answer because he was not aware of what he lived through, and does not remember many of the more significant moments...

'You will astonish him by your description of his acting. He will gradually come to realise things about his performance of which he had been entirely unconscious.

'We may conclude from this that *if* is also a stimulus to the creative subconscious. Besides, it helps us to carry out another fundamental principle of our art: "unconscious creativeness through conscious technique."

'Up to this point I have explained the uses of *if* in connection with two of the main principles... It is even more strongly bound up with a third. Our great poet Pushkin wrote about it in his unfinished article on the drama.

'Among other things he said: "Sincerity of emotions, feelings that seem true in given circumstances – that is what we ask of a dramatist."

'I add from myself that this is exactly what we ask of an actor...

'Just what', asked Paul, 'does the expression "given circumstances" mean?'

'It means the story of the play, its facts, events, epoch, time and place of action, conditions of life, the actors' and *regisseur's* interpretation, the *mise en scene*, the production, the sets, the costumes, properties, lighting and sound effects – all the circumstances that are given to an actor to take into account as he creates his role.

'*If* is the starting point, the given circumstances, the development. The one cannot exist without the other, if it is to possess a necessary stimulating quality. However, their functions differ somewhat: *if* gives the push to dormant imagination, whereas the *given circumstances* build the basis for *if* itself. And they both, together and separately, help to create an inner stimulus.

'And what,' asked Vanya, with interest, 'does "sincerity of emotions" mean?'

'Just what it says – living human emotions, feelings which the actor himself has experienced.'

'Well then,' Vanya went on, 'what are "feelings that seem true"?'

'By true seeming we refer not to actual feelings themselves but to something nearly akin to them, to emotions reproduced indirectly, under the prompting of true inner feelings.

'In practice, this is approximately what you will have to do: first, you will have to imagine in your own way "the given circumstances" offered by the play, the regisseur's production and your own artistic conception. All of this material will provide a general outline for the life of the character you are to enact, and the circumstances surrounding him. It is necessary that you really believe in the general possibilities of such a life, and then become so accustomed to it that you feel yourself close to it. If you are successful in this, you will find that "sincere emotions", or "feelings that seem true" will spontaneously grow in you.

'However, when you use this third principle of acting, forget about your feelings, because they are largely of subconscious origin, and not subject to direct command. Direct all of your attention to the "given circumstances". They are always within reach.

Towards the end of the lesson he said: 'I can now supplement what I said earlier about *if*. Its power depends not only on its own keenness, but also on the sharpness of outline of the given circumstances.'

'But,' broke in Grisha, 'what is left for the actor since everything is prepared by others? Just trifles?'

'What do you mean, trifles?' said the Director indignantly. 'Do you think that to believe in the imaginative fiction of another person, and bring it to life, is a trifle? Don't you know that to compose on a theme suggested by someone else, is much more difficult than to invent one yourself? We know of cases where a bad play has achieved world fame because of having been re-created by a great actor. We know that Shakespeare re-created stories by others. That is what we do to the work of the dramatist; we bring to life what is hidden under the words; we put our own thoughts into the author's lines, and we establish our own relationships to other characters in the play, and the conditions of their lives; we filter through ourselves all the materials that we receive from the author and the director; we work over them, supplementing them out of our own imagination. That material becomes part of us, spiritually, and even physically; our emotions are sincere, and as a final result we have truly productive activity – all of which is closely interwoven with the implications of the play.

'And that tremendous work you tell me is just trifles!'

'No, indeed. That is creativeness and art.'

With these words he ended the lesson.

Taken from: *An Actor Prepares* by Konstantin Stanislavski, translated by Elizabeth Hapgood, London: Geoffrey Bles, 1948, pages 46–53.

Stanislavski developed a method for breaking a scene down into its constituent parts, which he called units of action. This kind of systematic analysis of the component parts enables the actor to examine and study the play's structure; but, according to Stanislavski, its benefits go well beyond this.

21: Units and Objectives

'You have divided the play into its main... episodes – its largest units. Now draw from each of these units its essential content and you will have the inner outline of the whole play. Each large unit is in turn divided into... medium and small parts which, together, compose it...

*

'The division of a play into units, to study its structure, has one purpose,' explained the Director... 'There is another, far more important inner reason. At the heart of every unit lies a *creative objective*.

'Each objective is an organic part of the unit, or, conversely, it creates the unit which surrounds it.

'It is just as impossible to inject extraneous objectives into a play as it is to put in units which are not related to it, because the objectives must form a logical and coherent stream...

'The mistake most actors make is that they think about the result instead of about the action that must prepare it. By avoiding action and aiming straight at the result you get a forced product which can lead to nothing but ham acting.

'Try to avoid straining after the result. Act with truth, fullness and integrity of purpose. You can develop this type of action by choosing lively objectives...

'We find innumerable objectives on the stage and not all of them are either necessary or good; in fact, many are harmful. An actor must learn to recognise quality, to avoid the useless, and to choose essentially right objectives.'

'How can we know them?' I asked.

'I should define right objectives as follows,' said he:

'(1) They must be on our side of the footlights. They must be directed towards the other actors, and not toward the spectators.

'(2) They should be personal yet analogous to those of the character you are portraying.

'(3) They must be creative and artistic because their function should be to fulfil the main purpose of our art: to create the life of a human soul and render it in artistic form.

'(4) They should be real, live, and human, not dead, conventional or theatrical.

'(5) They should be truthful so that you yourself, the actors playing with you, and your audience can believe in them.

'(6) They should have the quality of attracting and moving you.

'(7) They must be clear cut and typical of the role you are playing. They must tolerate no vagueness. They must be distinctly woven into the fabric of your part.

'(8) They should have value and content, to correspond to the inner body of your part. They must not be shallow, or skim along the surface.

'(9) They should be active, to push your role ahead and not let it stagnate.

'Let me warn against a dangerous form of objective, purely motor, which is prevalent in the theatre and leads to mechanical performance.

'We admit three types of objectives: the external or physical, the inner or psychological, and the rudimentary psychological type.'

Vanya expressed dismay at these big words and the Director explained his meaning by an example.

'Suppose you come into the room,' he began, 'and greet me, nod your head, shake my hand. That is an ordinary *mechanical* objective. It has nothing to do with psychology.'

'Is that wrong?' broke in Vanya.

The Director hastened to disabuse him.

'Of course you may say how do you do, but you may not love, suffer, hate or carry out any living, human objective in a purely mechanical way, without experiencing any feeling.

'A different case,' he continued, 'is holding out your hand and trying to express sentiments of love, respect, gratitude through your grasp and the look in your eye. That is how we execute an *ordinary objective* and yet there is a psychological element in it, so we, in our jargon, define it as a rudimentary type.

'Now here is a third way. Yesterday you and I had a quarrel. I insulted you publicly. Today, when we meet, I want to go up to you and offer my hand, indicating by this gesture that I wish to apologise, admit that I was wrong and beg you to forgive the incident. To stretch out my hand to my enemy of yesterday is not a simple problem. I will have to think it over carefully, go through and overcome many emotions before I can do it. That is what we call a *psychological* objective.

'Another important point about an objective is that besides being believable, it should have attraction for the actor, make him wish to carry it out…

'Objectives which contain these necessary qualities we call creative. It is difficult to cull them out. Rehearsals are taken up, in the main, with the task of finding the right objectives, getting control of them and living with them…

*

The important question today was: how to draw an objective from a unit of work. The method is simple. It consists of finding the most appropriate name for the unit, one which characterises its inner essence.

'Why all these christenings?' asked Grisha, ironically.

The Director replied: 'Have you any conception of what a really good name for a unit represents? It stands for its essential quality. To obtain it you must subject the unit to a process of crystallisation. From that crystal you find a name.

'The right name, which crystallizes the essence of a unit, discovers its fundamental objective.'...

'... you should not try to express the meaning of your objective in terms of a noun... the objective must always be a *verb...*

'This is because a noun calls forth an intellectual concept of a state of mind, a form, a phenomenon, but can only define what is presented by an image without indicating motion or action. *Every objective must carry in itself the germ of action...'*

Taken from: *An Actor Prepares* by Konstantin Stanislavski, translated by Elizabeth Hapgood, London: Geoffrey Bles, 1948, pages 116–123.

As we have seen, the essential goal of Stanislavski's system is to arouse the subconscious by conscious means. Stanislavski was particularly interested in the subconscious because, for him, this is where emotional life resides. The secret of acting truthfully lies in creating the spiritual life of the role; this is achieved by the actor experiencing feelings that are analogous to those of the character. In order to help actors achieve this measure of truthfulness in their performances, Stanislavski developed the concept of **emotion memory.**

22: Emotion Memory

'Do you remember,' asked the Director, 'that you once told me about the great impression Moskvin made on you when he came to your town on a tour? Can you recall his performance vividly enough so that the very thought of it now, six years later, brings back the flush of enthusiasm you felt at the time?'

'Perhaps the feelings are not as keen as they once were,' I replied, 'but certainly I am moved by them very much even now.'

'Are they strong enough to make you blush and feel your heart pound?'

'Perhaps, if I let myself go entirely, they would.'

'What do you feel, either spiritually or physically, when you recall the tragic death of the intimate friend you told me about?'

'I try to avoid that memory, because it depresses me so much.'

'That type of memory, which makes you relive the sensations you once felt when seeing Moskvin act, or when your friend died, is what we call *emotion memory*. Just as your visual memory can reconstruct an inner image of some forgotten thing, place or person, your emotion memory can bring back feelings you have already experienced. They may seem to be beyond recall, when suddenly a suggestion, a thought, a familiar object will bring them back in full force. Sometimes the emotions are as strong as ever, sometimes weaker, sometimes the same strong feelings will come back in a somewhat different guise.

'Since you are still capable of blushing or growing pale at the recollection of an experience, since you still fear to recall a certain tragic happening, we can conclude that you possess an emotion memory...'

Next Tortsov made the distinction between sensation memory, based on experiences, connected with our five senses, and emotion memory...

When he was asked to what extent an actor uses his sensation memories, and what the varying value of the five senses is, he said...

'Of our five senses sight is the most receptive of impressions. Hearing is also extremely sensitive. That is why impressions are readily made through our eyes and ears...

'Although our senses of smell, taste and touch are useful, and even sometimes important, in our art, their role is merely auxiliary and for the purpose of influencing our emotion memory...'

*

'Can you picture to yourself what our emotion memory is really like? Imagine a number of houses, with many rooms in each house, in each room innumerable cupboards, shelves, boxes, and somewhere, in one of them, a tiny bead. It is easy enough to find the right house, room cupboard and shelf. But it is more difficult to find the right box. And where is the sharp eye that will find that tiny bead that rolled out today, glittered for a moment, and then disappeared from sight? – only luck will ever find it again.

'That is what it is like in the archives of memory. It has all those divisions and sub-divisions. Some are more accessible than others. The problem is to recapture the emotion that once flashed by like a meteor. If it remains near the surface and comes back to you, you may thank your stars. But do not count on always recovering the same impression. Tomorrow something quite different may appear in its place... If you learn how to be receptive to these recurring memories, then the new ones as they form will be more capable of stirring your feelings repeatedly. Your soul in turn will be more responsive and will react with new warmth to parts of your role whose appeal had worn thin from constant repetition.

'When the actor's reactions are more powerful, inspiration can appear. On the other hand, don't spend your time chasing after an inspiration that once chanced your way. It is as unrecoverable as yesterday, as the joys of childhood, as first love. Bend your efforts to creating a new and fresh inspiration for today. There is no reason to suppose that it will be less good than yesterday's. It may not be as brilliant. But you have the advantage of possessing it today…

'… an artist does not build his role out of the first thing at hand. He chooses very carefully from among his memories and culls out of his living experience the ones that are most enticing. He weaves the soul of the person he is to portray out of emotions that are dearer to him than his everyday sensations. Can you imagine a more fertile field for inspiration? An artist takes the best that is in him and carries it over on to the stage…

*

'The broader your emotion memory, the richer your material for inner creativeness… It is, however, necessary, in addition to the richness of the emotion memory, to distinguish certain other characteristics; namely, its power, keenness and exactness of our memory…

'Theoretically you might suppose that the ideal type of emotion memory would be one that could retain and reproduce impressions in all the exact details of their first occurrence, that they would be revived just as they really were experienced. Yet if that were the case what would become of our nervous systems? How would they stand the repetition of horrors with all the original painful realistic details? Human nature could not stand it.

'Fortunately things actually happen in a different way. Our emotion memories are not exact copies of reality – occasionally some are more vivid, but usually they are less so, than the original. Sometimes impressions once received continue to live in us, grow and become deeper. They even stimulate new processes and either fill out unfinished details or else suggest altogether new ones.

'In a case of this kind a person can be perfectly calm in a dangerous situation and then faint away when he remembers it later. That is an example of the increased power of the memory over the original happening and of the continuing growth of an impression once had.

'There remains now – in addition to the power and intensity of these memories – their quality. Suppose that instead of being the person to whom something happened, you are merely an onlooker. It is one thing to receive an insult in public yourself and to experience a keen sense of embarrassment on your own account, and it is quite another thing to see this happen to someone else, to be upset by it, to be in a position to side freely with the aggressor or his victim.

'There is, of course, no reason why the onlooker should not experience very strong emotions. He may even feel the incident more keenly than the participating parties...

'There is another possibility – a person might not participate in an incident either as a principal or an onlooker. He might only hear or read about it. Even that would not prevent his receiving deep and powerful impressions. It would all depend on the strength of the imagination of the person who wrote the description or told about it, and also on that of the person reading or hearing the story.

'Again, the emotions of the reader or hearer differ in quality from those of an onlooker or principal in such an event.

'An actor has to deal with all these types of emotional material. He works it over and adjusts it to the needs of the person whom he portrays.

'Now let us suppose that you were a witness when that man was slapped in public, and that the incident left strong traces in your memory. It would be easier for you to reproduce those feelings if on the stage you played the part of a witness. But imagine that, instead, you were called upon to play the man who was slapped. How would you adapt the emotion you experienced as a witness to the role of the man insulted?'

'The principal feels the insult; the witness can share only sympathetic feelings. But sympathy then might be transformed into direct reaction. That is exactly what happens to us when we are working on a role. From the very moment when the actor feels that change take place in him he becomes an active principal in the life of the play – real human feelings are born in him – *often this transformation from human sympathy into the real feelings of the person in the part occurs spontaneously.*

'The actor may feel the situation of the person in the part so keenly, and respond to it so actively, that he actually puts himself in the place of that person. From that point of view he then sees the occurrence through the eyes of the person who was slapped. He wants to act, to participate in the situation, to resent the insult, just as though it were a matter of personal honour with him. In that case the transformation of the emotions of the witness to those of the principal takes place so completely that the strength and quality of the feelings involved are not diminished.

'You can see from this that we use not only our own past emotions as creative material but we use feelings that we have had in sympathising with the emotions of others. It is easy to state *a priori* that it is utterly impossible that we should have sufficient emotional material of our own to supply the needs of all the parts we shall be called upon to play in a whole lifetime on the stage. No one person can be the universal soul in Chekhov's *Seagull*, which has had all human experiences, including murder and one's own death. Yet we have to live all these things on the stage. So we must study other people, and get as close to them emotionally as we can, until sympathy for them is transformed into feelings of our own.

'Isn't that what happens to us every time we begin the study of a new role?'

*

'Our artistic emotions are, at first, as shy as wild animals and they hide in the depths of our souls. If they do not come to the surface spontaneously you cannot go after them and find them. All you can do is to concentrate your attention on the most effective kind of lure for them...

'The bond between the lure and the feeling is natural and normal and one that should be extensively employed. The more you test its effect and analyse its results in emotions aroused, the better you will be able to judge what your sensation memory retains, and you will be in a stronger position to develop it.

'At the same time we must not overlook the question of the quantity of your reserves in this respect. You should remember that you must constantly be adding to your store. For this purpose you draw, of course, principally upon your own impressions, feelings and experiences. You also acquire material from life around you, real and imaginary, from reminiscences, books, art, science, knowledge of all kinds, from journeys, museums and above all from communication with other human beings.

'Do you realise, now that you know what is required of an actor, why a real artist must lead a full, interesting, beautiful, varied, exciting and inspiring life? He should know, not only what is going on in the big cities, but in the provincial towns, far-away villages, factories, and the big cultural centres of the world as well. He should study the life and psychology of the people who surround him, of various other parts of the population, both at home and abroad.

'We need a broad point of view to act the plays of our times and of many peoples. We are asked to interpret the life of human souls from all over the world. An actor creates not only the life of his times but that of the past and future as well. That is why he needs to observe, to conjecture, to experience, to be carried away with emotions. In some cases his problem is even more complex. If his creation is to interpret current life he can observe his surroundings. But if he has to interpret the past, the future, or an imaginary epoch, he has either to reconstruct or to recreate something out of his own imagination – a complicated process.

'Our ideal should always be to strive for what is *eternal* in art, that which will never die, which will always remain young and close to human hearts.

'Our goal should be the heights of accomplishment built by the great classics. Study them and learn to use living emotional material for their rendering...'

Taken from: *An Actor Prepares* by Konstantin Stanislavski, translated by Elizabeth Hapgood, London: Geoffrey Bles, 1948, pages 167–192.

Everything in Stanislavski's system is directed towards the truthful realisation of the playwright's intentions; and, in this final extract from An Actor Prepares, *we begin to see how all of the creative work of the actor is harnessed to this end.*

23: The Super-Objective

Tortsov began the lesson today with the following remarks: 'Dostoyevski was impelled to write *The Brothers Karamazov* by his life-long *search for God*. Tolstoy spent all of his life struggling for *self-perfection*. Anton Chekhov wrestled with the triviality of bourgeois life and it became the *leit motiv* of the majority of his literary productions.

'Can you feel how these larger, vital purposes of great writers have the power to draw all of an actor's creative faculties and to absorb all the details and smaller units of a play or part?

'In a play the whole stream of individual, minor objectives, all the imaginative thoughts, feelings and actions of an actor, should converge to carry out the *super-objective* of the plot. The common bond must be so strong that even the most insignificant detail, if it is not related to the *super-objective*, will stand out as superfluous or wrong.

'Also this impetus towards the super-objective must be continuous throughout the whole play. When its origin is *theatrical* or *perfunctory* it will give only an approximately correct direction to the play. If it is human and directed towards the accomplishment of the basic purpose of the play it will be like a main artery, providing nourishment and life to both it and the actors.

'Naturally, too, the greater the literary work, the greater the pull of its super-objective.'

'But if a play lacks the touch of genius?'

'Then the pull will be distinctly weaker.'

'And in a bad play?'

'Then the actor has to point up the super-objective himself, make it deeper and sharper. In doing that the name he gives to it will be extremely significant.

'You already know how important it is to choose the right name for an objective. You remember that we found the verb form preferable because it gave more impetus to action. The same is true to an even greater extent in defining the super-objective...

'In my own experience I have had some... vivid proofs of the importance of choosing the right name for the super-theme. One instance was when I was playing *La Malade Imaginaire* of Moliere. Our first approach was elementary and we chose the theme "I wish to be sick". But the more effort I put into it and the more successful I was, the more evident it became that we were turning a jolly, satisfying comedy into a pathological tragedy. We soon saw the error of our ways and changed to: "I wish to be thought sick". Then the whole comic side came to the fore and the ground was prepared to show up the way in which the charlatans of the medical world exploited the stupid Argan, which was what Moliere meant to do...

'The main theme must be firmly fixed in an actor's mind throughout the performance. It gave birth to the writing of the play. It should also be the fountain-head of the actor's artistic creation.'

*

The Director began today by telling us that the main inner current of a play produces a state of inner grasp and power in which actors can develop all the intricacies and then come to a clear conclusion as to its underlying, fundamental purpose.

'That inner line of effort that guides the actors from the beginning to the end of the play we call the *continuity* or the *through-going action*. This through line galvanises all the small units and objectives of the play and directs them toward the super-objective. From then on they all serve the common purpose...

'Everything that we have undertaken in this first course has been directed towards enabling you to obtain control of the three most important features in our creative process:

> (1) Inner grasp
> (2) The through line of action
> (3) The super-objective

There was silence for a while and then Tortsov brought the lesson to a close by saying:

'We have covered all these points in general terms. Now you know what we mean by our "system".'

Taken from: *An Actor Prepares* by Konstantin Stanislavski, translated by Elizabeth Hapgood, London: Geoffrey Bles, 1948, pages 271–279.

We have seen how, in An Actor Prepares, **emotion memory** *is a cornerstone of Stanislavski's system. Increasingly, Stanislavski became dissatisfied with the effectiveness of emotion memory and, by the time he came to write* Creating a Role, *his thinking had undergone something of a transformation.*

24: The Method of Physical Actions

Disappointed in the results of his earlier developments, Stanislavski continued his search for the "conscious means towards the subconscious" – that is, a conscious means which would stir the actor's emotions.

It is not clear whether Stanislavski studied the work of the neurophysiologist Ivan Pavlov or whether his final discovery was the logical and natural result of his forty-year study of human behaviour. There is proof, however, that Stanislavski studied the work of the neurophysiologist I.M. Sechenov.

Stanislavski discovered that internal experiences and their physical expression are unbreakably united. "The first fact," said Stanislavski, "is that the elements of the human soul and the particles of a human body are indivisible." The thesis of Stanislavski, that human psychological life – moods, desires, feelings, intentions, ambitions – is expressed through simple physical actions, has been confirmed by such scientists as Ivan Pavlov and I.M. Sechenov.

There is no inner experience without external physical expression; our bodies transmit to others our inner experiences. Science has confirmed that neural pathways connect our physical actions with the inner mechanism of emotions, the innumerable nuances in human experience. The most profound processes of one's inner life are expressed through phsyical actions. A shrug of the shoulders, a movement of the spine, a complete immobility express the mental processes. Sechenov said that our bodies express what we are thinking and experiencing before we are aware of it. It is impossible to separate an experience from its physical expression. Stanislavski realised that when an actor on stage executes only physical movements, he violates the psycho-physical union and his performance is mechanical, dead. And if the actor does not express his thoughts and feelings physically, he is equally dead. It is impossible to understand a person or character without comprehending the person's or the character's thoughts and emotions.

It is impossible to build a character only with the body. Thoughts and emotions are essential in building a functioning individual. But we cannot underestimate the importance of training an actor's body. The body provides a great deal of information through visual transmission.

Stanislavski realised that to be natural the actor must be capable of grasping every reaction on stage in a psycho-physical way. He realises

that there is a break between the intellectual and the physical preparation in the actor's work on the character. He concludes that from the
very beginning the performer must include the physical life – his body
– in the psychological process in order to make this break disappear.

Due to the break between the mental and the physical behaviour of the
actor and owing to the scientific fact that emotions respond only when
there is a real reason, Stanislavski faced great difficulty in stirring the
actor's emotions. There is nothing real on stage. He understood the
mutual influence of psychological and physical behaviour and began to
think about stirring the actor's creativity on stage from the physical
side of the psycho-physical process. Stanislavski found his point of
departure in a process which without fail leads the actor from the "conscious to the subconscious." He developed his ultimate technique, "the
method of physical actions," which is the solution to spontaneous
behaviour on stage. Instead of forcing an emotion before going on
stage, the actor fulfils a simple, concrete, purposeful physical action
which stirs the psychological side of the psycho-physical act, thus
achieving psycho-physical involvement.

It must be clearly understood that Stanislavski does not mean that the
actor goes on stage to fulfil any physical movement. Physical movement
is a mechanical act. Physical action has a purpose; it has a psychology.
Human action – an act of human behaviour – is conditioned by the
environment. The circumstances created by the playwright add nuance
and colour to the scenic action. Science established that every nuance of
emotion is connected with a particular physical action. Therefore, that
action must be carefully selected on the basis of the play's circumstances. It must be the indispensable physical action connected with the
emotion that the actor must bring out. Only when the actor finds the
correct physical action will he achieve psycho-physical involvement.
The building of the character's logic of physical actions is simultaneously the building of the character's logic and consecutiveness of emotions.
All the elements of the system, which were important in their own right
at the time when Stanislavski was developing them, now contribute to
the truthful execution of a physical action.

The process by which an actor finds such physical action is as complex
as that by which a composer finds the correct harmonious sound for
his chord. It requires a great deal of experimentation through
improvisation. But when the actor finds such an action, he achieves psycho-physical involvement. Through a great deal of preparatory work,
the actor can achieve spontaneity. Then, during the performance, he is

in an improvisational state when none of the preparatory work is seen, because he behaves as in life. With the method of physical actions, Stanislavski reversed a human process: in life, we experience an emotion, and the body expresses it. Stanislavski achieves the experience of an emotion through a physical action. He superseded the system of "expressive movement" formulated by Francois Delsarte (1811–1871), who suggested that an emotion could be expressed with a "prescribed" gesture established beforehand. A human gesture depends on numerous factors, such as individual traits, the tempo-rhythm in which the individual is acting at the given moment, and other circumstances.

The only man in the theatre world who studied theatre through science and who studied the creative work of the great actors of his time, Stanislavski determined laws by means of which an actor restirs in himself at every performance the true emotions of the character he portrays.

In life, people often conceal what they experience. In theatre, real experiences must be expressed. The great Russian singer Chaliapin was known to have his voice tonality conditioned by the gestures which he found. It "flowed" from the gestures of his body in his roles. The gestures of the actor's body expressing mental experience such as thoughts, emotions, evaluations, decisions, are a gift of genius. Stanislavski made them possible for all capable actors. The actor's body must "speak" where there are no words, projecting in silence the inner monologue and other mental processes and creating an uninterrupted flow of life on stage.

Obviously, words are very important elements in theatre, but equally important are gestures of the body and the *mise en scene*. Stanislavski said, "Verbal action depends on the physical action." Words alone cannot project everything. Human relationships are expressed by gestures, poses, glances, silences. Gesture is an integral part of the action and gives the spectator visual information. It expresses, during pauses in the actor's own lines or while others are speaking, what words cannot express. Every gesture of the actor's body must be absolutely essential and easily understood. Everything else must be cut as superfluous. Through the art of the actor, the logic of the body reflects the logic of emotions. In theatre, there must be a mutual influence of words and pantomime.

G.A. Tovstonogov, the eminent Russian director, has said, "The method of physical actions is now the only one and there is nothing in the world theatre to equal it in the field of the actor's art." Most important in the actor's art is achieving the experience of a true emotion. The method of physical actions gives the actor the possibility of such an achievement...

In addition to giving the actor the possibility of achieving lifelike behaviour on stage, "the method of physical actions" is the most subtle means of analysing a play. The period of analysis while sitting around the table has not been entirely abandoned, but it has been shortened. Now actors continue analysis of the play through improvisations on actions. It is impossible to select an action without a thorough analysis of its motivation. To understand the motivation, the actor must study the play and refer to his own associations. The search for the logic and consecutiveness of actions is the most subtle analysis of the role, in which the actor's mind, his senses, his intuition, the muscles of his body – his whole spiritual and physical nature – participate...

Taken from: *The Stanislavski System* by Sonia Moore, London: Gollancz, 1966, pages 17–22.

Stanislavski's ideas on acting became extremely influential and in 1922, Richard Boleslavsky and Maria Ouspenskaya, who had both worked with Stanislavski at the Moscow Art Theatre, went to the United States where they founded the American Laboratory Theatre to pass on the fundamentals of Stanislavski's system. Among their students were Lee Strasbreg, Harold Clurman and Stella Adler, responsible for setting up the Group Theatre *which evolved its own approach to actor training in the United States.*

Following the success of Group Theatre*, Strasberg was instrumental in setting up the Actors' Studio which developed an intensive programme of actor training in what came to be known as the 'Method'. This programme was based on elements of Stanislavski's system, principally emotion memory. But, not having access to* Creating a Role*, Strasberg was unaware of the change that had taken place in Stanislavski's thinking; and it is probably true to say that 'Method Acting' is based on a fundamental misunderstanding of the basic principles of Stanislavski's mature system. The 'Method' was built around 'sense memory', Strasberg's version of Stanislavski's emotion memory.*

25: Sense Memory

The training of the senses to react to imaginary stimuli as they do to real objects is one of the major tasks in the training of the actor. This is accomplished through the use of *affective memory*, i.e. sense memory, or memory of experience. Every human being possesses not only mental memory (like the memorising of lines), muscular memory (like the handling of a certain tool or machine), but also *sense memory*. We experience sense memory when, for instance, we smell smoke without seeing it, or when in coming into a room where something unpleasant had once occurred we re-experience the original feeling.

Taken from: 'The Actor in the Theatre' by Lee Strasberg in *Producing the Play* edited by John Gassner, New York: Holt, Rhinehart and Winston, 1953, page 144.

The emphasis that Stanislavski had placed on emotion was, of course, inappropriate for the epic style of theatre that Bertolt Brecht was try-ing to create. A substantial part of Brecht's thinking is devoted to the problems of developing an acting style in keeping with the principles of the epic. He understood that the problem was double-sided. Of course, he needed a new kind of actor; but he also needed an audience that was prepared to accept the style of acting demanded by epic theatre.

26: A Dialogue about Acting

The actors always score great successes in your plays. Are you yourself satisfied with them?

No.

Because they act badly?

No. Because they act wrong.

How ought they to act then?

For an audience of the scientific age.

What does that mean?

Demonstrating their knowledge.

Knowledge of what?

Of human relations, of human behaviour, of human capacities.

All right; that's what they need to know. But how are they to demon-strate it?

Consciously, suggestively, descriptively.

How do they do it at present?

By means of hypnosis. They go into a trance and take the audience with them.

Give an example.

Suppose they have to act a leave-taking. They put themselves in a leave-taking mood. They want to induce a leave-taking mood in the audience. If the séance is successful it ends up with nobody seeing anything further, nobody learning any lessons, at best everyone recollecting. In short, everybody feels.

That sounds almost like some erotic process. What ought it to be like, then?

Witty. Ceremonious. Ritual. Spectator and actor ought not to approach one another but to move apart. Each ought to move away from himself. Otherwise the element of terror necessary to all recognition is lacking.

Just now you used the expression 'scientific'... Are we to see science in the theatre then?

No. Theatre.

I see: scientific man is to have his theatre like everybody else.

Yes. Only the theatre has already got scientific man for its audience, even if it doesn't do anything to acknowledge the fact. For this audience hangs its brains up in the cloakroom along with its coat.

Can't you tell the actor then how he ought to perform?

No. At present he is entirely dependent on the audience, blindly subject to it.

Haven't you ever tried?

Indeed. Again and again...

Give an example.

When an actress of this new sort was playing the servant in *Oedipus* she announced the death of her mistress by calling out her 'dead, dead' in a wholly unemotional and penetrating voice, her 'Jocasta has died' without any sorrow but so firmly and definitely that the bare fact of her mistress's death carried more weight at that precise moment than could have been generated by any grief of her own. She did not abandon her voice to horror, but perhaps her face, for she used white make-up to show the impact which a death makes on all who are present at it. Her announcement that the suicide had collapsed as if before a beater was made up less of pity for this collapse than of pride in the beater's achievement, so that it became plain to even the most emotionally punch-drunk spectator that here a decision had been carried out which called for his acquiescence. With astonishment she described in a single clear sentence the dying woman's ranting and apparent irrationality, and there was no mistaking her 'and how she ended, we do not know' with which, as a meagre but inflexible tribute, she refused to give any further information about this death. But as she descended the few steps she took such paces that this slight figure seemed to be covering an immense distance from the scene of the tragedy to the people on the lower stage. And as she held up her arms in conventional lamentation she was begging at the same time for pity for herself who had seen the disaster, and with her loud 'now you may weep' she seemed to deny the justice of any previous and less well-founded regrets.

What sort of reception did she have?

Moderate, except for a few connoisseurs. Plunged in self-identification with the protagonist's feelings, virtually the whole audience failed to take part in the moral decision of which the plot is made up. The immense decision which she had communicated had almost no effect on those who regarded it as an opportunity for new sensations.

Taken from: 'A Dialogue about Acting' by Bertolt Brecht in *Brecht on Theatre*, translated by John Willett, London: Eyre Methuen, 1964, pages 26–28.

In developing his new acting style, Brecht was much influenced by the Chinese Theatre which made extensive use of 'strange-making' devices. Brecht absorbed this device into his epic theatre, under the name of the verfremdungseffekt.

27: The *Verfremdungseffekt* in Chinese Acting

The following is intended to refer briefly to the use of the alienation effect in traditional Chinese acting. This method was most recently used in Germany for plays of a non-aristotelian (not dependent on empathy) type as part of the attempts being made to evolve an epic theatre. The efforts in question were directed to playing in such a way that the audience was hindered from simply identifying itself with the characters in the play. Acceptance or rejection of their actions and utterances was meant to take place on a conscious plane, instead of, as hitherto, in the audience's subconscious...

Traditional Chinese acting... knows the *verfremdungseffekt*, and applies it most subtly. It is well known that the Chinese theatre uses a lot of symbols. Thus a general will carry little pennants on his shoulder, corresponding to the number of regiments under his command. Poverty is shown by patching the silken costumes with irregular shapes of different colours, likewise silken, to indicate that they have been mended. Characters are distinguished by particular masks, i.e. simply by painting. Certain gestures of the two hands signify the forcible opening of a door, etc. The stage itself remains the same, but articles of furniture are carried in during the action...

It is not all that simple to break with the habit of assimilating a work of art as a whole But this has to be done if just one of a large number of effects is to be singled out and studied. The *verfremdungseffekt* is achieved in the Chinese theatre in the following way.

Above all, the Chinese artist never acts as if there were a fourth wall besides the three surrounding him. He expresses his awareness of being watched. This immediately removes one of the European stage's characteristic illusions. The audience can no longer have the illusion of being the unseen spectator at an event which is really taking place. A whole elaborate European stage technique, which helps to conceal the fact that the scenes are so arranged that the audience can view them in the easiest way, is thereby made unnecessary. The actors openly choose those positions which will best show them off to the audience, just as if they were *acrobats*. A further means is that the artist observes himself. Thus if he is representing a cloud, perhaps, showing its unexpected appearance, its soft and strong growth, its rapid yet gradual transformation, he will occasionally look at the audience as if to say: isn't it just like that? At the same time he also observes his own arms and legs, adducing them, testing them and perhaps finally approving them. An obvious glance at the floor, so as to judge the space available for him for his act, does not strike him as liable to break the illusion. In this way the artist separates mime (showing observation) from gesture (showing a cloud), but without detracting from the latter, since the body's attitude is reflected in the face and is wholly responsible for its expression. At one moment the expression is of well-managed restraint; at another, of utter triumph. The artist has been using his countenance as a blank sheet, to be inscribed by the *gestus* of the body.

The artist's object is to appear strange and even surprising to the audience. He achieves this by looking strangely at himself and his work. As a result everything put forward by him has a touch of the amazing. Everyday things are thereby raised above the level of the obvious and automatic...

The Chinese artist's performance often strikes the Western actor as cold. That does not mean that the Chinese theatre rejects all representation of feelings. The performer portrays incidents of utmost passion, but without his delivery becoming heated. At those points where the character portrayal is deeply excited the performer takes a lock of hair between his lips and chews it. But this is like a ritual, there is nothing eruptive about it. It is quite clearly somebody else's repetition of the incident: a representation, even though an artistic one. The performer shows that this man is not in control of himself, and he points to the outward signs. And so lack of control is decorously expressed, or if not decorously at any rate decorously for the stage. Among all the possible signs certain particular ones are picked out, with careful and visible consideration. Anger is naturally different from sulkiness, hatred from distaste, love from liking; but the corresponding fluctuations of feeling are portrayed economically. The coldness comes from the actor's holding himself remote from the character portrayed, along the lines described. He is careful not to make its sensations into those of the spectator. Nobody gets raped by the individual he portrays; this individual is not the spectator himself but his neighbour.

The Western actor does all he can to bring his spectator into the closest proximity to the events and the character he has to portray. To this end he persuades him to identify with him (the actor) and uses every energy to convert himself as completely as possible into a different type, that of the character in question. If this complete conversion succeeds then his art has been more or less expended. Once he has become the bank-clerk, doctor or general concerned he will need no more art than any of these people need 'in real life'.

This complete conversion operation is extremely exhausting. Stanislavski puts forward a series of means – a complete system – by which what he calls 'creative mood' can repeatedly be manufactured afresh at every performance. For the actor cannot usually manage to feel for very long on end that he really is the other person; he soon gets exhausted and begins just to copy various superficialities of the other person's speech and hearing, whereupon the effect on the public drops off alarmingly. This is certainly due to the fact that the other person has been created by an 'intuitive' and accordingly murky process which takes place in the subconscious. The subconscious is not at all responsive to guidance; it has as it were a bad memory.

These problems are unknown to the Chinese performer, for he rejects complete conversion. He limits himself from the start to simply quoting the character played. But with what art he does this! He only needs a minimum of illusion...

For the actor it is difficult and taxing to conjure up particular inner moods or emotions night after night; it is simpler to exhibit the outer signs which accompany these emotions and identify them. In this case, however, there is not the same automatic transfer of emotions to the spectator, the same emotional infection. The *verfremdungseffekt* intervenes, not in the form of absence of emotion, but in the form of emotions which need not correspond to those of the character portrayed. On seeing worry the spectator may feel a sensation of joy; on seeing anger, one of disgust. When we speak of exhibiting the outer signs of emotion we do not mean such an exhibition and such a choice of signs that the emotional transference does in fact take place because the actor has managed to infect himself with the emotions portrayed, by exhibiting the outer signs; thus, by letting his voice rise, holding his breath and tightening his neck muscles so that the blood shoots to his head, the actor can easily conjure up a rage. In such a case of course the effect does not occur. But it does occur if the actor at a particular point unexpectedly shows a completely white face, which he has produced mechanically by holding his face in his hands with some white make-up on them. If the actor at the same time displays an apparently composed character, then his terror at this point (as a result of this message, or that discovery) will give rise to a *verfremdungseffekt*. Acting like this is healthier and in our view less unworthy of a thinking being; it demands a considerable knowledge of humanity and worldly wisdom, and a keen eye for what is socially important. In this case too there is of course a creative process at work; but it is a higher one, because it is raised to the conscious level.

The *verfremdungseffekt* does not in any way demand an unnatural way of acting. It has nothing whatever to do with ordinary stylization. On the contrary, the achievement of a *verfremdungseffekt* absolutely depends on lightness and naturalness of performance. But when the actor checks the truth of his performance (a necessary operation, which Stanislavski is much concerned with in his system) he is not just thrown back on his 'natural sensibilities', but can always be corrected by a comparison with reality (is that how an angry man really speaks? is that how an offended man really sits down?) and so from outside, by other people. He acts in such a way that nearly every sentence could be followed by a verdict of the audience and practically every gesture is submitted for the public's approval.

The Chinese performer is in no trance. He can be interrupted at any moment. He won't have to 'come round'. After an interruption he will go on with his exposition from that point. We are not disturbing him at the 'mystic moment of creation'; when he steps on to the stage before us the process of creation is already over. He does not mind if the setting is changed around him as he plays...

Taken from: 'The *Verfremdungseffekt* in Chinese Acting' by Bertolt Brecht in *Brecht on Theatre*, translated by John Willett, London: Eyre Methuen, 1964, pages 91–95.

Brecht went on to develop a model for the acting required in his epic theatre; it was based on an everyday street scene.

28: The Street Scene
A basic model for an epic theatre

It is comparatively easy to set up a basic model for epic theatre. For practical experiments I usually picked as my example of completely simple, 'natural' epic theatre an incident such as can be seen at any street corner: an eyewitness demonstrating to a collection of people how a traffic accident took place. The bystanders may not have observed what happened, or they may simply not agree with him, may 'see things a different way'; the point is that the demonstrator acts the behaviour of a driver or victim or both in such a way that the bystanders are able to form an opinion about the accident.

Such an example of the most primitive type of epic theatre seems easy to understand. Yet experience has shown that it presents astounding difficulties to the reader or listener as soon as he is asked to see the implications of treating this kind of street corner demonstration as a basic form of major theatre, theatre for a scientific age. What this means of course is that the epic theatre may appear richer, more intricate and complex in every particular, yet to be major theatre it need at bottom only contain the same elements as a street-corner demonstration of this sort; nor could it any longer be termed epic theatre if any of the main elements of the street-corner demonstration were lacking. Until this is understood it is impossible to understand what follows. Until one understands the novelty, unfamiliarity and direct challenge to the critical faculties of the suggestion that street-corner demonstration of this sort can serve as a satisfactory basic model of major theatre one cannot really understand what follows.

Consider: the incident is clearly very far from what we mean by an artistic one. The demonstrator need not be an artist. The capacities he needs to achieve his aim are in effect universal. Suppose he cannot carry out some particular movement as quickly as the victim he is imitating; all he needs to do is explain that *he* moves three times as fast, and the demonstration neither suffers in essentials nor loses its point. On the contrary it is important that he should not be too perfect. His demonstration would be spoilt if the bystanders' attention were drawn to his powers of transformation. He has to avoid presenting himself in such a way that someone calls out 'What a lifelike portrayal of a chauffeur!' He must not 'cast a spell' over anyone. He should not transport people from normality to 'higher realms'. He need not dispose of any special powers of suggestion.

It is most important that one of the main features of the ordinary theatre should be excluded from our street scene: the engendering of illusion. The street demonstrator's performance is essentially repetitive. The event has taken place; what you are seeing now is a repeat. If the scene in the theatre follows the street scene in this respect then the theatre will stop pretending not to be a theatre, just as the street-corner demonstration admits it is a demonstration (and does not pretend to be the actual event). The element of rehearsal in the acting and of learning by heart the text, the whole machinery and the whole process of preparation: it all becomes plainly apparent. What room is left for experience? Is the reality portrayed still experienced in any sense?

The street scene determines what kind of experience is to be prepared for the spectator. There is no question but that the street-corner demonstrator has been through an 'experience', but he is not out to make his demonstration serve as an 'experience' for the audience. Even the experience of the driver and the victim is only partially communicated by him, and he by no means tries to turn it into an enjoyable experience for the spectator, however lifelike he may make his demonstration. The demonstration would become no less valid if he did not reproduce the fear caused by the accident; on the contrary it would lose validity if he did. He is not interested in creating pure emotions. It is important to understand that a theatre which follows his lead in this respect undergoes a positive change of function.

One essential element of the street scene must also be present in the theatrical scene if this is to qualify as epic, namely that the demonstration should have a socially practical significance. Whether our street demonstrator is out to show that one attitude on the part of driver or pedestrian makes an accident inevitable where another would not, or whether he is demonstrating with a view to fixing the responsibility, his demonstration has a practical purpose, intervenes socially.

The demonstrator's purpose determines how thoroughly he has to imitate. Our demonstrator need not imitate every aspect of his character's behaviour, but only so much as gives a picture. Generally the theatre scene will give much fuller pictures, corresponding to its more extensive range of interest. How do street scene and theatre scene link up here? To take a point of detail, the victim's voice may have played no immediate part in the accident. Eye-witnesses may disagree as to whether a cry they heard ('Look out!') came from the victim or from someone else, and this may give our demonstrator a motive for imitating the voice. The question can be settled by demonstrating whether the voice was an old man's or a woman's, or merely whether it was high or low. Again, the answer may depend on whether it was that of an educated person or not. Loud or soft may play a great part, as the driver could be correspondingly more or less guilty. A whole series of characteristics of the victim ask to be portrayed. Was he absent-minded? Was his attention distracted? If so, by what? What, on the evidence of his behaviour, could have made him liable to be distracted by just that circumstance and no other? Etc., etc. It can be seen that our street-corner demonstration provides opportunities for a pretty rich and varied portrayal of human types. Yet a theatre which tries to restrict its essential elements to those provided by our street scene will have to acknowledge certain limits to imitation. It must be able to justify any outlay in terms of its purpose.

The demonstration may for instance be dominated by the question of compensation for the victim, etc. The driver risks being sacked from his job, losing his licence, going to prison; the victim risks a heavy hospital bill, loss of job, permanent disfigurement, possibly unfitness for work. This is the area within which the demonstrator builds up his characters. The victim may have had a companion; the driver may have had his girl sitting alongside him. That would bring out the social element better and allow the characters to be more fully drawn.

Another essential element in the street scene is that the demonstrator should derive his characters entirely from their actions. He imitates their actions and so allows conclusions to be drawn about them. A theatre that follows him in this will be largely breaking with the orthodox theatre's habit of basing the actions on the characters and having the former exempted from criticism by presenting them as an unavoidable consequence deriving by natural law from the characters who perform them. To the street demonstrator the character of the man being demonstrated remains a quantity that need not be completely defined. Within certain limits he may be like this or like that; it doesn't matter. What the demonstrator is concerned with are his accident-prone and accident-proof qualities. The theatrical scene may show more fully-defined individuals. But it must then be in a position to treat their individuality as a special case and outline the field within which, once more, its most socially relevant effects are produced. Our street demonstrator's possibilities of demonstration are narrowly restricted (indeed, we chose this model so that the limits should be as narrow as possible). If the essential elements of the theatrical scene are limited to those of the street scene then its greater richness must be an enrichment only. The question of border-line cases becomes acute...

One essential element of the street scene lies in the natural attitude adopted by the demonstrator, which is two-fold; he is always taking two situations into account. He behaves naturally as a demonstrator, and he lets the subject of the demonstration behave naturally too. He never forgets, nor does he allow it to be forgotten, that he is not the subject but the demonstrator. That is to say, what the audience sees is not a fusion between demonstrator and subject, not some third, independent, uncontradictory entity with isolated features of (a) demonstrator and (b) subject, such as the orthodox theatre puts before us in its productions. The feelings and opinions of demonstrator and demonstrated are not merged into one.

We now come to one of those elements that are peculiar to the epic theatre, the so-called *verfremdungseffekt*. What is involved here is, briefly, a technique of taking the human social incidents to be portrayed and labelling them as something striking, something that calls for explanation, is not to be taken for granted, not just natural. The object of this 'effect' is to allow the spectator to criticise constructively from a social point of view. Can we show that this *verfremdungseffekt* is significant for our street demonstrator.

We can picture what happens if he fails to make use of it. The following situation could occur. One of the spectators might say: 'But if the victim stepped off the kerb with his right foot, as you showed him doing -' The demonstrator might interrupt saying: 'I showed him stepping off with his left foot'. By arguing which foot he really stepped off with in his demonstration, and, even more, how the victim himself acted, the demonstration can be so transformed that the *verfremdungseffekt* occurs. The demonstrator achieves it by paying exact attention this time to his movements, executing them carefully, probably in slow motion; in this way he defamiliarises the little sub-incident, emphasises its importance and makes it worthy of notice. And so the epic theatre's *verfremdungseffekt* proves to have its uses for our street demonstrator too; in other words it is also to be found in this small everyday scene of natural street-corner theatre, which has little to do with art. The direct changeover from representation to commentary that is so characteristic of the epic theatre is still more easily recognised as one element of any street demonstration. Wherever he feels he can the demonstrator breaks off his imitation in order to give explanations. The epic theatre's choruses and documentary projections, the direct addressing of the audience by its actors, are at bottom just this.

It will have been observed, not without astonishment I hope, that I have not named any strictly artistic elements as characterising our street scene and, with it, that of epic theatre. The street demonstrator can carry out a successful demonstration with no greater abilities than, in effect, anybody has....

The epic theatre wants to establish its basic model at the street corner, i.e. to return to the very simplest 'natural' theatre, a social enterprise whose origins, means and ends are practical and earthly.

Taken from: 'The Street Scene: A Basic Model for an Epic Theatre' by Bertolt Brecht in *Brecht on Theatre*, translated by John Willett, London: Eyre Methuen, 1964, pages 121–126.

*By now, we should have a sense of Brecht's preferred acting style. But it is important to realise that the epic theatre has an overt **social purpose**. Throughout his description of the street scene, he constantly alludes to this social function: the aim of the* verfremdungseffekt *is to allow the spectator to criticise constructively from a **social point of view**.*

29: The Social *Gestus*

… Whatever the actor offers in the way of gesture, verse structure, etc., must be finished and bear the hallmarks of something rehearsed and rounded-off. The impression to be given is one of ease, which is at the same time one of difficulties overcome. The actor must make it possible for the audience to take his own art, his mastery of technique, lightly too. He puts an incident before the spectator with perfection and as he thinks it really happened or might have happened. He does not conceal the fact that he has rehearsed it, any more than an acrobat conceals his training, and he emphasises that it is his own (actor's) account, view, version of the incident.

Because he doesn't identify himself with him he can pick a definite attitude to adopt towards the character whom he portrays, can show what he thinks of him and invite the spectator, who is likewise not asked to identify himself, to criticise the character portrayed.

The attitude which he adopts is a socially critical one. In his exposition of the incidents and in his characterisation of the person he tries to bring out those features which come within society's sphere. In this way his performance becomes a discussion (about social conditions) with the audience he is addressing. He prompts the spectator to justify or abolish these conditions according to what class he belongs to.

The object of the *verfremdungseffekt* is to defamiliarise the *gestus* underlying every incident. By *gestus* is meant the mimetic and gestural expression of the social relationships prevailing between people of a given period.

It helps to formulate the incident for society, and to put it across in such a way that society is given the key…

Taken from: 'Short Description of a New Technique of Acting which Produces a *Verfremdungseffekt*' by Bertolt Brecht in *Brecht on Theatre*, translated by John Willett, London: Eyre Methuen, 1964, pages 139–140.

*Brecht's concept of gestus is, then, an expression of the **social relationship** that exists between people. But additionally, Brecht wanted this gestus to contain a **contradiction**. Probably the best known gestus is Helene Weigel's 'silent scream' in the Berlin production of* Mother Courage. *The contradiction is contained in the idea of a scream that is silent; and the physical action indicates Courage's powerless social position.*

30: The Silent Scream

At the end of the third scene in Brecht's *Mother Courage*, the soldiers carry Schweizerka's body onstage. They suspect that he is the son of Mother Courage and want her to identify the body. According to Brecht's text, when her son's body is laid before her, Mother Courage shakes her head twice, indicating that she doesn't recognise him. The soldiers then carry the body away to bury him in a common grave.

When Helene Weigel, the greatest performer of female Brechtian characters, played this scene, she remained immobile; she moved only her head, signalling to the soldiers that the body was not that of her son. When they forced her to look at the body one more time, she again refused to recognise it, maintaining a fixed and absent expression. But when the body was carried away, Weigel turned her head in the opposite direction and opened her mouth wide, in a 'silent scream'.

George Steiner, who saw Weigel at the *Berliner Ensemble*, relates:

> She turned her head the other way and stretched her mouth wide open, just like the screaming horse in Picasso's *Guernica*. A harsh and terrifying, indescribable sound issued from her mouth. But, in fact, there was no sound. Nothing. It was the sound of absolute silence. A silence which screamed and screamed throughout the theatre, making the audience bow their heads as if they had been hit by a blast of wind.
>
> (G. Steiner, *The Death of Tragedy*, 1961)

This was a spectator's impression. Now here is how the same work is described by a theatre historian:

> Weigel found that she was to perform in the midst of symbols, onstage with a cart which was partly a war-machine, partly a bazaar, mounted on a revolve which represented Mother Courage's world and which carried her around the stage in her various scenes. She managed to avoid being overwhelmed by all of this because, as an actress who had worked with Piscator, she knew that she could combat the abstract by exploiting her character's physicality and the creativity of her own body in the situation.
>
> She began to rehearse, using a criterion which Brecht had established in the *Berliner Ensemble*: she worked through the whole part over and over again, concentrating only on

approximated interpretative sketches. By the time of the opening, Weigel had at her disposal about a hundred different details and narrative poses which she could have used to reveal the relationship between Mother Courage and the other characters; and she developed other details and poses in subsequent performances. The pose of tremendous suffering, the unforgettable image of Weigel standing with her mouth stretched wide open but emitting no sound, first appeared after many performances, when out of her subconscious came an image she had once seen in a newspaper photo, that of an Indian woman crying over the murder of her son.

(Claude Meldolesi, *Brecht in Rehearsal* in C. Meldolesi, L. Olivi, *Brecht Regista, Brecht the Director*)

Apropos of the same performance – in the same book, in the diary kept by Hans Bunge, Brecht's assistant – one reads: 'Weigel, for example, had worked out Mother Courage's way of walking not by theorising, but by wearing the character's dress and shoes from the very first rehearsal'...

Weigel's 'silent scream' is based on tension in the spinal column by means of which she conveys an energy equivalent to that of a scream.

The understanding of the emotive effect of the spinal column and especially the attention given to concrete physical details, is also clear in the following episode, told by Helene Weigel to Ekkehard Schall, one of her colleagues at the *Berliner Ensemble*:

Helene Weigel once told me the following story. As a young actress she once played at the side of the great Albert Bassermann in one of Ibsen's plays, I think. In one scene in which she was on the stage with him, he received one piece of catastrophic news after another: father dead, mother dead, children dead. (Laughter) To take in these catastrophic bits of news, Bassermann chose to stand with his back to the audience. One day Helene complained to him that his face, turned away from the audience, did not show any emotion, and what was worse, took on some private expressions. And she quoted him as having replied: "So what, the audience doesn't see my face." He played everything with his back: he played every shock he received with his back.

Taken from: *The Secret Art of The Performer* **by Eugenio Barba and Nicola Savarese: Routledge, 1991, pages 234–235.**

By juxtaposing the extracts from An Actor Prepares *with those from* Brecht on Theatre *it quickly becomes apparent that Stanislavski and Brecht occupied very different positions on the question of acting style. Although Brecht's theories were developed largely in reaction to Stanislavski's 'Aristotelian' concept of theatre, it is always important to remember that Brecht did not reject **everything** that Stanislavski had worked for.*

31: Some of the Things that can be Learnt from Stanislavski

1. *The feeling for a play's poetry*
Even when S.'s theatre had to put on naturalistic plays to satisfy the taste of the time the production endowed them with poetic features; it never descended to mere reportage. Whereas here in Germany even classical plays acquire no kind of splendour.

2. *The sense of responsibility to society*
S. showed the actors the social meaning of their craft. Art was not an end in itself to him, but he knew that no end is attained in the theatre except through art.

3. *The stars' ensemble playing*
S.'s theatre consisted only of stars, great and small. He proved that individual playing only reaches full effectiveness by means of ensemble playing.

4. *Importance of the broad conception and of details*
In the Moscow Art Theatre every play acquired a carefully thought-out shape and a wealth of subtly elaborated detail. The one is useless without the other.

5. *Truthfulness as a duty*
S. taught that the actor must have exact knowledge of himself and of the men he sets out to portray. Nothing that is not taken from the actor's observation, or confirmed by observation, is fit to be observed by the audience.

6. *Unity of naturalness and style*
In S.'s theatre a splendid naturalness went arm-in-arm with deep significance. As a realist he never hesitated to portray ugliness, but he did so gracefully.

7. *Representation of reality as full of contradictions*

S. grasped the diversity and complexity of social life and knew how to represent it without getting entangled.

8. *The importance of man*

S. was a convinced humanist, and as such conducted his theatre along the road to socialism.

9. *The significance of art's further development*

The Moscow Art Theatre never rested on its laurels. S. invented new artistic methods for every production. From his theatre came such important artists as Vakhtangov, who in turn developed their teacher's art further in complete freedom.

Taken from: 'Some of the Things that can be Learnt from Stanislavski' by Bertolt Brecht in *Brecht on Theatre*, **translated by John Willett, London: Eyre Methuen, 1964, pages 236–237.**

The question of how best to portray emotion is central to both Stanislavski's system and to Brechtian acting. Although each came to a very different conclusion, they are united in their recognition that the truthful presentation of feelings and emotions is a crucial concern for the actor. In recent years, this view has increasingly come into question. Roland Barthes, the French post-structuralist critic, is in no doubt that the passionate portrayals of the actor are produced by the audience's perception that self-sacrifice and hard labour are essential ingredients of the actor's art.

32: A Myth of the New Theatre

If we are to judge by a recent festival of young companies, the new theatre angrily inherits the myths of the old (so that it is hard to tell what it is that distinguishes the one from the other). We know, for example, that in the bourgeois theatre the actor, "devoured" by his role, is supposed to seem fired by a veritable conflagration of passion. He must seethe at any price, i.e. burn and at the same time spill over; whence the moist forms of this combustion. In one play (which won a prize), the two male partners spread themselves in liquids of all kinds, tears, sweat and saliva. It was as if we were watching a dreadful psychological labour, a monstrous torsion of the internal tissues, as if passion were a huge wet sponge squeezed by the playwright's implacable hand. The intention of this visceral tempest is comprehensible enough: to make "psychology" into a quantitative phenomenon, to compel laughter or suffering to assume simple metrical forms, so that passion, too, becomes a merchandise like any other, an object of commerce, inserted in a numerical system of exchange: I give my money to the theatre, in return for which I demand a clearly visible, almost computable passion; and if the actor gives full measure, if he can make his body work before my eyes without cheating, if I cannot doubt the trouble he takes, then I shall declare the actor to be excellent, I shall evidence my joy at having invested my money in a talent worthy of it, returning it to me a hundredfold in the form of real tears, real sweat. Combustion's great advantage is of an economic order: my spectator's money has a certifiable yield at last.

Naturally, the actor's combustion decks itself out in spiritualised justifications: the actor gives himself over to the demon of the theatre, he sacrifices himself, allows himself to be eaten up from inside by his role: his generosity, the gift of his body to Art, his physical labour are worthy of pity and admiration; this muscular labour is acknowledged, and when, exhausted, drained of all his humours, he appears in front of the curtain at the end, we applaud him like a champion weight lifter or hunger artist, and we secretly suggest he go and restore himself somewhere, renew his inner substance, replace all that water by which he has measured out the passion we have bought from him. No bourgeois public resists so obvious a "sacrifice", and I suppose that an actor who knows how to weep or sweat on stage is always certain to triumph: the obviousness of his labour makes it unnecessary to judge further.

Taken from: 'Two Myths of the New Theatre' in *The Eiffel Tower and Other Mythologies* by Roland Barthes, translated by R. Howard, New York: Noonday Press, 1979, pages 75–76.

We end this section with two extracts from David Mamet's recent book, True and False. *In the first, he echoes some of Barthes' concerns.*

33: Ancestor Worship

Stanislavski was essentially an amateur. He was a member of a very wealthy merchant family, and he came to the theatre as a rich man. I do not mean to denigrate either his fervour or his accomplishments – I merely note his antecedents.

The busker, the gypsy, the mountebank, come to the theatre to support themselves. As their support depends directly on the favour of the audience, they study to obtain that favour. Those who have, in the perhaps overused phrase, "come up from the streets", have little interest in their own performance, save as it relates to their ability to please an audience. This is, I believe, as it should be.

I do not assume that the doctor, or the musician or dancer or painter, strives first to bring himself to a "state", and only then directs his efforts outward. I assume that practitioners of these crafts put their attention on the legitimate demands of their profession and of their clients; and I, as a client, patient, audience member, do not expect these professionals to burden me with their life story.

The actor is onstage to communicate the play to the audience. That is the beginning and the end of his and her job. To do so the actor needs a strong voice, superb diction, a supple, well-proportioned body, and a rudimentary understanding of the play.

The actor does not need to "become" the character. That phrase, in fact, has no meaning. There *is* no character. There are only lines upon a page. They are lines of dialogue meant to be said by the actor. When he or she says them simply, in an attempt to achieve an object more or less like that suggested by the author, the audience sees an *illusion* of a character upon a stage.

To create this illusion the actor has to undergo nothing whatever. He or she is as free of the necessity of "feeling" as the magician is free of the necessity of actually summoning supernormal powers. The magician creates an illusion in the mind of the audience. So does the actor…

Most acting training is directed at recapitulating the script. Actors are told to learn how to "be happy," "be sad," "be distracted," at those points in the script or performance where it would seem the "character" would so be. Such behaviour is not only unnecessary, it is harmful both to the actor and to the audience.

My philosophical bent and thirty years' experience inform me that nothing in the world is less interesting than an actor on the stage involved in his or her own emotions. The very act of striving to create an emotional state in oneself takes one out of the play. It is the ultimate self-consciousness, and though it may be self-consciousness in the service of an ideal, it is no less boring for that.

The actor on the stage, looking or striving to create a "state" in himself can think only one of two things: (a) I have not reached the required state yet; I am deficient and must try harder; or (b) I *have* reached the required state, how proficient I am! (at which point the mind, ever jealous of its prerogatives, will reduce the actor to (a)).

Both (a) and (b) take the actor right out of the play. For the mind cannot be forced. It can be suggested but it cannot be forced. An actor onstage can no more act upon the order "Be happy" than she can upon the order "Do not think of a hippopotamus."

Our emotional-psychological makeup is such that our only response to an order to think or feel anything is rebellion. Think of the times someone suggested you "cheer up," of the perfect young person your friends wanted to fix you up with, of the director who suggested you "relax." There is no exception. If one were truly able to command one's conscious thoughts, to summon emotion at will, there would be no neurosis, no psychosis, no psychoanalysis, no sadness.

We cannot control our thoughts, nor can we control our emotions. But perhaps "control of emotion" has a special case-specific meaning on the stage. Indeed it does. It means "pretending".

I don't care to see a musician concentrating on what he or she feels while performing. Nor do I care to see an actor do so. As a playwright and as a lover of good writing, I know that the good play does not *need* the support of the actor, in effect, narrating its psychological undertones, and that the bad play will not benefit from it.

"Emotional memory," "sense memory," and the tenets of the Method back to and including Stanislavski's trilogy are a lot of hogwash. This "method" does not work; it cannot be practised; it is, in theory, design, and supposed execution supererogatory – it is as useless as teaching pilots to flap their arms while in the cockpit in order to increase the lift of the plane.

The plane is designed to fly; the pilot is trained to direct it. Likewise, the play is designed, if correctly designed, as a series of incidents in which and through which the protagonist struggles toward his or her goal. It is the job of the actor to show up, and use the lines and his or her will and common sense, to attempt to achieve a goal similar to that of the protagonist. And that is the end of the actor's job…

Taken from: 'Ancestor Worship' in *True and False: Heresy and Common Sense for the Actor* by David Mamet, London: Faber and Faber, 1997, pages 8–12.

Having attempted to demolish some of the mythology surrounding the process of acting, Mamet then subjects it to what he would probably call some common-sense scrutiny. In this final extract, he offers some straightforward, but useful advice to the aspiring actor.

34: Find Your Mark

***Find your mark, look the other fellow in the eye,
And tell the truth.***

James Cagney

Why accept the second-rate in yourself or in others? Why laugh at the unfunny? Why sigh at the hackneyed? Why gasp at the predictable? Why do we do that? We do it because we need to laugh, to sigh, to gasp.

And in the absence of the real stimulus we are capable of being manipulated and of manipulating ourselves, to take the form for the substance. To take cheap, degraded thrills for fear of having no thrills at all. Because, remember, it is the audience that goes to the theatre to exercise its emotion – not the actor, the audience. And when they go, having paid to be moved, they exercise their right to their money's worth.

What moves them?

When we read the newspaper, we are most moved by the ordinary man or woman forced by circumstances to act in an extraordinary way. We are moved by heroism. We are not moved by the self-proclaimed emotions of the manipulative, or of the famous. We discount to the greatest extent these reports, as we fear, correctly, that they are only advertising themselves. Similarly, at the theatre or at the film, we are truly and only moved by the ordinary men or women (actors) doing their best under extraordinary circumstances, forced to act in an extraordinary way in order to achieve their goal. Just as when we read in the newspaper of the postman who rescues the invalid from the burning building. We are moved by the heroism of the ordinary person acting in an extraordinary way.

We enjoy the foibles of the great, their follies, and their self-proclamations, as it titillates both our own grandiose folly and our feeling of self-importance – as we feel ourselves, rightly, superior to them. But this thrill is cheap and it is as nothing compared to our enjoyment of real heroism. Why? Because when we see real heroism, the heroism of the ordinary person forced by circumstances to act bravely, we identify with that man or woman and we say, "If they can do it, then perhaps I could, too".

The actor who mugs, who hams it up, who lays claim to emotions which are false, or who uses these supposed emotions to make a demand upon the audience, can extort an unhappy admiration as he asks the audience in admiring him to admire itself. But the actor who tells the truth simply because the circumstances require it is like the postman who saves the invalid, the bicycle messenger who rides in the Olympics, an ordinary man or woman behaving with address and direction in extraordinary circumstances. And, at this, we, the audience, exercise a higher faculty than that of getting our money's worth: the faculty of admiration, of love for true nobility in human character. Now, I have spoken of "the situation". You say, "The postman was placed in a situation; Hamlet was placed in a situation. I might act *truthfully* perhaps, but cannot one act truthfully and be out of adjustment with the situation? How can I be true to the situation?"

Stanislavski said the actor should ask, "What would I do in that situation?" His student Vakhtangov said the question was more aptly put, "What must I do to do what I would do in that situation?" But I say you should ask not "What would I do in that situation," not "What must I do to do what I would do in that situation," but you should discard the idea of "the situation" altoghether.

None of us has any idea whatever what we would do in such a situation – Hamlet's or the postman's. How can we know? Only a fool or a liar would claim to know what they would do when called upon to act with courage.

Well, fine then, let's disavow foreknowledge of our capacity for bravery, for grace under pressure; and rather than idolising ourselves – which is what sense memory is all about, enthroning our power to feel and hoping that that includes the power to move – rather let us learn to submit, as it were, to stand the gaff, to face the audience, the casting director, the opponent on the stage, with, bravely, shoulders squared. And then, rather than pretending, we can *discover* whether or not we are courageous...

*

... Here's a hint. The opportunity for bravery is always there – it is always in the play itself.

Let me explain. The actor says to himself, "I can't play this scene because I am unprepared; I can't play it because I don't like the other actor, who is a swine; I feel that the moment is wrong as the director has interpreted it; I feel this flies in the face of my preparation; the script isn't as good as I thought it was," and so on.

All of these feelings are engendered by the *script* and they are always and only engendered by the script. The fantasy that the play brings to life supplies everything we need to act – and all our excuses, all those supposed "impediments" to acting are, if we listen closely, merely the play asserting itself. The actor creates excuses not to act and attributes her reluctance to everything in the world except the actual cause. The play itself has brought her to life in ways she has not foreseen, and she doesn't like it one small bit. I realise this observation may seem simplistic and even Pollyannaish, and I wouldn't credit it myself except that I have seen it to be true over too long a time spent in show business.

We say, "I can't play the scene in *Hamlet* because I am unprepared. I can't play the scene in *Othello* because I don't believe the fellow playing Othello would actually act that way. I can't play Bigger Thomas because I am furious at everyone around me. I can't play the Madame Ranyevskaya scene because I simply don't care about this project anymore".

All of the above and every other "I can't" excuse is engendered by the play because our suggestibility known no limits. Our minds work with unbelievable speed assembling and ordering information. That is our protective device as animals, and it has enabled us both to defeat the woolly mammoth and to vote for supply-side economics – we are infinitely suggestible.

As much as we theatre folk like to think of ourselves as intellectuals, we are not. Ours is not an intellectual profession. All the book learning in the world, all the "ideas" will not enable one to play Hedda Gabler, and all the gab about the "arc of the character" and "I based my performance on –" is gibberish. There is no arc of the character; and one can no more base a performance on an idea than one can base a love affair on an idea. These phrases are nothing but talismans of the actor to enable him or her to ward off evil, and the evil they attempt to ward off is the terrifying unforeseen.

The magic phrases and procedures are incantations to lessen the terror of going out there naked. But that's how the actor goes out there, like it or not.

And all the emotions and sense memory and emotional checkpoints will not create certainty. On the contrary, they will only dull the actor to the one certainty onstage, which is that the moment is going to unfold as it will and in spite of the actor's desires. The actor cannot control it; he or she can only ignore it.

To return to suggestibility. The script is going to live in its own unforeseeable ways. Therefore you the actor, as you will be dealing with both the script and the others, as you are *seeing* something you did not expect, will likely be feeling something you did not expect. You will be brought to feel as I said, "I cannot play that scene in *Hamlet* because I am unsure; I thought I understood it and now I just don't know. Also, the other actors seem to want something from me I am not in the position to deliver" – which is, of course, the same situation in which the audience discovers Hamlet – what a coincidence.

How can the actor know that that which he or she is feeling in the moment is not only acceptable but an eloquent and beautiful part of the play? The actor cannot. When onstage it's not only necessary but impossible to attribute one's feelings, to say, "I feel A because I am overtired, and I feel B because the 'character' should feel it, and I feel C because the fellow playing the king opposite me is a ham," and so on.

Actors like to attribute their feelings, as this gives them the illusion of control over them. Everything they try to wish away is the unexpected; which is to say again, the *play*.

The question is, how can an actor know or remember that? And the answer is, the actor can't. Time onstage moves too quickly; and the moment, if one has time to consider it, is long gone by the time the consideration begins.

So wisdom consists in this: do not attribute feelings, act on them before attributing them, before negotiating with them, before saying, "This is engendered by the play; this is not engendered by the play." Act on them. First, although you won't believe it, they're *all* engendered by the play; and second, even if they were not, by the time you feel something, the audience has already seen it. It happened and you might as well have acted on it. (If you didn't, the audience saw not "nothing," but you, the actor, denying something).

The above is true and it's difficult to do. It calls on the actor not to do more, not to believe more, not to work harder as part of an industrial effort, but to *act*, to speak out bravely although unprepared and frightened.

The middle-class work ethic: "But I did my preparation. It is not my fault if the truth of the moment does not conform." That ethic is not going to avail. Nobody cares how hard you worked. Nor should they.

Acting, which takes place, for an audience, is not as the academic model would have us believe. It is not a test. It is an art, and it requires not tidiness, not paint-by-numbers intellectuality, but immediacy and courage.

We are of course trained in our culture to hold our tongue and control our emotions and to behave in a reasonable manner. So, to act one has to unlearn these habits, to train oneself to speak out, to respond quickly, to act forcefully, irrespective of what one feels and in so doing to create the habit, not of "understanding," not of "attributing," the moment, but of giving up control and, in so doing, giving oneself up to the play.

Acting in my lifetime has grown steadily away from performance and toward what for want of a better term can only be called oral interpretation, which is to say a pageantlike presentation in which actors present to the audience a prepared monologue complete with all the Funny Voices. And they call the Funny Voices emotional preparation.

In life there is no emotional preparation for loss, grief, surprise, betrayal, discovery; and there is none onstage either.

Forget the Funny Voices, pick up your cue, and speak out *even though* frightened.

Taken from: 'Find Your Mark' in *True and False: Heresy and Common Sense for the Actor* **by David Mamet, London: Faber and Faber, 1997, pages 25–33.**

Part Four: The Director

The role of the theatre director, as we understand it today, began to evolve during the last quarter of the nineteenth century. Previously, the playwright or the 'star' actor had been responsible for supervising the production. It was only with the appearance of the Saxe-Meiningen Company, under the direction of Duke Georg II and Ludwig Chronekg, that all aspects of production were integrated into a coherent and unified whole.

May 1st 1874, represents a landmark in the early history of the director. This was the date that the Duke brought his unknown company to Berlin to provide us with the first real example of a director's theatre. The hallmarks of the company were intensive rehearsals, disciplined acting and meticulous attention to the detailed composition of the stage picture, especially where crowd scenes were involved.

35: Pictorial Motion in the Meiningen Theatre

In composing a stage effect, it is important to keep the middle of the picture from being congruent with the middle of the stage. If one follows the geometric principle of the golden mean, the stage divides into two even parts, which is likely to lead to monotony in the distribution and grouping. Assimilation in the total picture becomes more or less symmetrical, creating a wooden, stiff and boring impression...

(The charm of Japanese art can be largely attributed to their avoidance of symmetry...)

The exception proves the rule: the grouping of the principal figure – or the principal mass of figures – in the centre can work out if the neighbouring figures or groups are placed on the side at more or less regular intervals. It can create a happy artistic effect, particularly is a powerfully exalted mood is desired. (One is reminded of the Sistine Chapel. There the picture is one of leisurely rest.) But the stage must always depict movement, the continuous unfolding of a story. That is why this method is to be generally avoided, as it creates a lifeless effect and holds up the action.

It rarely works to have a figure dead centre. Scenery and other objects are to be placed whenever possible on the sides, of course at a certain distance from the wings, and so as to be visible to the audience.

The actor must never stand dead centre directly in front of the prompter, but always slightly to the left or right of his box.

The middle foreground of the stage, about the width of the prompter's box, from the footlights to the background, should be considered by the actor merely as a passageway from right to left or vice versa; otherwise he has no business there.

Likewise, two actors should avoid standing in similar relation to the prompter's box.

One should give special attention, also, to the relative position of the actor and the scenery. That relation must be correct...

Generally, the first rehearsals of a new play with crowd scenes and a large cast make the director's hair stand on end. He almost doubts the possibility of bringing to life and moulding this rigid, inflexible mass. It helps him a great deal in this task to have the scenery unchanged from the beginning. Changing the sets, rehanging certain parts of the scenery, moving the furniture during rehearsals slows up everything, gets on the director's nerves, bores his co-workers and puts them to sleep.

In costume plays, weapons, helmets, arms, swords, etc., must be used as soon as possible, so that the actor is not encumbered by the unusual handling of heavy armour during the performance.

With these plays it is obligatory that the actors rehearse in costume even before the dress rehearsal, which only differs from opening night by the exclusion of the public... The performance should not present the actor with any unforeseen or surprising situation...

Carriage and gestures are influenced by changing from modern clothes to those of the past. Our perfectly familiar way of standing with heels together, which is the accepted one for the military at a halt, and which civilians also use in greeting superior and notable people, looks out of place in older costumes – from the ancient Greek period to the Renaissance – and is completely wrong. This position, heel to heel, seems to have been introduced along with the step of the minuet. A peasant leader cannot stand like an *Abbe galant* from the time of wigs, or with clicked heels, like a lieutenant in a modern drawing room.

The natural, correct and visually satisfying posture in costume from the days of pigtails on, is feet apart and placed one in front of the other.

The general rule is: all parallels on the stage are to be avoided as much as possible. This applies to costume plays in certain ways as well...

The use of parallels is particularly bad in relating the position of one actor with another. Since the parallel position of a single person, facing the footlights squarely, is bad; so two or three actors of approximately the same height doing likewise will give a most disagreeable impression.

Nor should an actor move in a parallel line. For example, an actor moving from forward right to left forward should, by imperceptible and subtle means, break the straight line, not the best on the stage, by moving on a diagonal.

If three or more actors play a scene together, they should never be placed in a straight line. They must stand at angles to each other. The space between the individual actors must always be uneven. Regular intervals create a sense of boredom and lifelessness like figures on a chessboard.

It is always an advantage to have an actor touch a piece of furniture or some other near-by object naturally. That enhances the impression of reality.

Should the stage have different levels – steps, an uneven floor strewn with rocks, and the like – the actor must remember to give his posture a rhythmical, living line. He must never stand with both feet on the same step. He should, if there is a stone close by, stand with one foot on it. Should he be walking down stairs and for some reason – such as having to speak a line or notice some object – be obliged to stop, one foot should always be placed lower than the other. By this device, his entire appearance takes on freedom and ease...

The handling of crowds on the stage requires a special preparation...

It is the first job of the director to sort out of his crowd, and as soon as possible, the talented from the untalented, separating the goats from the sheep. The doubtful and naïve ones must only serve as padding.

The walk-ons should then he divided into small groups and trained separately.

Each group is then led by an experienced actor or member of the chorus, who acts as "cover" and stands in front of them on the stage. It is in a way the responsibility of this leader to see to it that the group entrusted to him follows orders. He is responsible to the director in seeing that the positions, gestures, etc. are taken at the right moment...

At Meiningen, various artists without exception are used as leaders of walk-ons. The amazing effectiveness of first-night performances at Meiningen can be largely attributed to the lively participation of the crowds. This is in contrast to the awkward, wooden apathy of the supers to which we had accustomed ourselves and which makes such a disastrous impression.

The ugly and erroneous positions of individual actors in relation to each other are particularly disturbing in crowd scenes. The chief charm of groups is in the line of the heads. Just as a similarity of posture is to be avoided, so a regularity of height in actors standing near each other is, wherever possible, to be shunned. When it can be done, individuals should stand on different levels... It is effective to have those looking at one person or situation form an uneven semi-circle whenever it can be done.

Care must be taken that the actors nearest to the public and seen most by the spectators stand so that their shoulders are in various relations to the footlights. One should remind a walk-on to change his position as soon as he notices himself standing like his neighbour. In a good picture, one finds few figures in the same position or facing the same way...

When the impression of a great crowd is desired, one should place the groups so that the people on the sides are lost in the shadows of the wings. No one in the audience can be permitted to see where the grouping stops. The grouping must give the illusion that other crowds are also forming behind the scene.

Quoted by Max Grube in *Geschicte der Meininger*, reprinted in *Directors on Directing*, edited by Toby Cole and Helen Krich Chinoy, Indianapolis, Ind: Bobbs-Merrill, 1976, pages 81–88.

The example of the Meiningen company, with its meticulous attention to detail, became an inspiration to the great naturalistic directors like Stanislavski in Russia, Otto Brahm in Germany and Andre Antoine, founder of Theatre Libre, in France.

36: Behind the Fourth Wall

... The first time I had to direct a play, I saw clearly that the work was divided into two distinct parts: one was quite tangible, that is, finding the right *décor* for the action and the proper way of grouping the characters; the other was impalpable, that is, the interpretation and flow of the dialogue.

First of all, therefore, I found it useful, in fact, indispensable, carefully to create the setting and the environment, without worrying at all about the events that were to occur on the stage. For it is the environment that determines the movements of the characters, not the movements of the characters that determine the environment.

This simple sentence does not seem to express anything very new; yet that is the whole secret of the impression of newness which came from the initial efforts of the *Theatre Libre*.

Since our theatre has the bad habit of assigning the actors to their first places in an empty theatre on a bare stage, before the sets are built, we are constantly thrown back on the four or five classic "positions," more or less elaborated according to the director's taste or the scene designer's talent, but always identically the same.

For a stage set to be original, striking and authentic, it should first be built in accordance with something seen – whether a landscape or an interior. If it is an interior, it should be built with its four sides, its four walls, without worrying about the fourth wall, which will later disappear so as to enable the audience to see what is going on.

Next, the logical exits should be taken care of, with due regard for architectural accuracy; and, outside the set proper, the halls and rooms connecting with these exits should be plainly indicated and sketched. Those rooms that will only partly be seen, when a door opens slightly, should be furnished on paper. In short, the whole house – and not just the part in which the action takes place – should be sketched.

Once this work is done, can you see how easy and interesting it is, after examining the landscape or an interior from every one of its angles, to choose the exact point at which we shall have to cut in order to remove the famous fourth wall, while retaining a set that it most authentic in character and best suited to the action?

It is very simple, is it not? Well, we do not always proceed in that manner – either through negligence, or lack of time, or because we press into service old sets that have been used in other plays. Yet it is only too true that you can never stage a play well in an old set.

Once we have sketched the four-sided plan, according to the method outlined above, it may be that the whole apartment is not absolutely necessary for the action. In modern life, in our living rooms, bedrooms, and studies, the floor plan as well as the nature of our occupations causes us unconsciously to live and work in certain places rather than in others. In winter, we are more apt to gather around a fireplace or stove; in summer, on the contrary, we are drawn toward the sunlit windows, and we instinctively go there to read or breathe.

You will understand how important these considerations gradually become when you have to build your set. The Germans and the English do not hesitate: they combine, cut and ingeniously break up space, so as to present in the central portion of the stage picture nothing but the fireplace, window, desk, or corner they need.

These settings – so picturesque, so alive, with such novel and intimate charm – are sadly neglected in France because our scene designers are still influenced, in spite of everything, by the traditional heritage of our classical theatre. They feel that the eye will not tolerate a lack of symmetry.

Their hidebound timidity is all the more inexcusable in that our architects, within the small land areas at their disposal, have built modern houses with unusual designs and broken lines; and to the scene designer these can be an inexhaustible source of picturesqueness and variety…

Taken from: 'Causerie sur la mise en scene' in *La Revue de Paris, Vol X*; reprinted in *Directors on Directing*, edited by Toby Cole and Helen Krich Chinoy, Indianapolis, Ind: Bobbs-Merrill, 1976, pages 94–96.

At the same time that Antoine and Stanislavski were trying to forge an ever closer relationship between theatre and reality; another group of directors were avidly seeking to exploit all of the resources that theatre has to offer in the creation of what came to be known as a 'new theatricality'. A leading light in this group was Edward Gordon Craig, who argued that a new kind of theatre artist was needed; a master who could bring together all of the diverse elements of theatre into a harmonious whole, bringing about a renaissance in the art of the theatre.

37: On the Art of the Theatre

PLAYGOER

… You consider that the stage director is a craftsman and not an artist?

STAGE DIRECTOR

When he interprets the plays of the dramatist by means of his actors, his scene-painters, and his other craftsmen, then he is a craftsman – a master craftsman; when he will have mastered the uses of actions, words, line, colour and rhythm, then he may become an artist. Then we shall no longer require the assistance of the playwright – for our art will then be self-reliant.

PLAYGOER

Is your belief in a Renaissance of the art based on your belief in the Renaissance of the stage director?

STAGE DIRECTOR

Yes, certainly, most certainly...

PLAYGOER

What are his duties?

STAGE DIRECTOR

What is his craft? I will tell you. His work as interpreter of the play of the dramatist is something like this: he takes the copy of the play from the hands of the dramatist and promises faithfully to interpret it as indicated in the text (remember I am speaking only of the very best of stage directors). He then reads the play, and during the first reading the entire colour, tone, movement and rhythm that the work must assume comes clearly before him. As for the stage director, descriptions of the scenes, etc. with which the author may interlard his copy, these are not to be considered by him, for if he is master of his craft he can learn nothing from them... He then puts the play aside for some time, and in his mind's eye mixes his palette (to use a painter's expression) with the colour which the impression of the play has called up. Therefore, on sitting down a second time to read through the play, he is surrounded by an atmosphere which he proposes to test. At the end of the second reading he will find that his more definite impressions have received clear and unmistakable corroboration, and that some of his impressions which were less positive have disappeared... It is possible even now to commence to suggest, in line and colour, some of the scenes and ideas which are filling his head, but this is more likely to be delayed until he has re-read the play at least a dozen times.

PLAYGOER

But I thought the stage-manager always left that part of the play – the scene designing – to the scene painter?

STAGE DIRECTOR

So he does, generally. First blunder of the modern theatre.

PLAYGOER

How is it a blunder?

STAGE DIRECTOR

This way: *A* has written a play which *B* promises to interpret faithfully. In so delicate a matter as the interpretation of so elusive a thing as the spirit of a play, which, do you think, will be the surest way to preserve the unity of that spirit? Will it be best if *B* does all the work himself? or will it do to give the work into the hands of *C*, *D*, and *E*, each of whom see or think differently to *B* or *A*?

PLAYGOER

Of course the former would be best. But is it possible for one man to do the work of three men?

STAGE DIRECTOR

That is the only way the work can be done, if unity, the one thing vital to a work of art, is to be obtained.

PLAYGOER

So, then, the stage director does not call in a scene painter and ask him to design a scene, but he designs one himself?

STAGE DIRECTOR

Certainly. And remember he does not merely sit down and draw a pretty or historically accurate design, with enough doors and windows in picturesque places, but he first of all chooses certain colours which seem to him to be in harmony with the spirit of the play, rejecting other colours as out of tune. He then weaves into a pattern certain objects – an arch, a fountain, a balcony, a bed – using the chosen object as the centre of his design. Then he adds to this all the objects which are mentioned in the play, and which are necessary to be seen. To these he adds, one by one, each character which appears in the play, and gradually each movement of each character, and each costume. He is as likely as not to make several mistakes in his pattern. If so, he must, as it were, unpick the design, and rectify the blunder even if he has to go right back to the beginning and start the pattern all over again – or he may even have to begin a new pattern. At any rate, slowly, harmoniously, must the whole design develop, so that the eye of the beholder shall be satisfied. While this pattern for the eye is being devised, the designer is being guided as much by the sound of the verse or prose as by the sense or spirit. And shortly all is prepared, and the actual work can be commenced.

PLAYGOER

What actual work? ...

STAGE DIRECTOR

… the stage director's most interesting work is just beginning. His scene is set and his characters are clothed. He has, in short, a kind of dream picture in front of him. He clears the stage of all but the one, two or more characters who are to commence the play, and he begins the scheme of lighting these figures and the scene… Being… a man of some intelligence and training, he has devised a special way of lighting his scene… just as he has devised a special way of painting the scene and costuming the figures. If the word "harmony" held no significance for him, he would of course leave it to the first comer.

PLAYGOER

Then do you actually mean that he has made so close a study of nature that he can direct his electricians how to make it appear as if the sun were shining at such and such an altitude, or as if the moonlight were flooding the interior of the room with such and such intensity?

STAGE DIRECTOR

No, I should not like to suggest that, because the reproduction of nature's lights is not what my stage director ever attempts. Neither should he attempt such an impossibility. Not to *reproduce* nature, but to *suggest* some of her most beautiful and most living ways – that is what my stage director shall attempt…

PLAYGOER

… in what way does he set to work? What guides him in his task of lighting the scene and costumes which we are speaking about?

STAGE DIRECTOR

… Why the scene and the costumes, and the verse and the prose, and the sense of the play. All these things, as I told you, have now been brought into harmony, the one with the other – all goes smoothly – what simpler, then, that it should so continue, and that the director should be the only one to know how to preserve this harmony which he has commenced to create… We… come to the most interesting part, that of the manipulation of the figures in all their movements and speeches… Consider… the nature of this work… Some actors have the right instincts… and some have none whatever. But even those whose instincts are most keen cannot remain in the pattern, cannot be har-monious, without following the directions of the stage director.

PLAYGOER

Then you do not even permit the leading actor and actress to move and act as their instincts and reason dictate?

STAGE DIRECTOR

No, rather must they be the very first to follow the directions of the stage director, so often do they become the very centre of the pattern – the very heart of the emotional design.

PLAYGOER

And is that understood and appreciated by them?

STAGE DIRECTOR

Yes, but only when they realise and appreciate at the same time that the play, and the right and just interpretation of the play, is the all-important thing in the modern theatre... the finer the actor the finer his intelligence, and therefore the more easily controlled...

PLAYGOER

But are you not asking these intelligent actors almost to become puppets?

STAGE DIRECTOR

A sensitive question! Which one would expect from an actor who felt uncertain about his powers. A puppet is at present only a doll, delightful enough for a puppet show. But for a theatre we need more than a doll. Yet that is the feeling which some actors have about their relationship with the stage director. They feel they are having their strings pulled, and resent it, and show they feel hurt – insulted...

PLAYGOER

... you would allow no one to rule on the stage except the stage director?

STAGE DIRECTOR

The nature of the work permits nothing else.

PLAYGOER

Not even the playwright?

STAGE DIRECTOR

Only when the playwright has practised and studied the crafts of acting, scene painting, costume, lighting, and dance, not otherwise... I look for a Renaissance.

PLAYGOER

How will that come?

STAGE DIRECTOR

Through the advent of a man who shall contain in him all the qualities which go to make up a master of the theatre, and through the reform of the theatre as an instrument. When that is accomplished, when the theatre has become a masterpiece of mechanism, when it has invented a technique, it will without any effort develop a *creative art* of its own... There are already some theatre men at work on the building of the the-atres; some are reforming the acting, some the scenery. But the very first thing to be realised is that little or no result can come from the reforming of a single craft of the theatre without at the same time, in the same theatre, reforming all the other crafts. *The whole renaissance of the Art of the Theatre depends upon the extent that this is realised...* it must be realised at the commencement that ENTIRE, not PART reform is needed; and it must be realised that *one* part, one craft, has a *direct* bear-ing upon each of the other crafts in the theatre, and that no result can come from fitful, uneven reform, but only from a systematic progres-sion. Therefore, the reform of the Art of the Theatre is possible to those men alone who have studied and practised all the crafts of the theatre.

PLAYGOER

In other words, your ideal stage director.

STAGE DIRECTOR

Yes... I told you my belief in the Renaissance of the Art of the Theatre was based in my belief in the Renaissance of the stage director, and when he had understood the right use of actors, scene, costume, light-ing and dance, and by means of these had mastered the crafts of interpretation, he would then gradually acquire the mastery of action, line, colour, rhythm and words, this last strength developing out of all the rest... Then I said the Art of the Theatre would have won back its rights, and its work would stand self-reliant as a creative art, and no longer as an interpretative craft...

...I am now going to tell you out of what material an artist of the the-atre of the future will create his masterpieces. Out of ACTION, SCENE, and VOICE. Is it not very simple?

And when I say *action*, I mean both gesture and dancing, the prose and poetry of action.

When I say *scene*, I mean all which comes before the eye, such as the lighting, costume, as well as the scenery.

When I say *voice*, I mean the spoken word or the word which is sung, in contradiction to the word which is read, for the word written to be spo-ken and the word written to be read are two entirely different things...

Taken from: *On the Art of the Theatre* by Edward Gordon Craig, London: Heinemann, 1968, pages 148–181.

The other key figure in the move towards the 'new theatricality' was the Russian director, Vsevolod Meyerhold. In common with Craig, Meyerhold wanted to see the rebirth of what he called 'the universal theatre'; but, as one might expect from someone who had been one of the original members of the Moscow Art Theatre (MAT) and acted in many of Stanislavski's early naturalistic productions, Meyerhold sees the function of the actor in very different terms to Craig. On leaving MAT, Meyerhold set about creating a new theatre based on the symbolic, 'theatrical' theatres of the past.

38: The Stylised Theatre

'I call for the calculated stylisation of the theatre of antiquity to replace the irrelevant truth of the modern stage', said Valery Bryusov. Vyacheslav Ivanov, too, awaits its revival. Bryusov makes only a passing reference to the phenomenon of stylisation in the antique theatres; Ivanov however reveals a coherent plan for a Dionysian festival.

It is taking an excessively narrow view of Ivanov's project to interpret it as a repertoire composed exclusively of Greek tragedies and plays written in the style of Greek tragedy... In order to demonstrate that Ivanov had a far broader repertoire in mind, we should need to examine everything which he has written. Unfortunately we are not concerned primarily with him; I want to draw on his insight in order to show more clearly the advantages of the stylistic technique, and to show that it alone makes it possible for the theatre to embrace the diverse repertoire advocated by Ivanov and the variegated bouquet of plays which our modern dramatists are presenting to the Russian stage.

Drama proceeded from the dynamic to the static pole. Drama was born 'of the spirit of music, out of the dynamic energy of the choric dithyramb'...

Having originated in the dithyrambic homage paid to Dionysus, drama gradually receded from its religious origins. The mask of the tragic hero, the recognisable embodiment of the spectator's own fate, the mask of a single tragic fate which embodied the universal 'I', became slowly objectivised over the course of centuries. Shakespeare explored characterisation. Corneille and Racine made their heroes dependent on the morality of a particular age, thereby transforming them into materialistic formulae.

The stage has become estranged from its communal-religious origins; it has alienated the spectator by its objectivity. The stage is no longer *infectious*, it no longer has the power of *transfiguration*.

But thanks to such dramatists as Ibsen, Maeterlinck, Verhaeren and Wagner, the theatre is moving back towards its dynamic origins. We are rediscovering the precepts of antiquity. Just as the sacred ritual of Greek tragedy was a form of Dionysian *catharsis*, so today we demand of the artist that he heal and purify us.

In the New Drama external action, the revelation of character, is becoming incidental. 'We are striving to penetrate *behind* the mask, *beyond* the action into the character as perceived by the mind; we want to penetrate to the *inner mask*.'

The New Drama rejects the external in favour of the internal, not in order to penetrate man's soul and thus renounce this earth and ascend to the heavens (*theatre esoterique*), but to intoxicate the spectator with the Dionysian cup of eternal sacrifice.

'If the New Theatre is once again dynamic, then let it be totally dynamic.' If the theatre is finally to rediscover its dynamic essence, it must cease to be 'theatre' in the sense of mere 'spectacle'. We intend the audience not merely to observe, but to participate in a *corporate* creative act.

Ivanov asks: 'What is a fit subject for the drama of the future?' – and replies: 'Everything must be on a grand scale: tragedy, comedy, the mystery, the popular tale, the myth and the social drama.' The symbolical drama which is no longer obscure but 'strikes an answering chord in the popular soul'; the exalted, heroic tragedy which resembles the tragedies of antiquity (not, of course, a resemblance in dramatic structure – we are referring to Fate and Satire as the fundamental elements of Tragedy and Comedy); the mystery which is broadly analogous to the medieval mystery play; somedy in the manner of Aristophanes – this is the range of plays envisaged by Vyacheslav Ivanov.

Could the naturalistic theatre possibly cope with such a varied repertoire? No! The leading exponent of the naturalistic style, the Moscow Art Theatre, tried to embrace Greek classical theatre... Shakespeare... Ibsen.... and Maeterlinck. Even though it had Stanislavski, the most talented director in Russia, at its head, plus a host of outstanding actors and actresses... it was powerless to cope with such a wide repertoire.

I maintain that its efforts were frustrated by its obsession with the Meiningen style, with *naturalistic* method. The Moscow Art Theatre succeeded in mastering only Chekhov, and remained finally an 'intimate theatre'. The intimate theatres and all those which rely on the Meiningen method or on the 'atmosphere' of Chekhov's theatre have proved incapable of broadening their repertoire, and consequently have been unable to attract a wider audience.

With the passing of each century the antique theatre has become progressively transformed, and the intimate theatre represents its ultimate guise, its last offshoot. The theatre today is split into tragedy and comedy, wheras the antique theatre was a single, unified theatre.

I regard this fragmentation of the theatre into intimate theatres as the obstacle which is obstructing the rebirth of the universal theatre, the truly *dramatic* theatre, the festive theatre.

The offensive launched against naturalistic methods by certain theatres and directors is no coincidence, but a direct outcome of historical evolution. Experiments with new theatrical forms have been provoked not by idle whim or fashion, by the desire to introduce a new production method (stylisation), nor by the need to satisfy the taste of the crowd for more and more acute sensations. The experimental theatres and their directors are seeking to create a stylised theatre in order to arrest the dissolution of the stage into *intimate* theatres, and in order to restore *the unified theatre*.

The stylised theatre embodies a technique so simplified that it will be possible to stage Maeterlinck as well as Wedekind, Andreyev as well as Sologub, Blok as well as Przybyszewski, Ibsen as well as Remizov.

The stylised theatre liberates the actor from all scenery, creating a three-dimensional area in which he can employ natural, sculptural plasticity. Thanks to stylisation, we can do away with complicated stage machinery, and mount simple productions in which the actor can interpret his role free from all scenery and specifically *theatrical* properties – free from all purely incidental trappings.

In Ancient Greece at the time of Sophocles and Euripides, the competition amongst tragic actors gave rise to the art of the creative actor. Later with the development of technical devices, the creative powers of the actor declined; with the further refinement of technical devices in our day, the independent function of the actor has declined still further. In this connection, Chekhov is right when he says – 'nowadays there are few outstandingly gifted actors, but the average actor has improved enormously' (*The Seagull*). By freeing the actor from the haphazard conglomeration of irrelevant stage properties, and by reducing technical devices to the minimum, the stylised theatre avoids the 'mood' of Chekhovian theatre, which transforms acting into the passive experience of emotions and reduces the actor's creative intensity.

Having removed the footlights, the stylised theatre aims to place the stage on a level with the auditorium. By giving diction and movement a rhythmical basis, it hopes to bring about the revival of the *dance*. In such a theatre, dialogue can easily merge into melodic declamation and melodic silence.

The task of the director in the stylised theatre is to direct the actor rather than control him (unlike the Meiningen director). He serves purely as a bridge, linking the soul of the author with the soul of the actor. Having assimilated the author's creation, the actor is left *alone*, face to face with the spectator, and from the friction between these two unadulterated elements, the actor's creativity and the spectator's imagination, a clear flame is kindled.

Taken from: 'The Stylised Theatre' by Vsevolod Meyerhold in *Meyerhold on Theatre*, edited by Edward Braun, London: Methuen, 1991, pages 58–62.

In Meyerhold's theatre, it is the actor who holds the key; Meyerhold wanted to see a breaking down of the barrier between performer and spectator. His goal was to create an unbroken circle of creative energy which would bring both sides together in an act of communion. This aim was shared with the Polish director Jerzy Grotowski, who, in his Theatre Laboratory, *undertook the most thorough investigation of acting since Stanislavski.*

39: The Theatre's New Testament

… one must ask oneself what is indispensable to theatre. Let's see.

Can the theatre exist without costumes and sets? Yes, it can.

Can it exist without music to accompany the plot? Yes.

Can it exist without lighting effects? Of course.

And without a text? Yes; the history of the theatre confirms this. In the evolution of the theatrical art the text was one of the last elements to be added. If we place some people on a stage with a scenario they themselves have put together and let them improvise their parts as in the Commedia dell'Arte, the performance will be equally good even if the words are not articulated but simply muttered.

But can the theatre exist without actors? I know of no example of this. One could mention the puppet-show. Even here, however, an actor is to be found behind the scenes, although of another kind.

Can the theatre exist without an audience? At least one spectator is needed to make it a performance. So we are left with the actor and the spectator. We can thus define the theatre as "what takes place between spectator and actor". All the other things are supplementary – perhaps necessary, but nevertheless supplementary. It is no mere coincidence that our own theatre laboratory has developed from a theatre rich in resources... into the ascetic theatre we have become in recent years: an ascetic theatre in which the actors and audience are all that is left. All the other visual elements... are constructed by means of the actor's body, the acoustic and musical effects by his voice... Since our theatre consists only of actors and audience, we make special demands on both parties...

The actor is a man who works in public with his body, offering it publicly. If this body restricts itself to demonstrating what it is – something that any average person can do – then it is not an obedient instrument capable of performing a spiritual act...

What strikes one when looking at the work of an actor as practised these days is the wretchedness of it: the bargaining over a body which is exploited by its protectors... creating in return an atmosphere of intrigue and revolt.

Just as only a great sinner can become a saint according to the theologians... In the same way the actor's wretchedness can be transformed into a kind of holiness. The history of the theatre has numerous examples of this.

Don't get me wrong, I speak about "holiness" as an unbeliever. I mean a "secular holiness". If the actor, by setting himself a challenge publicly challenges others, and through excess, profanation and outrageous sacrilege reveals himself by casting off his everyday mask, he makes it possible for the spectator to undertake a similar process of self-penetration...

There is a myth telling how an actor with a considerable fund of experience can build up what we might call his own "arsenal" – i.e. an accumulation of methods, artifices and tricks. From these he can pick out a certain number of combinations for each part and thus attain the expressiveness necessary for him to grip his audience. This "arsenal" or store may be nothing but a collection of cliches, in which case such a method is inseparable from the conception of the "courtesan actor".

The difference between the "courtesan actor" and the "holy actor" is the difference between the skill of a courtesan and the attitude of giving and receiving which springs from true love; in other words, self-sacrifice. The essential thing in this second case is to be able to eliminate any disturbing elements in order to be able to overstep every conceivable limit. In the first case it is a question of the existence of the body; in the other, rather of its non-existence. The technique of the "holy actor" is an **inductive technique** (i.e. a technique of elimination), whereas that of the "courtesan actor" is a **deductive technique** (i.e. an accumulation of skills).

The actor who undertakes an act of self-penetration, who reveals himself, and sacrifices the innermost part of himself – the most painful, that which is not intended for the eyes of the world – must be able to manifest the least impulse. He must be able to express, through sound and movement, those impulses which waver on the borderline between dream and reality...

We are concerned with the spectator who has genuine spiritual needs and who really wishes through confrontation with the performance, to analyse himself. We are concerned with the spectator who does not stop at an elementary stage of psychic integration, content with his own petty, geometrical, spiritual stability, knowing exactly what is good and what is evil, and never in doubt. For it was not to him that El Greco, Norwid, Thomas Mann and Dostoyevsky spoke, but to him who undergoes an endless process of self development, whose unrest is not general but directed towards a search for the truth about himself and his mission in life...

The theatre must recognise its own limitations. If it cannot be richer than the cinema, then let it be poor. If it cannot be as lavish as television, let it be ascetic. If it cannot be a technical attraction, let it renounce all outward technique. Thus we are left with a "holy actor" in a poor theatre.

There is only one element of which film and television cannot rob the theatre: the closeness of the living organism. Because of this, each challenge from the actor, each of his magical acts... becomes something great, something extraordinary, something close to ecstasy. It is therefore necessary to abolish the distance between actor and audience by eliminating the stage, removing all frontiers. Let the most drastic scenes happen, face to face with the spectator so that he is within an arm's reach of the actor, can feel his breathing and smell the perspiration. This implies the necessity for a chamber theatre...

In order that the spectator may be stimulated into self-analysis when confronted with the actor, there must be some common ground already existing in both of them, something they can either dismiss in one gesture or jointly worship. Therefore the theatre must attack what might be called the collective complexes of society, the core of the collective subconscious... the myths which are not an invention of the mind but are, so to speak, inherited through one's blood, religion, culture and climate...

To spark off this particular process of provocation in the audience, one must break away from the trampoline represented by the text and which is already overloaded with a number of general associations. For this we need either a classical text to which, through a sort of profanation, we simultaneously restore its truth, or a modern text which might well be banal and stereotyped in its content, but nevertheless rooted in the psyche of society...

The actor, who, in this special process of... self-sacrifice, self-penetration, is not afraid to go beyond all normally accepted limits, attains a kind of inner harmony and peace of mind. He literally becomes much sounder in mind and body... If we only engage ourselves superficially in this process of analysis and exposure... if we retain our daily mask of lies, then we witness a conflict between this mask and ourselves. But, if this process is followed through to its extreme limit, we can in full consciousness put back our everyday mask, knowing now what purpose it serves and what it conceals beneath it. This is a confirmation not of the negative in us but of the positive, not of what is poorest but of what is richest. It also leads to a liberation from complexes in much the same way as psycho-analytic therapy.

The same also applies to the spectator. The member of an audience who accepts the actor's invitation and to a certain extent follows his example by activating himself in the same way, leaves the theatre in a state of greater inner harmony. But he who fights to keep his mask of lies intact at all costs, leaves the performance even more confused...

The performance engages a sort of psychic conflict with the spectator. It is a challenge and an excess, but can only have any effect if based on human interest and, more than that, on a feeling of sympathy, a feeling of acceptance. In the same way the producer can help the actor in this complex and agonising process only if he is just as emotionally and warmly open to the actor as the actor is in regard to him. A kind of warmth towards one's fellow men is essential – an understanding of the contradictions in man, and that he is a suffering creature but not one to be scorned...

The producer's job demands a certain tactical **savoir faire**, namely in the art of leading. Generally speaking, this kind of power demoralises. It entails the necessity of learning how to handle people. It demands a gift for diplomacy, a cold and inhuman talent for dealing with intrigues. These characteristics follow the producer like his shadow even in the poor theatre. What one might call the masochistic component in the actor is the negative variant of what is creative in the director in the form of a sadistic component. Here, as everywhere, the dark is inseparable from the light.

When I take sides against half-heartedness, mediocrity and the easy-come-easy-go attitude which takes everything for granted, it is simply because we must create things which are firmly oriented towards either light or darkness. But we must remember that around that which is luminous within us, there exists a shroud of darkness which we can penetrate but not annihilate...

I do not think that the crisis in the theatre can be separated from certain other crisis processes in contemporary culture. One of its essential elements - namely, the disappearance of the sacred and of its ritual function in the theatre – is a result of the obvious and probably inevitable decline of religion. What we are talking about is the possibility of creating a secular **sacrum** in the theatre. The question is, can the current pace in the development of civilisation make a reality of this postulate on a collective scale? I have no answer to this. One must contribute to its realisation, for a secular consciousness in place of the religious one seems to be a psycho-social necessity for society...

In any case, I am sure that this renewal will not come from the dominating theatre. Yet, at the same time, there are and have been a few people in the official theatre who must be considered as secular saints: Stanislavski, for example. He maintained that the successive stages of awakening and renewal in the theatre had found their beginnings amongst amateurs and not in the circles of hardened, demoralised professionals... or to take an example from quite another culture, the Japanese No theatre which, owing to the technical ability it demands, might almost be described as a "super-profession"… From where can this renewal come? From a people who are dissatisfied with conditions in the normal theatre, and who take it on themselves to create poor theatres with few actors, "chamber ensembles" which they might transform into institutes for the education of actors; or else from amateurs working on the boundaries of the professional theatre and who, on their own, achieve a technical standard which is far superior to that demanded by the prevailing theatre: in short, a few madmen who have nothing to lose and are not afraid of hard work.

Taken from: 'The Theatre's New Testament', an interview with Grotowski conducted by Eugenio Barba; reprinted in *Towards A Poor Theatre* by Jerzy Grotowski, London: Methuen, 1968, pages 32–50.

This concern with the renaissance and renovation of the theatre was also shared by Brecht of course. But whereas Grotowski saw theatre operating almost therapeutically, Brecht wanted a theatre that was political from top to bottom. Grotowski sought to strip theatre down to its absolute essentials – the fundamental encounter between actor and spectator; but Brecht argued that actors were merely cyphers serving a political end. For the theatre to be relevant to the modern world, it had to follow the lead given by Piscator and make use of all the available technology to present matters of pressing political and social concern.

40: A Theatre for Modern Times

… In Germany… the real front-line battles were fought out mainly by Piscator, whose Theater am Nollendorfplatz was based on Marxist principles, and by myself at my Theater am Schiffbauerdamm. We denied ourselves nothing. We wrote our own texts – and I also wrote plays – or sliced up other people's in all directions, then stuck them together quite differently till they were unrecognisable. We introduced music and film and turned everything top to bottom; we made comedy out of what had originally been tragic, and vice versa. We had our characters bursting into song at the most uncalled-for moments. In short, we thoroughly muddled up people's idea of the drama.

I myself took part in it all. I spent many years training my actors; I had my own composers who knew how to write exactly in my style: Eisler, Kurt Weill and Hindemith (who was the best known). But then I was one of the few modern German playwrights who knew their way about the theatre. Most members of this profession never set foot on a stage, but I've learnt my business from the bottom, having been a producer long before any of my plays were staged. I can build a set and at a pinch take charge of my own lighting. But it's an effort, particularly when you come up against such disastrous shortcomings on the technical side as Piscator and I did...

But we put our schemes into effect. We built planes at various levels on the stage, and often made them move up or down. Piscator liked to include a kind of broad treadmill in the stage, with another one rotating in the opposite direction; these would bring on his characters. Or he would hoist his actors up and down in space; now and again they would break a leg, but we were patient with them.

But then of course we had to make use of complicated machinery if we were to show modern processes on the stage. E.g. there was a play called *Petroleum*, originally written by Leo Lania but adapted by us, in which we wanted to show exactly how oil is drilled and treated. The people here were quite secondary; they were just cyphers serving a cause. And we performed a number of other plays which needed quite a complex apparatus...

I don't think the traditional form of theatre means anything any longer. Its significance is purely historic; it can illuminate the way in which earlier ages regarded human relationships, and particularly relationships between men and women. Works by such people as Ibsen and Strindberg remain important historical documents but they no longer move anybody. A modern spectator can't learn anything from them.

In modern society the motions of the individual psyche are utterly uninteresting; it was only in feudal times that a king's or leader's passions meant anything. Today they don't. Not even Hitler's personal passions...

So the theatre has outlived its usefulness; it is no more able to represent modern phenomena and processes with the means available to it than the traditional kind of novelist can describe such everyday occurrences as housing shortage, export of pigs or speculation in coffee. Seen through its eyes, a little middling business man who despite all his care and effort loses his money through an unlucky stroke of business, would inevitably become a 'speculator'. He would 'go bankrupt', just like that, without comment, and it would be a kind of inexplicable blow of fate, much as if a man had been struck down by pneumonia.

No, in its own field the theatre must keep up with the times and all the advances of the times, and not lag several thousand miles behind as it does at present. In the old days there was no more need for the artist to bother about science than for science to concern itself with him. But now he has to, for science has progressed so much further. Look at an aeroplane and then look at a theatrical performance. People have acquired new motives for their actions; science has found new dimensions by which to measure them; its time for art to find new expressions...

Such is our time, and the theatre must be acquainted with it and go along with it, and work out an entirely new sort of art such as will be capable of influencing modern people. The main subject of the drama must be relationships between one man and another as they exist today, and that is what I'm primarily concerned to investigate and find means of expression for. Once I've found out what modes of behaviour are most useful to the human race I show them to people and underline them. I show them in parables: if you act this way the following will happen, but if you act like that then they opposite will take place. This isn't the same thing as committed art. At most pedagogics.

But ever since the days of Bacon, the great pioneer of practical thinking, people have worked to find out how man can improve his condition, and today we know that he cannot do this purely privately. It's only by banding together and joining forces that he stands a chance. Once I take that into consideration my plays are forced to deal with political matters. Thus when a family is ruined I don't seek the reason in an inexorable fate, in hereditary weaknesses or special characteristics – it isn't only the exceptional families that get ruined – but try rather to establish how it could have been avoided by human action, how the external conditions could be altered; and that lands me back in politics again...

Taken from: 'Interview with an Exile' by Bertolt Brecht in *Brecht on Theatre*, translated by John Willett, London: Eyre Methuen, 1964, pages 65–68.

So far, we have examined the general approaches of the leading twentieth century directors to the art of making theatre; and now we turn our attentions to some of the more practical aspects of directing. We begin with the making of an important distinction.

41: Two Kinds of Director

There are two kinds of director: the one who expects everything from the play, for whom the play itself is essential; and the one who expects nothing except from himself, for whom the play is a starting point. That is to say – perhaps too summarily, but in order to be clear – there are two sorts of dramatic works, and two sorts of playwrights.

There is the spectacular or theatrical theatre in which entertainment, rhythm, music, lines and appeal to the eye – all of the spectacular elements – are the important things, and here the director can indulge himself to his heart's content. In this theatrical theatre there can be included the mimes of Roman decadence, the theatre of the market-place, a good part of opera and all operetta, ballet, fair-plays, melodrama and the productions of the majority of present-day foreign directors, in which the actor, the singer, the setting, the machinery, are the essentials of the entertainment.

Then there is the theatre of dramatists and poets which makes of dramatic art a literary form of the highest order. Here the important thing is the text, and the spectacular elements are admitted only as side-issues and supplements. The literary theatre includes the Greek and Roman dramatists (Aeschylus, Sophocles, Euripides, Seneca); the humanistic renaissance with Shakespeare; the classic with Corneille, Racine, Moliere; then Marivaux, Beaumarchais, Musset. These peaks of dramatic art have been defined by one of our directors, somewhat cavalierly, as "men of letters who wrote for the theatre".

There are works of lasting character, and others whose value is only momentary. It is an accepted fact that fashion affects the writing of plays and their conception; but whenever one attains universality, where the characters are dealt with purely as human beings, we have what the text-books call a classic. This type of play contains within itself its own method of staging; that is, the work of the director is to observe how the play responds to his suggestions, to make his devices disappear into the text, so incorporating them that the play absorbs his directions without being deformed by them.

In the spectacular theatre, on the other hand, external direction is required; the work is swathed in personal contributions and inventions. The text is no more than a pretext or a support for the setting, the actors and the stage devices; and the director, relying heavily on the storehouse of the theatre or of his imagination, often rivals the leader of a cotillion. So true is that that we can say that the text of a classic or literary play is written for the audience, the text of the other kind for the actors and the director.

The natural tendency of a director is to see his plays with a definite personal bias that is the index of his temperament. Almost all directors, after a few years of modest service, dream of showing their own stature and the scale of their imagination. And, like the apprentice who thought himself a past master of his trade, like the shoemaker whom the painter Apelles put in his place by advising him not to criticise anything above shoes, they are seized with a violent desire to make over masterpieces and to express at last their own personal conceptions.

As an illustration of this mentality, this professional deformity, I should like to quote a sentence that has been in print, on the film production of *A Midsummer Night's Dream*: one of the greatest directors wrote it: "The dream of my life was to produce a work without having anything hamper my imagination." That in itself is not bad for a man whose profession is to serve others. But he adds, "I have set the condition that this work should represent Shakespeare, and nothing but Shakespeare." I hope you can feel in this avowal both the homage he intended to pay to Shakespeare and the opinion he held – comparatively – of himself. And, as a final touch, he adds, "My dream has just been realised." That is, his dream is at your disposal in the motion-picture houses. You may see Shakespeare adapted to the use of commercial New York calendars.

The greatest director will never be able to equal in his achievement the dreams and imagination of the most humble of his audience.

In reality, a play stages itself: the only necessity is to be attentive and not too personal in order to see it take on its own movement and begin to manipulate the actors. Acting on them, mysteriously, it tests them, magnifies or diminishes them, embraces or rejects them, nourishes them, transforms and deforms them. From its first rehearsal a true play comes alive, just as wood warps, wine ferments and dough rises. It gathers impetus and gradually the director, like the sorcerer's apprentice, terrified and enraptured at the same time, sees it sweep over the actors and bring them to life, rejecting or carrying away all his directions like straws in the wind, in a kind of blossoming or birth.

The profession of the director suffers from the disease of immodesty, and even the most sincere do not escape it. Their licence to work freely with the plays of other people, to dabble with them and make them over, is an established and accepted convention, and after a few hours of conversation with himself or with a colleague a man must have a steady head and a firm foothold to resist the dizziness in which, convinced of what he would like to believe, he approaches the conclusion that Shakespeare and Goethe understood nothing of the theatre. Great dramatic art is a mystery. No work can be judged outside of its age, and its transportation into another atmosphere requires long adaptation and very great respect. But here is a formula:

One can recognise a great dramatic work with certainty when the director, deciding in all good faith that it should be otherwise constructed or written, has, nevertheless, nothing more to say; when, in spite of all his desire to make over the play, he accepts it practically as it is written. A conversation I had with a director who confided to me that he was in despair because he had just been working for two months, without any result, on *La Malade Imaginaire* illustrates this definition. When I expressed astonishment, he said, "Yes, I've just spent my whole summer at it. I've tried lighting it from above, and below, and from the side; I've experimented with settings and movement on the stage. There's nothing, nothing, to be done. It's the perfect play. It is a work of genius."

This was the same man, moreover, who one day defined for me his ideas on staging the play: "My work begins and the play interests me at the moment when the text ends".

I have also heard one of the greatest directors declare, in an impulse of revolt and disgust, "I've had enough! All plays are the same. I get tired and disheartened by my work. I am greater than what I do".

If I had space I would speak here in praise of restraint and success in the theatre, and say too that the inner joy necessary to good work should not be confused with the taste for indulging one's own pleasure.

In general, the director follows his instinct and directs the play as he feels and loves, and distorts most of the others to his personal taste. That is the fundamental fault with this authorised intermediary who is so valuable when he directs a theatre. It is not because I have a taste for disparagement that I say these things, but because I want to point out everything in the director's function that can be an obstacle to the free development of the theatre.

*

If there is any conclusion to be drawn to this subject... it should be a commendation of the profession. To be professional is to be authentic.

It is the only way of being real, to possess and practice the virtue of truth. For nothing counts unless it be true, unless it has roots. Nothing counts but honesty...

Taken from: 'The Profession of the Director' by Louis Jouvet; reprinted in *Directors on Directing*, edited by Toby Cole and Helen Krich Chinoy, Indianapolis, Ind: Bobbs-Merrill, 1976, pages 229–232.

*Jouvet makes an important distinction between the director of what he calls the **spectacular** theatre, and the director whose main concern is to realise, as faithfully as possible, the playwright's work. He leaves us in little doubt about his own preference; so we will begin by looking at a section of the production notebook of a playwright's director.*

*Arguably one of the best **playwright's directors** is the American, Elia Kazan whose production of Tennesses Williams'* A Streetcar Named Desire *is legendary. Kazan was originally an actor with Strasberg's Group Theatre, but it is as a director that he is best known. In his analysis of Williams' text, Kazan applied the Stanislavskian principle of trying to establish the 'spine' of each of the characters in the play; in this extract, he examines the main character, Blanche.*

42: Notebook for a *Streetcar Named Desire*

A thought – directing finally consists of turning Psychology into Behaviour.

Theme – this is a message from the dark interior. This little twisted, pathetic, confused bit of light and culture puts out a cry. It is snuffed out by the crude forces of violence, insensibility and vulgarity which exist in our South – and this cry is the play.

Style – one reason a "style", a stylised production is necessary is that a subjective factor – Blanche's memories, inner life, emotions, are a real factor. We cannot really understand her behaviour unless we see the effect of her past on her present behaviour.

This play is a poetic tragedy. We are shown the final dissolution of a person of worth, who once had great potential, and who, even as she goes down, has worth exceeding that of the "healthy", coarse-grained figures who kill her.

Blanche is a social type, an emblem of a dying civilisation, making its last curlicued and romantic exit. All her behaviour patterns are those of the dying civilisation she represents. In other words her behaviour is *social*. Therefore find social modes! This is the source of the play's stylisation and the production's style and colour. Likewise Stanley's behaviour is *social* too. It is the basic animal cynicism of today. "Get what's coming to you! Don't waste a day! Eat, drink, get yours!" This is the basis of his stylisation, of the choice of his props. All props should be stylised: they should have a colour, shape and weight that spell: style.

An effort to put poetic names to edge me into stylisations and physicalisations. Try to keep each scene in terms of Blanche.

1. Blanche comes to the last stop at the end of the line.
2. Blanche tries to make a place for herself.
3. Blanche breaks them apart, but when they come together, Blanche is more alone than ever!
4. Blanche, more desperate because more excluded, tries the direct attack and makes the enemy who will finish her.
5. Blanche finds that she is being tracked down for the kill. She must work fast.
6. Blanche suddenly finds, suddenly makes for herself, the only possible, perfect man for her.
7. Blanche comes out of the happy bathroom to find that her own doom has caught up with her.
8. Blanche fights her last fight. Breaks down. Even Stella deserts her.
9. Blanche's last desperate effort to save herself by telling the whole truth. The *truth dooms her.*
10. Blanche escapes out of this world. She is brought back by Stanley and destroyed.
11. Blanche is disposed of.

The style – the real deep style – consists of one thing only: to find behaviour that's truly social, significantly typical, at each moment. It's not so much what Blanche has done – it's how she does it – with such style, grace, manners, old-world trappings and effects, props, tricks, swirls, etc., that they seem anything but vulgar.

And for the other characters, too, you face the same problem. To find the Don Quixote character for them. *This is a poetic tragedy, not a realistic or a naturalistic one. So you must find a Don Quixote scheme of things for each.*

Stylised acting and directing is to realistic acting and direction as poetry is to prose. The acting must be styled, not in the obvious sense.

(Say nothing about it to the producer and actors.) But you will fail unless you find this kind of poetic realisation for the behaviour of these people.

Blanche

"Blanche is desperate"

"This is the End of the Line for the Streetcar Named Desire"

Spine – find Protection: the tradition of the old South says that it must be through another person.

Her problem has to do with her tradition. Her notion of what a woman should be. She is stuck with this "ideal". It is her. It is her ego. Unless she lives by it, she cannot live; in fact her whole life has been for nothing. Even the Alan Gray incident as she now tells it and believes it to have been, is a necessary piece of romanticism. Essentially, in outline, she tells what happened, but it also serves the demands of her notion of herself, to make her *special* and different, out of the tradition of the romantic ladies of the past: Swinburne, Wm Morris, Pre-Raphaelites, etc. This way it serves as an excuse for a great deal of her behaviour.

Because this image of herself cannot be accomplished in reality, certainly not in the South of our day and time, it is her effort and practice to *accomplish it in fantasy.* Everything that she does in *reality* too is coloured by this necessity, this compulsion to be *special.* So, in fact, *reality becomes fantasy too.* She makes it so!

The variety essential to the play, and to Blanche's playing and to Jessica Tandy's achieving the role demands that she be a "heavy" at the beginning. For instance: contemplate the inner character contradiction: bossy yet helpless, domineering yet shaky, etc. The audience at the beginning should see her bad effect on Stella, want Stanley to tell her off. He does. He exposes her and then gradually, as they see how genuinely in pain, how actually desperate she is, how warm, tender and loving she can be (the Mitch story), how freighted with need she is – then they begin to go with her. They begin to realise that they are sitting in at the death of something extraordinary... colourful, varied, passionate, lost, witty, imaginative, of her own integrity... and then they feel the tragedy. In the playing too there can be a growing sincerity and directness.

The thing about the "tradition" in the nineteenth century was that *it worked then.* It made a woman feel important, with her own secure positions and functions, her own special worth. It also made a woman at that time *one with her society*. But *today* the tradition is an anachronism which simply does not function. *It does not work.* So while Blanche must believe it because it makes her special, because it makes her sticking by Belle Reve an act of heroism, rather than an absurd romanticism, still *it does not work*. It makes Blanche feel *alone, outside of her society*. Left out, insecure, shaky. The airs the "tradition" demands isolate her further, and every once in a while, her resistance weakened by drink, she breaks down and seeks human warmth and contact where she can find it, not on her terms, on theirs; the merchant, the travelling salesman and the others... among whom the vulgar adolescent soldiers seem the most innocent. Since she cannot integrate these episodes, she rejects them, begins to forget them, begins to live in fantasy, begins to rationalise and explain them to herself thus: "I never was hard or self-sufficient enough... men don't see women unless they are in bed with them. They don't admit their existence except when they're love-making. You've got to have your existence admitted by someone if you are going to receive someone's protection," etc. As if you had to apologise for needing human contact! Also n.b. above – the word: protection. That is what she, as a woman in the tradition, so desperately needs. That's what she comes to Stella for, Stella and her husband. Not finding it from them she tries to get it from Mitch. *Protection.* A haven, a *harbour*. She is a refugee, punch drunk, and on the ropes, making her last stand, trying to keep up a gallant front, because she is a proud person. But really if Stella doesn't provide her haven, *where is she to go*. She's a misfit, a liar, her "airs" alienate people, she must act superior to them which alienates them further. She doesn't know how to work. So she can't make a living. She's really helpless. She needs someone to help her. Protection. She's a last dying relic of the last century now adrift in our unfriendly day. From time to time, for reasons of simple human loneliness and need she goes to pieces, smashes her tradition... then goes back to it. This conflict has developed into a terrible crisis. All she wants is a haven: "I want to rest! I want to breathe quietly again... just think! If it happens! I can leave her and have a home of my own..."

*

If this is a romantic tragedy, what is its inevitability and what is the tragic flaw? In the Aristotelian sense, the flaw is the need to be superior, special (or *her* need for protection and what it means to her), the "tradition". This creates an apartness so intense, a loneliness so gnawing that only a complete breakdown, a refusal, as it were, to contemplate what she's doing, a *binge* as it were, a destruction of all her standards, a desperate violent ride on the Streetcar Named Desire can break through the walls of her tradition. The tragic flaw creates the circumstances, inevitably, that destroy her. More later.

Try to find an entirely different character, a self-dramatised and self-romanticised character for Blanche to play in each scene. She is playing 11 different people. This will give it a kind of changeable and shimmering surface as it should have. And all these 11 self-dramatised and romantic characters should be out of the romantic tradition of the Pre-Bellum South, etc. Example: Sc 2 Gay Miss Devil-may-care.

There is another, simpler and equally terrible contradiction in her own nature. She won't face her physical or sensual side. She calls it "brutal desire." She thinks she sins when she gives in to it, out of loneliness... but by calling it "brutal desire," she is able to separate it from her "real self," her "cultured," refined self. Her tradition makes no allowance, allows no space for this very real part of herself. So she is constantly in conflict, not at ease, sinning. *She's still looking for something that doesn't exist today, a gentleman*, who will treat her like a virgin, marry her, protect her, defend and maintain her honour, etc. She wants an old-fashioned wedding dressed in white... and still she does things out of "brutal desire" that makes this impossible. *All this too is tradition.*

She has worth too – she is better than Stella. She says: "There has been some kind of progress... Such things as art – as poetry and music – such kinds of new light have come into the world... in some kinds of people some kinds of tenderer feelings have had some little beginning that we've got to make *grow*! And cling to, and hold as our flag! In this dark march toward whatever it is we're approaching... don't... don't hang back with the brutes!" And though the direct psychological motivation for this is jealousy and personal frustration, still she, alone and abandoned in the crude society of New Orleans back streets, is the *only voice of light*. It is flickering and, in the course of the play, goes out. But it is valuable because it is unique.

Blanche is a butterfly in a jungle looking for just a little momentary protection, doomed to a sudden, early, violent death. The more I work on Blanche, incidentally, the less insane she seems. She is caught in a fatal inner contradiction, but in another society, she *would* work. In Stanley's society, no!

This is like a classic tragedy. Blanche is Medea or someone pursued by the Harpies, the Harpies being *her own nature*. Her inner sickness pursues her like *doom* and makes it impossible for her to attain the one thing she needs, the only thing she needs: a safe harbour.

An effort to phrase Blanche's spine: to find *protection*, to find something to hold on to, some strength in whose protection she can live, like a sucker shark or a parasite. The tradition of *woman* (or all women) can only live through the strength of someone else. Blanche is entirely dependent. Finally the doctor!

Blanche is an outdated creature, approaching extinction... like the dinosaur. She is about to be pushed off the edge of the earth. On the other hand she is a heightened version, an artistic intensification of all women. That is what makes the play universal. Blanche's special relation to all women is that she is at that critical point where *the one thing above all else that she is dependent on: her attraction for men, is beginning to go*. Blanche is like all women, dependent on a man, looking for one to hang onto: only *more so*!

So beyond being deeply desperate, Blanche is in a hurry. She'll be pushed off the earth soon. She carries her doom in her character. Also, her past is chasing her, catching up with her. Is it any wonder that she tries to attract each and every man she meets. She'll even take that protected feeling, that needed feeling, that superior feeling, for a moment. Because, at least for a moment, that anxiety, the hurt and the pain will be quenched. The sex act is the opposite of loneliness. Desire is the opposite of Death. For a moment the anxiety is still, for a moment the complete desire and concentration of a man is on her. He clings to you. He may say I love you. All else is anxiety, loneliness and being adrift.

Compelled by her nature (she must be special, superior) she makes it impossible with Stanley and Stella. She acts in a way that succeeds in being destructive. But the last bit of luck is with her. She finds the only man on earth whom she suits, a man who is looking for a dominant woman. For an instant she is happy. But her past catches up with her. Stanley, whom she's antagonised by her destructiveness aimed at his home, but especially by her need to be superior, uses her past, which he digs up, to destroy her. Finally she takes refuge in fantasy. She must have protection, closeness, love, safe harbour. The only place she can obtain them any longer is in her own mind. She "goes crazy".

Blanche is a stylised character, she should be played, should be dressed, should move like a stylised figure. What is the physicalisation of an aristocratic woman pregnant with her own doom? ... Behaving by a tradition that dooms her in this civilisation, in this "culture"? All her behaviour patterns are *old-fashioned, pure tradition*. All as if jellied in rote...

Why does the "Blues" music fit the play? The Blues is an expression of the loneliness and rejection, the exclusion and isolation of the Negro and their (opposite) longing for love and connection. Blanche too is "looking for a home," abandoned, friendless. "I don't know where I'm going, but I'm going." Thus the Blues piano catches the soul of Blanche, the miserable unusual human side of the girl which is beneath her frenetic duplicity, her trickery, lies, etc. It tells, it emotionally reminds you what all the fireworks are caused by.

Blanche-Physically. Must at all times give a single impression: her social mask is: *the High-Bred Genteel Lady in Distress*. Her past, her destiny, her falling from grace is just a surprise... then a tragic contradiction. But the mask never breaks down.

The only way to understand any character is through yourself. Everyone is much more alike than they willingly admit. Even as frantic and fantastic a creature as Blanche is created by things you have felt and known, *if only you'll dig for them and be honest about what you see*.

Taken from: "Notebook for *A Streetcar Named Desire*, by Elia Kazan; reprinted in *Director's On Directing*, edited by Toby Cole and Helen Krich Chinoy, Indianapolis, Ind: Bobbs-Merrill, 1976, pages 364–371.

*In this extract from Kazan's notebook, we can see the director's search- ing, critical eye subjecting Williams' text to enormously detailed analysis in order to realise, as faithfully as possible, the world of the cen- tral character, Blanche. But, returning to Jouvet's distinction, there is also the director of the 'spectacular' theatre; the director who uses the text as a springboard, or pretext, for a radical new interpretation. The production of such a director would be (to borrow Jouvet's own phrase) 'swathed in' her/his own 'personal contributions and inventions'. Today we would call such a director an **auteur**, implying that the new interpretation is so distinctive that it has actually been 're-written'.*

*Max Reinhardt's well-known production of The Miracle was based on a wordless play by Karl Vollmoeller. Here is an extract from Reinhardt's Regiebuch ('Director's Book') that contains an introducto- ry statement and details how he '**authored**' the first scene. The size, scale and scope of this 'spectacle' (and Reinhardt's vision) are breath- taking.*

43: *The Miracle*, Scene 1

... the true mission of the theatre... is to lift the word out of the sepulchre of the book, to breathe life into it, to fill it with blood, with the blood of today, and thus to bring it into living contact with ourselves, so that we may receive it and let it bear fruit in us... Life is the incomparable and most valuable possession of the theatre. Dress it up in any manner you wish, the cloak will have to fall when the eternal human comes to the fore, when, in the height of ecstasy, we find and embrace each other...

Therefore, do not write out prescriptions, but give to the actor and his work the atmosphere in which they can breathe more freely and more deeply... Our standard must not be to act a play as it was acted in the days of its author. To establish such facts is the task of the learned historian, and is of value only for the museum. How to make a play live in our time, that is decisive for us. The Catholic Church which aims at the most spiritual, the most supernatural, does so by means which appeal directly to the senses. It overwhelms us with the pathos of its temples towering in the sky; it surrounds us with the mystical dimness of its cathedrals; it charms our eye with wonderful masterpieces of art, with the brilliancy of its coloured windows, with the lustre of thousands of candles, which reflect their light in golden objects and vessels. It fills our ears with music and song and the sound of the thundering organ. It stupefies us by the odour of incense. Its priests stride in rich and precious robes. And in such a sphere of sensuousness, the highest and the most holy reveals itself to us. We reveal ourselves, and we find the way to our innermost being, the way to concentration, to exaltation, to spiritualization...

Scene 1... Cathedral

Characters

The Nun	*The Lame Piper*
The Abbess	*The Knight*
The Old Sacristan	*The Madonna*

Nuns and Novices, Peasants, Townsfolk and Children, Bishops, Priests, Monks and Pilgrims, Cripples, Blind, Lame and Lepers, Patricians of the Town, Knights and Troops of Soldiers.

1. The interior of an early Gothic Church.
2. High, massive columns rise into mystic darkness.

3. Gothic arches, stone ornaments representing tendrils and lace work, a richly decorated iron grating, entangled scrolls and figures.
4. Narrow, high church windows in deep, rich colouring.
5. Aisles, corridors, doors, an unsymmetrical arrangement of mysterious openings, windows, stairways.
6. Votive statues on columns, small statues with candles and flowers before them, crucifixes, offerings brought by grateful people, wax flowers, embroideries, jewels, a child's doll, decoratively painted candles.
7. In the background a richly carved altar, with a golden shrine and candles seen through a grilled screen.
8. The eternal lamp burns before it.
9. A Cardinal's hat hangs above.
10. Altar, with table, to divide and open, with steps through it.
11. The floor is of large grey stones, some of which are tombstones. In the centre of the floor the stones are to be glass with lamps below, so wired as to spread the light from the middle outwards.
12. Flickering light from behind columns as from invisible candles throws fantastic shadows.
13. Shafts of sunlight, coming through the high windows at the right, project patterns on the floor.
14. At left and right of auditorium, cloisters with vaulted ceilings and stone floors.
15. Chandeliers of various sizes in the auditorium to cast light downwards only, adding depth and mystery to the ceiling.
16. Several poles for flags and lanterns fastened to the seat ends in aisles of auditorium.
17. Panelling of balcony rail to show here and there between flags.
18. A clock above pulpit. The clock is to strike at various times during the dream parts, to suggest the existence of the church. Remember the sound before the clock strikes.
19. On top of the clock two figures to mark the hours, by striking a large bell beneath them. One of these figures symbolises life; the other death.
20. Clerestory windows around upper part of auditorium. Choir stands and triforium openings below windows.
21. All doors have heavy bolts, locks and knockers to create business and noise.
22. Large keys on rings for various doors.
23. The doors immediately behind proscenium lead to sacristy.
24. The doors below the loges lead to exterior.

25. Small midnight Mass bell, near top of tower, to be rung from rope on stage floor.
26. Wind machines, thunder drums and voices also to be there.
27. When audience take their seats everything is dark.
28. The sound of a storm far away.
29. Soft candlelight in the auditorium, only where it is absolutely necessary, and flickering around the columns behind the altar screen.
30. Clusters of candlelights in distant places in the auditorium and stage, high up in the tower to produce an effect of tremendous size and of incredible distance.
31. There are to be candles around the altar screen and on the altar itself. The candles should be of various lengths and the bulbs of very low voltage and of various pale colours.
32. In chapels tiny candles suggest side-altars against darkness. Prominent clusters of them unsymmetrically chosen. Flickering candles on the columns in the apse and cloisters throwing shadows.
33. Candles on altar, altar screen and in chapels to be wired individually and lighted or extinguished by nuns. Candle bulbs to be no larger than one-half inch in diameter. The bulb must not show.
34. Candle extinguishers and wax tapers.
35. The large altar is dark.
36. One recognises gradually among the towering columns several dark figures huddled together absorbed in prayer.
37. From a distant tower a bell sounds.
38. Large bells are located in ventilating shaft over auditorium and controlled from orchestra gallery.
39. A praying voice from behind the triforium windows is indistinctly heard; now and then a Latin word is audible.
40. Chairs are pushed about, some one blows his nose, others cough. The echo resounds through the church.
41. After that, silence.
42. An old sexton appears carrying a lantern.
43. His stick taps the pavement, and his steps drag over the stone floor.
44. He pulls back the green curtain over the Madonna statue.
45. He goes to the tower. Up the winding staircase the lantern shows through little windows and finally at the top.
46. He crosses a bridge and disappears through a doorway in the wall.
47. The organ starts and bells ring high above the church.

48. Nuns in pairs march through the cloisters toward the altar in two long columns, to take part in the coming ceremony.
49. The windows of the church become more brilliant from sunlight without.
50. Outside a young bright spring morning has awakened.
51. Sixty nuns dressed in ivory-coloured garments trimmed with black. They all wear ropes. The black nuns' costumes appear like shadows passing in the dark and must be cut in such a way that the white undergarments show conspicuously when the nuns flutter like white doves in their excitement at the loss of the Madonna.
52. The chin cloths must be drawn very tightly, so that they never look slovenly. In fact they are to be made so that they can not be worn otherwise.
53. One column is headed by the Abbess.
54. The Abbess may be dressed either in white or in black, wears a crown and carries a silver staff, like the Bishop's but smaller.
55. In this column the aged feeble Sacristan of the convent is carried in on a chair by four nuns.
56. In the other column a young nun, still but a child, is led in. She takes a tearful farewell of her mother, father, and grandmother who are seated at the right.
57. In an impressive ceremony the young Nun is dressed in an over-garment similar to that of the old Sacristan and receives the keys and office.
58. The Abbess sits in a special chair during the ceremony. She sings while one nun holds a music book for her and another holds a lighted candle.
59. This is accompanied by responses without music from the choir gallery.
60. In front are the holy pictures and the statue of the Madonna which stands on a column. It is a stone statue, painted in blue tempera and gold-leaf and wearing a crown set with precious stones.
61. The statue is to look as stonelike as possible and heavy, even if clumsy.
62. She must wear the white muslin nun's garb, as an undergarment.
63. The white head-cloth always has to remain on and be drawn as tightly as possible.
64. The Madonna holds the child in her arms.

65. The pedestal is decorated with many flowers, and large and small candles.
66. Crutches stacked around the base.
67. This pedestal altar conceals steps, covered with soft rubber. There must be supports for the Madonna under her armpits, at her waist, a seat, and recesses cut in floor for her feet. Her shoes are rubber-soled.
68. There are five statues of saints at other positions.
69. Large bells in the distance begin to sound as the Convent Church is revealed in its full glow of light.
70. The Nun, for the first time as the new Sacristan, opens all the doors with her keys.
71. A great commotion and the hum of voices can be heard from without
72. The sound of music grows nearer, the organ starts with massive tones.
73. A great procession pours into the church through all the doors. Men and women who are making the pilgrimage to the celebrated miracle-working statue of the Madonna.
74. First come the visiting orders of nuns in white.
75. Then peasants with banners.
76. Women in vivid-coloured clothes, some barefooted.
77. Townspeople following, carrying banners with coats of arms of towns.
78. Tradesmen carrying various emblems of their trade on poles.
79. A group of peasants bring in an enormous cross.
80. A great crowd of children with a Maypole.
81. Priests carrying church banners.
82. Acolytes swinging incense.
83. Choirboys with their large books.
84. The Archbishop carries his staff and walks beneath a canopy carried by four men.
85. Under another canopy is carried the monstrance. Church dignitaries follow.
86. Then monks carrying wooden statues of saints on poles.
87. A great mass of cripples on primitive crutches and stretchers, wearing dirty ragged clothes.
88. Blind people, who are led.
89. Widows in mourning.
90. Mothers carrying sick children on their backs, in their arms, and with others clinging to their skirts.

91. Lepers with clappers.
92. Pilgrims with broad-brimmed hats, staves, bundles and flasks.
93. Finally the knights in vivid colour.
94. Followed by heralds, squires, men-at-arms, in full dress.
95. No one comes empty-handed. All who have nothing else to carry bring full-leafed birch branches.
96. The procession fills the whole stage and all the aisles in the auditorium.
97. There is much singing and waving of the yellow green branches. It looks almost like a green forest, waving to and fro.
98. The voice of a priest, whom no one hears, is heard.
99. The music stops.
100. A bell rings at the altar.
101. A white vapour begins to rise from the vessels containing the incense.
102. The crowd falls onto its knees.
103. The sick crowd up to the statue of the Madonna and pray without halt. The Archbishop leads the prayers from the pulpit.
104. The tension grows. A breathless silence.
105. Finally there arises in the audience a completely lamed man, who has been carried in on a stretcher. He gets heavily to his feet, with convulsive twitching, and raising his arms high in ecstasy strides to the figure of the Mother of God, where he dances with joy.
106. A cry, the organ, rejoicing of the crowd.
107. The pilgrims leave the church singing.
108. The candles are extinguished and the nuns slowly pass out.
109. The young Sacristan goes about her duties of locking the doors.
110. In the last doorway there stands the healed fellow blowing harmlessly upon a flute. This demoniac figure, who runs through the play and has an evil influence upon the fate of the young Nun, is the lure of sensual life. At this moment his appearance resembles that of the Pied Piper. He wears a broad-brimmed hat over his faunlike ears.
111. Children surround him in their curiosity and listen to his music.
112. The Nun stands still as if under a spell and hears his tunes with the same astonishment and naïve joy as the children.
113. The children, unable to resist longer, fall into the rhythm, crowd into the church and force the Nun, who resists, into their ranks.
114. An unconscious yearning for the spring without causes her momentarily to forget her new office.
115. In her childishness, the Nun lets herself be forced into their dance.

116. She lets her keys fall and dances joyfully.
117. In the meantime, the Piper's tune has attracted a young Knight, who quietly enters and is fascinated by the graceful dancing of the Nun.
118. Suddenly, on seeing him, she becomes frightened and rooted to the spot as they exchange glances.
119. The Nun hears nothing as the bell rings for vespers.
120. Nuns approach in a column, the Abbess at their head.
121. They become enraged on seeing this pair in the church.
122. The children and the Piper slyly escape through the open door.
123. The Abbess rebukes the young Sacristan who stares about her, dazed.
124. At a nod from the angry Abbess the keys are taken away from her and the heavy bolts locked behind the Knight who has slowly gone out.
125. She is sentenced to spend the night in prayer before the statue of the Madonna.
126. The nuns again depart and the church sinks gradually into night and silence.
127. The Nun prays fervently before the statue of the Holy Virgin.
128. In her confusion she scarcely knows what is happening to her.
129. Her thoughts, which she seeks vainly to discipline, escape through the stone walls and wander tirelessly into the night in the direction of the young Knight.
130. The poor child returns again and again to her prayers.
131. Her youth, awakened for the first time, struggles against the cold discipline offered her.
132. She runs to the font and sprinkles herself madly with holy water.
133. Her heart beats wildly, she throws herself about on the steps leading to the miracle statue.
134. She wrings her hands and plunges desperately into passionate prayer.
135. At this moment something happens that can just as well be a raving dream of fever as a fantastic reality. With the rapid pace of dreams, one experience chases after another and drives the Nun back into the church after a moment of actual happiness through a martyrdom of indescribable suffering. Dream, or reality. It is intense, terrible, vital, as endlessly long as an intense dream, as horribly short as a full life.
136. Suddenly there is a light but insistent knocking at the gate. The Nun grows tense.

137. The knock is repeated. Is it her own heartbeat? She tries not to hear and prays aloud.
138. The knocking continues, always louder, and finally sounds from all sides and from all doors. Each door should have a heavy knocker.
139. She springs up involuntarily, takes several steps towards the door.
140. She stands still in fright, throws herself on her knees, wrings her hands, is torn back and forth.
141. Finally like an excited but caged bird, she flutters anxiously to and fro, beating her head against the cold walls.
142. The knocking grows wilder, her yearning more uncontrollable.
143. She shakes the locked doors with all her strength.
144. Throwing herself on her knees, she begs the Mother of God to set her free.
145. The moon shines through the windows.
146. As if mad, she dashes toward the Holy Virgin and points fiercely at the child in her arms. She is yearning for the child, for everything out there.
147. Completely out of her mind she finally takes the holy child from the arms of the Madonna and holds it high.
148. A warm glow radiates from it and then suddenly the child disappears in a flash of light.
149. Everything grows dark. A sound like thunder resounds through the high church.
150. When it is again light Mary has heard the passionate pleadings and has performed a miracle.
151. The high altar glittering with candles, slowly opens, forming a Gothic arch, with a knight in silver armour and a blue mantle, visible through the high candles on the altar tables.
152. The Knight and the Nun stand regarding each other.
153. The Nun shrinks back frightened and flees to the foot of the Madonna.
154. The Mother of God smiles as graciously as ever. Her will is plain.
155. The altar table, with the candles on it, opens slowly, exposing a flight of steps.
156. The Knight slowly approaches the Nun. She rises shyly.
157. He offers her his hand to lead her forth. She looks at her clothing and hesitates to go out in her holy costume.
158. She removes the black nun's veil, the white cape, the rosary with its large cross, the belt and finally her dark dress and lays them all tenderly on the steps of the miracle statue.

159. Rising, she shudders at the sight of her underdress, feeling that she is without clothes.
160. The Piper who was behind the Knight brings in the blue cloak of the Knight and covers the young Nun with the dress of life.
161. Again she kneels, and the Knight with her, at the foot of the Virgin.
162. Then he catches her in his arms and runs off with her into the world.
163. The church is deserted.
164. A sigh comes from somewhere within the walls.
165. The Madonna statue begins to glow with an unearthly light.
166. It seems as if she were opening her lips and smiling. The figure moves.
167. The light on her face changes from unearthly to the pink of life.
168. She opens her eyes.
169. She smiles
170. She turns her head.
171. She drops her robe.
172. She descends.
173. She lifts her arm.
174. She removes her crown.
175. She holds it up high.
176. She lays it on the pedestal.
177. Then she gives a sign for the altar to close, and it becomes as before.
178. The Virgin bends low, and in sweet humility puts on the simple costume of the Nun.
179. She goes to the tower and rings the bell.
180. Voices of singing nuns. The Virgin kneels and prays in front of her pedestal.
181. The nuns come into the church for mass.
182. The Abbess glances at the supposed Nun, sunk in prayer, and chuckles fondly at the repentance of her favourite.
183. By accident her glance falls on the spot where the miracle statue has stood, but now where only her cloak and crown lie. She does not trust her eyes, stares, consults the sister.
184. A terrible fear seizes all the nuns.
185. They scream, run around enraged, cry out, weep, threaten their supposed sister, fetch the priest and ring the alarm bell.
186. With clenched fist and swinging chords, all rush at the poor Nun, who has obviously permitted the theft of the precious treasure in her impious sin.

187. The Nun's head remains humbly bowed.
188. Whenever the threatening sisters surround her in a wild rush, she gently floats a short distance into the air without changing her position. This is done on a trap on the right.
189. In silent awe they draw back from her; staring at this miracle speechlessly, they recognise that a higher power is obviously at work here, and the young Nun is the chosen agent.
190. Returning to the earth, she goes about her duties like an ordinary nun, taking a jar of oil to fill the eternal lamp.
191. The nuns form open rows and follow their holy sister spreading their arms wide and singing in ecstasy.
192. The scene grows dark.

Taken from: *Regiebuch* of *The Miracle* by Max Reinhardt in *Max Reinhardt and His Theatre*, edited by Oliver M. Sayler, New York: Brentano's, 1924, pages 65–262.

*Reinhardt speaks of the need to make a play live **in our time**. The question of **how** and **why** a director is drawn to a particular play at a particular time, and how s/he approaches the work in hand is something we need to consider. Peter Brook has some interesting thoughts on this subject.*

44: The Formless Hunch

When I begin to work on a play, I start with a deep, formless hunch which is like a smell, a colour, a shadow. That's the basis of my job, my role – that's my preparation for rehearsals for any play I do. There's a formless hunch that is my relationship with the play. It's my conviction that this play must be done today, and without that conviction I can't do it. I'd have nowhere to start. I could produce a sort of synthetic technique and a few ideas built from my experience of doing plays, but it wouldn't be much good. I have no structure for doing a play, because I work from that amorphous non-formed feeling, and from that I start preparing.

Now, preparing means going toward that idea. I start making a set, destroying it, making it, destroying it, working it out. What kind of costumes? What kind of colours? All of those are a language for making that hunch a little more concrete. Until gradually, out of this comes the form, a form that must be modified and put to the test, but nevertheless it's a form that's emerging. Not a closed form, because it's only the set, and I say "only the set" because the set is only the basis, the platform. Then work starts with the actors.

The rehearsal work should create a climate in which the actors feel free to produce everything they can bring to the play. That's why in the early stages of rehearsal everything is open and I impose nothing at all. In a sense this is diametrically opposed to the technique in which, the first day, the director gives a speech on what the play's about and the way he's going to approach it. I used to do that years ago and I eventually found out that that's a rotten way of starting.

So, now we start with exercises, with a party, with anything, but not ideas. In some plays, for instance, with the *Marat/Sade*, for three-quarters of the rehearsal period I encouraged the actors, and encouraged myself – it's a two-way thing – to produce excess, simply because it was a very dynamic subject. There was such an outrageously baroque excess of ideas that, if you'd seen us three quarters of the way into the rehearsal period, you'd have thought the play was being submerged and destroyed by a surplus of what's called directorial invention. I encouraged other people to produce everything, good and bad. I censored nothing and no one, not even myself. I'd say, "Why don't you do this?" and there'd be gags, there'd be silly things. It didn't matter. All of it was for the purpose of having, out of that, such a lot of material that then, gradually, things could be shaped. To what criteria? Well, shaped to their relation to this formless hunch.

The formless hunch begins to take form by meeting that mass of material and emerging as the dominant factor from which some notions fall away. The director is continually provoking the actor, stimulating him, asking questions and creating an atmosphere in which the actor can dig, probe and investigate. And, in doing that, he turns over, both singly and together with the others, the whole fabric of the play. As he does so, you see forms emerging that you can begin to recognise, and in the last stages of rehearsal, the actor's work takes on a dark area which is the subterranean life of the play, and illuminates it; and as the subterranean area of the play is illuminated by the actor, the director is placed in a position to see the difference between the actor's ideas and the play itself.

In these last stages, the director cuts away all that's extraneous, all that belongs just to the actor and not to the actor's intuitive connection with the play. The director, because of his prior work, and because it is his role, and also because of his hunch, is in a better position to say then what belongs to the play and what belongs to that superstructure of rubbish that everybody brings with him.

The final stages of rehearsal are very important, because at that moment you push and encourage the actor to discard all that is superfluous, to edit and tighten. And you do it ruthlessly, even with yourself, because for every invention of the actor, there's something of your own. You've suggested, you've invented a bit of business, something to illustrate something. Those go, and what remains is an organic form. Because the form is not ideas imposed on a play, it is the play illuminated, and the play illuminated is the form. Therefore, when the results seem organic and unified, it's not because a unified conception has been found and has been put on the play from the outset, not at all.

When I did *Titus Andronicus*, there was a lot of praise for this production being better than the play. People said that here was a production that made something of this ridiculous and impossible play. That's very flattering, but it wasn't true, because I knew perfectly well that I couldn't have done that production with another play. That's where people so often misunderstand what the work of directing is. They think, in a way, that it's like being an interior decorator who can make something of any room, given enough money and enough things to put into it. It's not so. In *Titus Andronicus*, the whole work was to take the hints and the hidden strands of the play and wring the most from them, take what was embryonic perhaps, and bring it out. But if it isn't there to begin with it can't be done. You can give me a police thriller and say, "Do it like *Titus Andronicus*," and of course, I can't, because what's not there, what isn't latent, can't be found.

Taken from: 'The Formless Hunch' in *The Shifting Point* by Peter Brook, New York: Theatre Communication Group, 1994, pages 3–5.

Once the director has selected the play, and conceived her/his vision, the practical work in the rehearsal room begins. The following extract provides us with a sense of what the director's concerns are likely to be during this vital period (the author in this extract uses the word 'producer' when referring to the director).

45: An Audience of One

First of all, and very briefly, there is the question of organisation, discipline and that kind of thing. If the company is any good and the producer is any good, that is simply a matter of general convenience. I do not think the producer has any difficulty over discipline provided the rehearsals are not boring, and provided they are kept moving not at the pace of the very slowest person present but at a fairly decent tempo.

Then comes the question of coaching. How far is a producer to coach the interpretation? How much is he to say to the actors, "Do it this way"? I do not think one can give a complete answer to that. If you are taking the first production that has ever been done by the dramatic society attached to the Little Pifflington Women's Institute, you will probably have to do a great deal of coaching and coaxing to break down the self-conscious giggling of people who are quite unaccustomed to impersonation and pretending to be someone they are not.

But if you have a good professional cast the amount of coaching you have to do is very small.

I do not think one should be at all afraid of saying to actors in a quite dogmatic way, "Play this scene sitting on the sofa, and if you are not comfortable let me know later on, but don't decide until we have done it once or twice. Later on, maybe you would feel like getting up halfway through and going to the window." Otherwise if the actor is allowed to grope it out too much for himself, there is a waste of time, and the dominant personalities start bullying the milder, more unselfish and cooperative ones, which is what we have to be on the lookout for.

Then comes... the work of coordination... Where I think the producer's work of coordination requires the greatest amount of time and care spent upon it is in the vocal interpretation of the play... The performance of a play is, on a smaller scale, a performance of a musical work. The script is, as it were, sung, because speaking and singing are, after all, the same process... Every syllable I utter is on a certain pitch and a musician could say precisely where it was. Every sentence that I phrase is consciously phrased in a certain rhythm. The pauses, although I am not conscious of it, are expressing an instinctive need to pause, not merely to breathe, but for clarity and various other interpretative purposes. This is even more pronounced in the performance of a play, where all that has been most carefully thought out in terms of pace, rhythm, pitch, volume and all the rest of it, to make a certain expressive effect. That is particularly where the coordinating hand of the producer is required, joining up the various songs that are being sung and making them into a unit; and similarly, joining up the various patterns that are being danced, because even in the simplest realistic comedy, in the most ordinary kind of realistic set – the actors have to move, and their movements have to tot up to some kind of choreographic design which expresses the play, which has some meaning over and above the common-sense position in which one would pour tea or sugar into it...

Finally, I should like to discuss what to me is the most interesting part of the job, the blending of intuition with technique. If I may elaborate those terms, by intuition I mean the expression of a creative idea that comes straight from the subconscious, that is not arrived at by a process of ratiocination at all. It is my experience that all the best ideas in art just arrive, and it is absolutely no good concentrating on them and hoping for the best... Inspiration must be backed up by a very cast-iron technique.

It is the case that as one gets older one's technique, if one is an industrious and intelligent person, tends to become better; but there is also the danger that it becomes a little slick. I think not only artists, but anybody engaged in any activity must feel the same thing. The record begins to get worn, and we slip too easily into old grooves, the same association of ideas comes back too readily and easily. I notice with my own work in the theatre – and I have been at it now for nearly thirty years – that I have to check myself all the time from slipping into certain very obvious and to me now, rather dull choreographic mannerisms. I instinctively think, "Oh, the right place is so-and-so, and the right way to group this is such-and-such." Then I think, why do I think that? And usually the only reason is that one has done it that way a good many times before. That is obviously frightfully dangerous in any creative work. It is the negation of creation; it is just falling back into habit.

Yet there are certain very valuable things about experience and about technique. It is now comparatively easy for me, in late middle age, to establish a good relation with actors. They think because I have been at it for a long time that I know something about it, and they are readier to take suggestions from me now than they were twenty-five years ago when I was a beginner, though I am inclined to think that most of the suggestions are duller ones. Twenty-five years ago, intuition functioned oftener and more readily. That is, I think, one of the very difficult paradoxes about productions...

... the one really creative function of the producer... is to be at rehearsal a highly receptive, highly concentrated, highly critical sounding-board for the performance, an audience of one. He is not the drill-sergeant, not the schoolmaster, and he does not sweep in with a lot of verbiage and "Stand here and do it this way, darling, and move the right hand not the left." He is simply receiving the thing, transmuting it, and giving it back. When you come down to analysing what the creative part of acting is, it is the giving of impressions to the audience and then, on the part of the actor, the taking back of their impressions and doing something about them. The best simile that I can make is that the actor throws a thread, as it were, out into the house which, if the house is receptive, it will catch. Then it is the actor's business to hold that thread taut and to keep a varying and consequently interesting pressure on it, so that it is really pulled in moments of tension and allowed to go slack as possible in moments of relaxation, but never so slack that it falls and cannot be pulled up again. The producer at rehearsals can be that audience. He can perform that function, and if he is a good producer he will perform it better than the average audience; he will be more intelligently critical and alive, and the rehearsals will not be dreary learning of routine; they will be a creative act that is ultimately going to be a performance.

Taken from: 'An Audience of One'; a speech delivered to the Royal Society of Arts by Tyrone Guthrie; reprinted in *Director's On Directing*, edited by Toby Cole and Helen Krich Chinoy, Indianapolis, Ind: Bobbs-Merrill, 1976, pages 250–256.

It is a popular misconception that the director's work is finished once the show is in performance. The best directors understand that a production is never 'finished', in the sense of being complete at the end of the rehearsal process; it continues to live, changing and developing as a result of the audience's response. The director will continue to monitor these developments and will occasionally need to offer advice. The following notes were written by Joan Littlewood to her company, after the production had been running for a number of weeks.

46: Stick Your Behind Out, Dear

Dear Company,

As a young "actress" I was told "stick your behind out, dear, it's always good for a laugh." Well, this show of ours, at the moment is one big behind.

We may as well go the whole hog and start throwing whitewash at the audience and custard pies at the obtruding behinds, only that would need better timing.

Can we stop regarding the audience as morons, cut out the rubbish, get back a bit of tension, pace and atmosphere in Act II. Can we stop wriggling our anatomies all over the script, over-acting, *bullying* laughs out of the audience and playing alone, for approbation. This latter, which looks like selfishness, is mere insecurity and lack of trust in yourselves and each other. You cannot play alone, stop wanting the audience to adore you and you only, they do anyway. People love actors and actresses, so relax and let them have a look at a play for a change.

Taken from: 'Working with Joan', published in *Encore, Vol VII*, July–August 1960; reprinted in *Director's On Directing*, edited by Toby Cole and Helen Krich Chinoy, Indianapolis, Ind: Bobbs-Merrill, 1976, page 398.

Stanislavski would have approved wholeheartedly!

Part Five: Devising

Devising for performance is not new. We have already come across the mimed plays of the classical Greek period and the tradition of Commedia dell'Arte, *both of which allowed the actors to devise their own performances based on simple scenarios and stock characters. So the history of devising is at least as long as the history of tragedy.*

The twentieth century boasts many examples of devised work: that is, a performance developed collectively, with a specific, clearly defined purpose, and audience, in mind.

We will begin by considering the political agit-prop *('agitation-propaganda') movement, which got under way in the aftermath of the October Revolution in Russia in 1917. Piscator began his* agit-prop *work in 1919 with the* Proletarisches Theater, *and then in 1923* The Blue Blouses *were formed. Boris Yuzhanin set up* The Blue Blouses *(so-called in solidarity with the factory workers who wore loose-fitting blue blouses), the first Soviet* agit-prop *group, to offer their audiences, many of whom could not read, a Living Newspaper. The revue style performances consisted of material drawn from newspapers and magazines, and were played to assembled groups of workers in factory canteens, at worker's clubs and in the open air. During the next few years, the movement blossomed and eventually over five thousand Blue Blouse groups were active across the Soviet Union.*

47: Blue Blouse: Simple Advice to Participants

The Collective: Should be made up of twelve to twenty, two or three times as many men as women, with various skills: in voice, physical culture, speaking and playing.

Costume: All need a blue blouse, black trousers or skirts, black stockings and shoes. Down with naturalistic costumes, peasant shoes, blankets and birch [footwear] – folksy stuff, wigs – down with them. We use blue blouses and trousers to which things can be attached: stripes, leggings, cuffs, belts, bibs, etc.; head-gear: hats, top hats, peaked caps – to differentiate the characters.

The Stage: We are against bright beauty and realistic sets and decoration (no little birch trees and rivers), no clumsy props and set. On the stage there should only be a piano and a simple bough of a tree, only things necessary for demonstration.

Props: Tables, stools and other objects should only be put on the stage if they can be used in the play and in movement. If they are not useful, they slow down the tempo of movement and obstruct access to the stage. Things on stage must play with the actor.

Placards/Posters: Must be clear, letters and drawings visible from the last row.

Director/Producer: The organising centre of the collective, the theatrical master of the new formation which builds the action on the development of physical culture, mechanised movement, and on clear gestures and control of body and language.

Actor/BB Member: Must in accordance with the above possess all the skills of the new BB training and act without emotion, typical for BB members.

Souffleur [Prompter]: Does not exist – all texts must be learned by heart.

Stock Characters: 'Old Lovers', 'Slavonic Rag Wearers' don't exist in the BB any more – instead of these old-fashioned terms we have:

Masks: In the middle ages the comedy-masks presented a number of social types. BB uses masks for positive and negative types as defined by the new world and soviet economy: Capitalist, Banker, Premier, NEP-man, Kulak, Menshevik and Social Revolutionary, General, Lady, Female Worker, Female Komsomol, Red Army Man, the Peasant and Worker and many others not yet entirely defined.

Musical Illustration: Musicians must definitely be familiar with classical music, be able to read scores, and have good technique.

Music: The music featured in BB issues must be used all the time, must be applied to the appropriate texts in accordance with their sense so that little by little, the tunes boring everybody can be squeezed out.

Harmonica and Balalaika: In the mass scenes of the village type, i.e. *New Way of Life,* and in the accompaniment of *Chastushki* it is desirable to use harmonica and balalaika.

Tempo/Speed: The BB members must learn to work with industrial tempo, the march-parade, a definite beat. The leading role belongs to the accompanist. All little numbers, the satirical pieces and sketches (feuilleton) has medium speed, and at the finale the speed increases again, ending on a high note.

Text: On international and All-Soviet Union questions material must be taken from BB issues and needs to be conveniently divided among the members. Also material on local themes must definitely be used. If you have material on local themes it must be explained to those unfamiliar with it.

Literary Montage: (or the assembling of material). Should be used as developed by the centre first, but also performed and adapted in the provinces. Material for montage: Pathos – poems by proletarian and LEF poets, for humour – texts from humorous soviet journals and magazines can be used.

Organisation of Everyday Life: Not a photograph but a construction – BB not only shows our way of life like a mirror but influences the brain of the spectator with all scenic means and prepares him for the perception of the new social conditions.

Content and Form: Words in BB are everything, movement, music and acting add to them, make them more expressive, more meaningful, able quickly to organise the feelings and will of the audience – content and form are equally necessary.

Programme: a BB evening is made up of one and a half to two hours – this is the right length. Three quarters of the success depends on the following: 1) Parade, 2) *Oratoria*, 3) International survey, 4) Feuilleton, 5) Satirical sketch – village type, 6) *Lubok*-scene (living poster) three to four people, 7) Dialogue-Duet, 8) *Rayok* – quick-fire speech/tongue-twister/story, 9) *Chastushki*, two or four line folk verse, topical, humorous, satirical – sung in a lively manner, 10) A local theme, 11) Finale-march.

The lead articles/MC/Narrator: in two or three crisp phrases they should explain the content of the sequence of numbers and after a whistle and without any pause the pianist plays a chord and the action begins.

Reprinted in: *Twentieth Century Theatre: A Sourcebook*, edited by Richard Drain, London & New York: Routledge, 1995, pages 181–183.

The political purpose of the devised work of the Blue Blouses *is clearly evident in this 'Advice to Participants'. We have already come across the idea that, throughout history,* **oppositional** *forms of theatre have existed side by side with the theatrical* **mainstream**. *Although devised work usually falls within the former category, there are a few* *examples of devised mainstream productions: in England, the most famous is probably* Theatre Workshop's, Oh What A Lovely War, *directed by Joan Littlewood, and produced at the* Theatre Royal, Stratford East.

48: *Oh What a Lovely War*

Joan celebrated her return to Stratford in March 1963 with the enormously successful production of *Oh What A Lovely War*. Charles Chilton had written a radio programme called *A Long Trail* based on songs of the First World War, and Gerry Raffles had the idea of building a stage show around this theme. Advice was sought from those with first-hand knowledge of the war and Charles Chilton contributed research material. Both Gwyn Thomas and Ted Allan submitted scripts but they didn't fit in with Joan's conception of how the subject should be treated. The final version was based on factual data from official records and war memoirs, threaded through with popular songs of the period...

Joan rejected from the outset the notion that the actors should dress up as khaki-clad soldiers, imitating the appearance of those who had gone through the First World War. She thought khaki an ugly colour anyway. Instead she conceived the idea of presenting the Company as a pierrot troupe called 'The Merry Roosters' who had actually been performing at that time. Some of the Company still had qualms about being paid for portraying men who had actually died in the war, and Brian Murphy recalled Joan's answer:

> She said we were not doing a show about the First World War. We are finding a background for the songs, and these trace a period of history which can be presented without the realistic background that you would need in a film. Here we are, on the stage, The Clowns, and never in the course of the evening are we going to forget that the audience are out there. Tonight we are going to present to you 'The War Game'. We've got songs, dances, a few battles, a few jokes, and we start to put on Sam Browne belts and helmets. Some of the scenes were dealt with very realistically, we had to work for hours and hours pretending to be in the trenches, getting the feel of real boredom.

The cast were completely involved in building up the script. We improvised lots of different scenes, read books and came up with ideas. I read one of the few books written about the Great War by a Private, and out of it came the scene of the French Cavalry retreating in full glory with trumpets blowing.

A real inspiration was to use, behind the actors, a screen which ran the width of the stage on which were picked out in moving lights the terrifying facts, ten thousand men lost, a hundred yards gained, and so on. It was based on a similar principle to that used in advertising or for news flashes and, juxtaposed against the scenes on the stage, it made a tremendous impact.

The creation of an anti-war play was never in the minds of those connected with the production. *Lovely War* was a piece of social history showing the behaviour of men under certain conditions. Clive Barker takes up this point:

> The presumption was, you could reasonably expect everyone going into the theatre to think that war was horrible, there was no point in telling them that. That's why Joan rejected those realistic scripts that showed what life was really like in the trenches. Having been in the production, it's quite clear to me that *Lovely War* is a celebration of human resourcefulness in the face of the most appalling catastrophic conditions. So Joan celebrates courage, humour, comradeship, the triumph of life over death and the international solidarity between soldiers.

... Joan had brought together for *Lovely War* a group who were full of enthusiasm for the job in hand and who were ready and able to work closely together. There can be no doubting the part they played in its success and, in acknowledging this, Joan, as always, minimised her own contribution:

> Part of the good that has come out of this show is the way which a group of different people have worked together. Each brought a different point of view. They hated some of those songs. They didn't want to do propaganda, so they argued their way through each scene, and you've got, in the piece, the points of view of many people. This has been splendid. What you see is not a piece of direction by a producer. There were no rehearsals as they are known. There was a collection of individuals, more of an anti-group than a group, working on ideas, on songs, on settings, on facts. And if you get a few people with a sense of humour and brains together, you'll get theatre.

The critics were unanimous in their praise, no fewer than fifteen managements offered a transfer to the West End, and in June 1963, *Oh What A Lovely War* transferred to Wyndham's Theatre.

Taken from: *The Theatre Workshop Story* by Howard Goorney, London: Eyre Methuen, 1981, pages 125–127.

The production, which had originally been devised for the working-class community surrounding the theatre in London's East End, was an even bigger success with the middle-class theatre-going public. It is easy to see from the extract that the director's vision provided a particularly strong framework for the making of the piece; the devised work of Joint Stock Theatre Company *was much less strongly 'directed' or the result of a particular individual's vision. It sought to be a truly collaborative venture.*

49: Joint Stock

Joint Stock... has a reputation for ensemble work of the highest order, a certain notoriety for long company meetings (eight hours has been claimed although it probably seemed longer) and – rarest of all – it has established a unique approach to making plays: the *Joint Stock* method...

At the same time, *Joint Stock*'s method of work, both in creating the plays and in creating itself as an organisation, has attracted a lot of interest. Not all the attention has been friendly. Accusations of elitism, of writing plays by committee, of perversely pursuing a method for its own sake, have surfaced from time to time in the press and in theatre bars... However, the observation that the company's general way of working is as important a development in contemporary theatre as the achievements of the individual productions has been widely made. The key question, of course, is the relationship between the two, how the quality of the work is related to the conditions in which it is created. This is not just a matter of warm rehearsal rooms, genial company, chemistry. Such comforts have often proved elusive over the last twelve years... If the immediate circumstances differ very little from those endured by other theatre groups, the company have fashioned an approach to making plays that breaks with traditional patterns of production, extending the role of actors, writers, directors and technicians in the pursuit of the one goal that every *Joint Stock* member, on a good day, would agree upon: excellence.

This is hardly a novel objective – it is an achievement the Arts Council earnestly wishes for all its clients – and a commitment to excellence does not explain why writers like David Hare or Howard Brenton should have produced plays so strikingly different from their other work when writing for *Joint Stock*. But the amphasis on excellence, on aesthetic standards, is important if the impulse behind the creation of the company is to be correctly identified. The prominence of *Fanshen* – the show which above all else established *Joint Stock*'s identity – doubtless explains why it has been seen as a political theatre group. Here was a play about revolution, approached with an evident seriousness and played in a disciplined ensemble manner that surely sprung from a shared ideology. Brecht was mentioned by the critics; a degree of humourlessness – a sure sign of political conviction – noted. Moreover, having enacted the turning over to communism of the Chinese peasants, the company promptly applied the process to itself, eventually establishing a collective, abolishing the post of artistic director and subjecting all aspects of the work from get-ins and get-outs to the choice of future productions, to democratic discussion and control...

To those who subscribe to the notion that everything is political – now proving as disabling a perspective as it was liberating in the sixties – *Joint Stock* are clearly more political than the *Royal Shakespeare Company*... But attempting to establish the company's political credentials, to identify a programme that makes sense of the choice of plays, the style of production and the audience reached, will not get us very far. These issues have been discussed, often at great length, and many who have worked for the company have argued for a political assessment of its priorities. The evolution of *Joint Stock* however has been more marked by a refusal to adopt fixed principles governing the choice of projects than it has by any ambition to reach a shared political view. The point of departure of the company, the challenges it has set itself and the list of its achievements are, in the first instance, best understood in aesthetic terms. Max Stafford-Clark, the company's first and only artistic director, once described *Joint Stock* as a 'colourless company' in the sense that the group takes on the complexion of the material with which they are working...

(In)... the *Fanshen* workshop... Progress was slow, the subject seemed impossibly remote and there was real confusion and disagreement about what the objectives were. Success tends to glamourise hard work. In retrospect, a morning spent hawking and spitting like Chinese peasants can seem part of a necessary process of evolving a style. It can even sound like good fun. At the time, it seemed pointless, a blundering effort to find a way through a chaos of possibilities... (William) Hinton's book... (*Fanshen*)... is over 600 pages long. At the end of five weeks, few were convinced there was a play in it. (Bill) Gaskill's idea to set up the workshop as an exercise in democracy, however, began a process of self-enquiry that was to be decisive in the years ahead. In studying the existence of the Chinese peasants, the group equipped themselves to better understand their own. Actors directed, directors acted, all were entitled to question and criticise; pockets were emptied, earnings revealed, status and authority broken down and analysed. All this may not have achieved a play but it presented a challenge. The Long Bow villagers had improved their existence. *Joint Stock* would do the same...

The elements of the approach that grew from these beginnings are easily summarised. The essence is the insistence that good work requires time and a nucleus of people who are committed to the matter in hand. Again, commitment here should not be confused with a disposition to change the world. An actor with three lines and an evening of scene shifting may feel inclined to change the world but is better placed to take it out on the furniture... *Joint Stock*'s approach simply puts the actors' energy to better use, securing a commitment to the work by maximising the involvement of each. Eventually this was to extend to running the company, but initially it was more a matter of enriching the actor's work in rehearsal. An extended preparation period, typically ten weeks, is divided into a four week workshop and a six week rehearsal. During the workshop, actors, writer and director explore the subject matter, each contributing ideas and undertaking research. Improvisations, talks by experts (anything from 'The causes of the First World War' to 'The life of an English bookie'), interviews with character models, research trips, reading sessions , group discussions, a vast assortment of games and exercises (for analytical purposes rather than diversion), crash courses in professional skills – all are used to generate material for the play. In the second stage of the process – the gap between workshop and rehearsal – the writer composes the play. This is not, as is sometimes assumed, a question of scripting improvisations or following instructions drawn up by the group. The writer's work remains an independent creative act and the result may have no obvious relationship to the material yielded by the workshop: the *Fanshen* workshop did not produce the theme or narrative of the play, though it taught David Hare a great deal about Chinese prostitutes, peasant eating habits and the dramatic interest of dialectical debate... One of the many new experiences the process affords the writer is confronting a group of actors who know a great deal about the subject of the play. Allied with the actors' expectation that the piece will offer them the chance to show their skills across a range of parts or within a single substantial role – and this is the logical outcome of the whole approach – the gathering of the group for the final stage in the process – the rehearsal – can be terrifying. It is certainly never dull.

Taken from: *The Joint Stock Book: The Making of a Theatre Collective*, edited by Rob Ritchie, London: Methuen, 1987, pages 11–18.

If Joint Stock *could be described as a 'colourless company', taking its complexion, at any given moment, from the material it worked with, the work of many theatre in education companies is characterised by a full commitment to socialist politics. Some examples of the best devising practice are to be found in the work of the UK Theatre in Education (TiE) movement. The following extract shows how a TiE programme was developed as a result of a careful analysis of the prevailing political conditions in January 1990.*

50: *In Good Faith*: A Creative Process

He wishes for the cloths of Heaven

Had I the heavens embroidered cloths
Enwrought with golden and silver light,
The blue and the dim and the dark cloths
Of night and light and the half-light,
I would spread the cloths under your feet:
But I, being poor, have only my dreams;
I have spread my dreams under your feet;
Tread softly because you tread on my dreams.

W.B. Yeats

In the early stages of devising *In Good Faith* this poem was placed alongside a photograph of a young girl alone, at play, on a desolate stretch of Northumberland coastline. The photograph is from *In Flagrante* by Chris Killip. The resonance from the juxtaposition of the Yeats and the image of the girl was deep...

Early in our process the question 'How is it that a Capitalist society systematically kills its children?' became of very real affective significance.

Propelled in our thinking it became clear we were not only discussing the hundreds of thousands of young human beings literally killed or abused and stunted in their development – we were also focusing on the child who is us: the child in the adult, wronged, lied to and repressed in the distorted struggle to be whole human beings. We hope these concerns will become clearer to readers of the article as it progresses.

... In 1989, the company spent two weeks in New York City working with secondary school students and trainee teachers. In each and every moment of our time there, the obscene disparity in our wealth, resourcing and opportunity was having an enormous impact. Seward Park High School on the Lower East Side of Manhattan was an entirely new experience. Four thousand Chinese, Hispanic and Black American students are frisked by security guards on arrival; there is no playing field, no space, the building is literally collapsing. Racial tension and violence is commonplace; harrassment by the police viewed as quite natural.

The students were utterly committed to the very new experience of a dramatic exploration of their community. The work was richly disturbing. To meet and work with these people, at the sharpest end of economic and social crisis was a powerful experience.

A little over twelve months later, as we prepare this article, we read that the statue of Liberty, gateway to the city and the nation is closed. The state simply cannot afford the labour costs of its cleaning and maintenance. It is unsafe. Thinking back on our time there, and reflecting on the present machinations of US Imperialism, this is potent imagery.

On January 8th 1990 we began devising the new programme for 8–10 year-olds. We had no established line of enquiry. As a group of artists we struggled to 'own' the situation, to be fully, socially aware of ourselves meeting in the world with no pre-determined images of where our work would – or perhaps more dangerously 'should' take us. The company had a choice: to work from the premise that 'we had no ideas' – therefore we 'had to get one; or to understand that we were humans in a world undergoing the most rapid political transitions. Transitions that were sharply reflected in the company and ought to be in the work we would undertake. We wished to operate freely, truly and artistically as human beings both in and in conflict with the world.

> ... things, the environment, the world, exist independently of our sensations, of our consciousness, of our self and of man in general...

...our sensation, our consciousness is only an image of the external world and it is obvious that an image cannot exist without the thing imaged, and that the latter exists independently of that which images it...

In 'Living Contradiction and the Struggle to Recreate it Artistically' – *Theatre and Education Journal, No 3*, Tag McEntegart uses these formulations of Lenin's to explain that:

... it is the moment of direct connection through sensation which is both the basis for all human knowledge and the basis for all human error. Idealist philosophy.

This philosophical principle has been the subject of much discussion with the TiE (Theatre in Education) and YPT (Young People's Theatre) movement. We were attempting to be aware of, and employ this law in our work. To work, in and through, the art form; to use particulars to allow the content of the work to reveal itself *without* interposing our *ideas*; to allow the new in each moment to emerge, and not allow our sensation to become a wall or a barrier, between us and the world leading to the imposition of old images from the past.

... A decade ago, President Reagan was elected with a programme to balance the budget. But in the course of his two terms of office during which government expenditure on armaments and war tripled, whilst taxes, especially for the wealthy were slashed, the US was transformed from the world's largest creditor nation with a surplus of $141 billion in 1981 to the world's largest debtor with a $620 billion debt in 1989.

This was the crisis so powerfully at work on the Seward Park students, on the company, on the world. Co-incidentally we were (all) experiencing the deepening of the political revolutions in the Soviet Union and Eastern Europe. Every historical manifestation of Stalinism was under attack, and this struggle for the restoration of Soviet democracy interacts with the struggle of working people in every Capitalist country. In Britain, all the gains made by the working people over two centuries of struggle, were under increasingly brutal attack... This co-incidence; the crisis of Imperialism and the deepening of the struggle to smash Stalinism and establish the truth of 1917 has profound impact. As artists in January 1990, conscious or not, this impact was reverberating. The questions of historical truth: both individually and universally; the subjective fear of the drive to war; the future for youth, the species and the planet; all of these questions were deeply at work.

The attempt, then, to work artistically, to start with practice, 'from the standpoint of life' as Lenin explains, was at once both liberating and terrifying.

> ...There is no such thing as society, there are only individual men, women and children, and there are families...

> ... The dead clutches the living...

The now famous statement by Thatcher and the half remembered snippet from Lenin were given to the company. The task was to develop their resonance (if any) in the form of depictions. This was day one.

What emerged immediately were images which propelled the company out and into the material world.

A Romanian woman appealling to Western television cameras for a gun: 'a gun please, I need a gun'.

A Romanian mother and child make their way home through a park. The child focuses on dead bodies which lie at the side of the path, the mother looks ahead. The child is pulling, towards the dead. The tension between them.

Later, an image of pressing bodies toppling a statue; their weight wrenching it from its pedestal, overthrowing, tearing down and breaking up.

In these early depictions actors were exploring the enormous waves of revolt sweeping Eastern Europe. 'Spontaneous' action on the part of thousands; the weight of that action. The deeply felt sense of history in the making, and the dead present in the living makers of history.

As the work progressed, we were also drawn to images of crisis. With the introduction of the Killip photograph, we began to focus on children and what it is the world does to them.

A young girl's coat is unzipped. She is being 'prepared', as it were, for an appearance in a pornographic film. The image is held under the Yeats poem. The status and experience of young people today is brought sharply into focus. These images collide with our own images of life, our own expectations, our own memories.

The area the company was in now was both intriguing and disturbing.

The company however, had little understanding of a method with which to guide its practice in an evolving line of enquiry; and enquiry which felt rich and warm.

The conscious attempt to resist panic; to maintain the conditions that would leave the intuitive room to grow:

'The child plays in a zone of abandonment.'

'A mother waits in a zone of embarrassment and dependency.'

These explorations lay alongside further reflections on social and economic conditions experienced in the Britain of 1990.

'What is the border of the zone?'

'The child meets the border guard.'

Quickly the strong impulse to return to an analytic mode of working resurfaces.

'Why are we doing this? What is this exercise about? What is our teaching objective? Surely we must have a teaching objective?'

On reflection, this urge towards the analytical, points up the necessity to achieve the correct balance of the intuitive with the analytical. Also however, the emergence of these questions and a consequent fear of engaging in the work, manifested real philosophical and artistic difference. To enable the work to proceed creatively with the difference, required the development of forms.

The pressure was to rescind the exploration and hand over the contradictions to the writer who would provide the 'form' of a play and in so doing resolve the contradictions for the company. This was resisted. All of the objective scheduling requirements of the *Dukes Theatre* were negotiated back and the first offerings of the writer were rejected – because the contradictions and richness of the work were not evident; they did not resonate for the company, and so we knew would not resonate for the audience.

The company set about the creation of a garden. Visually, in written form, three dimensionally, we identified those 'seeds' in the material which we wished to cultivate, make room for, provide air, light and water for.

It was in this garden that central concerns to do with history, truth and the life and death of children were reflected back to us. The central image in *In Good Faith* is a derelict house. The derelict house grew slowly. In the garden it lay: bricks, old timber, torn wallpaper and dirt; certain 'lost objects', an apple, a child's knitted glove, a worn reproduction postcard of Botticelli's *Venus Rising from the Sea*.

The company knew that in this house a child has 'died'.

How was the 'dead' child found?

The child at the upstairs window – what is seen/unseen?

When was the last time (till now) the child entered the house?

When was the picture hung for the first time?

We would like to stress again that this exploration was almost entirely intuitive. The 'analytical' being brought to bear was, if anything, lacking.

The work had powerful ambience which held the company to the problem. We established

'Child as receiver'

The mother/the father

The man in the doorway watching

The radio

Outside the house, tension and great conflict. These were people in a true life and death struggle. The future of their world was somehow embodied in the future of the child. We were in rich ocean, with no real, reliable chart. We experienced a strong desire to wander more, and contradictorily to leave the ocean, or sink the ship.

Although we had a strong sense of them, we needed to concretely establish the objective class pressures on the lives that were emerging. The company's intuitive sense was demanding that the 'house' be located in pre-war Germany. We read widely, and consciously brought all of our cognitive understanding to the work. In continuing practical work the drama of these lives began to be played out in Bavaria, the Munich of 1929–1933. The period of the rise of Fascism and Stalinist betrayals, the defeat of the German working class.

Improvisation at this stage was unsatisfactory. It was general; the 'real time' pressures denied the company access to the essence of the 'event'. We decided to continue the exploration through the form of a photograph album: formal photos (the wedding, the christening), snaps, photos in which people 'appeared' but which they were unaware had been taken. Now the intuitive was beginning to be balanced alongside the analytical. Now the people began to rest securely in their time, in their place. Truth was knowable and artifice was detectable.

This process was joyous and painful. The company were not only confronting the truth within their own experience: Chris, Danie, for example as child, sometimes parent, worker, unionist, lover, they were (we were) also becoming able to place alongside an objective under-standing of the *historical conditions*, e.g. Trotsky's analysis of the Trade Union movement in pre-war Germany; the objective relationship of Stalinism with the victory of Fascism.

Though the 'drama' of the play was emerging in the past historically, the motivation for its uncovering were the actors engagement in the now. Eventually the full drama of the play emerged.

It is 1990 – Maria lives in East Germany, aged 64. Driven by the leaps made in the objective conditions of the East German working class, she crosses back and returns to her childhood home in Munich. She says:

> I saw the break in the wall, first a trickle, then a flood.

Maria confronts herself aged eight. What follows is not a remembering, it is a very real struggle. The child does battle in order that the adult confronts the truth, the whole truth, of her life and history. A life dis-torted on the one hand by the horrors of fascism, and on the other, later, by the deprivation and loss suffered under a Stalinist bureaucracy. A bureaucracy which was built upon the defeat of the working class.

> The child at the window; what is seen?

> ... Then my father went for his throat, and the hand with the club swung free, and down, down, down on my father's head. A single instant. The moment of truth. The pencil in my hand snapped and the lead rod slid ever so slowly on to the sill. And then Rolf bundled him into the van, lugging at his legs – because he was a big man...

The play which was written was performed to young people from the ages of seven to eleven. Daley, one of the actors, had remembered; 'when I was a child I could change the world before lunch, and then go out and change it all again'.

The play consistently held the audience at a very deep level of involvement. Children have such a burden of responsibility to 'parent their parents'.

> Probably everybody has a more or less concealed inner chamber that he hides from himself and in which the props of his childhood drama are to be found. These props may be his secret delusion, a secret perversion, or quite simply the unmastered aspects of his childhood suffering...

The last offering of the company to the writer Maureen Lawrence was Alice Miller's *For Your Own Good*. What was offered in return was and is a truly whole, material, and delicately balanced work of art. A play which spurred its audience to engage with an exploration of history and truth; which confirmed their appreciation of the objective importance of truth.

By the end of the creative process, leading to the writing of the play, one company member had lost, almost entirely, any connection with the process. Another, though recognising the power of the play, distrusted the process which led to its making. Although neither of these individuals were performers, we know, that the failure to make the process meaningful for the company *as a whole*, had effectively split the collective practice.

In the attempt to work in the art form were we merely indulging the sensibilities of the actors? Were we coming to know the world, or was our decision making arbitrary and idealist? These are risks. The true risk in a devising process is that *you will come to know*. You will be confronted with the necessity to change your life. The highest risk is the social risk.

There is no false separation between the human being in the world and the actor/deviser in the creative process. An actor in the company recently characterised the spring term of 1990 as a period in which the company:

> 'had so much to say to each other'.

All aspects of our lives, the financial, the emotional, the sexual, the political, the bereavements (one actor lost her father, the director a dear friend) were brought to bear. The people of the drama were not allowed to emerge as abstract images from another time and another place.

Today... the drive to war is actual; the political Revolution develops in all its contradicting aspects. The *knowability of the world* is of greater significance as a philosophical question than perhaps ever before. Cynicism, scepticism are the immensely strong opposites.

The young people we work with are makers and inheritors, they are *offensive*, but the state is *entirely offensive against them*. Each and every artist and educator is forced to confront what is at stake.

The struggle in art for the balance between the intuitive and the analytical is one we struggle to pursue. It is difficult. If this article offers anything… It is a collective recognition that the struggle bears fruit. Art is indeed a mode of knowing.

Taken from: '*In Good Faith:* A Creative Process' by Ian Yeoman with Chris Cooper, *SCYPT Journal, No 21*, 1991, pages 19–28.

In Good Faith was written by the writer, Maureen Lawrence whose collaborations with The Dukes' Company *have produced a number of theatre in education programmes. In the following extract, she offers a fascinating insight into the role of the writer in the devising process.*

51: Writing a Play with *The Dukes TiE Company*

When the company asked me to speak to a group of teachers about the current production, the devising of the piece was still fresh. Now, writing three months later, I turn to my notebooks to refurbish my meory and find that the forty or so pages of notes are so dense, so abbreviated and so dependent for interpretation upon shared experience that the prospect of further distillation is daunting. At first it seems impossible: to understand my notes even, one needs some knowledge of the company, its history, its individual members, their long-standing association with myself, to say nothing of the particular brief for this particular play and the larger social and political and educational issues that come to bear on the work.

If this seems like grandiosity – an absurd sense of expanding horizons around the tiny centre-piece of a children's play, then it must be admitted that, yes, there is at moments during the work an intense consciousness of its importance. In a sense that is the starting-point: a determination that a genuine communication shall take place between the company and the children. Underlying everything is the question: what is it that we need to say now to these children? This question is non-rhetorical; nobody in the group has a ready answer. To devise is to find the answer, the answer which evolves through dramatic play, through frozen images, through silence, through reflection, through argument, through imaginative leaps by the different members and ultimately through the shaping words that I as a writer give to these experiences.

Five actors, a stage-manager, an Education Development Officer, a director, a writer, and a designer, ten characters in search of a play constitutes a huge potential that may be creative or destructive, can sometimes be both those things, and sometimes yields nothing at all. It is true that on one occasion our collaboration did fail to produce the goods. However, the fact that the company is an extremely stable group, with performers who have worked together for several years is important here. The present play was my seventh with the *Dukes'*, which is a good starting point for me in terms of trust and confidence. After so long, much can be taken for granted. At the outset we can assume a certain common outlook. We may disagree about means, but we probably desire similar ends, at least in terms of social and economic change. My spells with the company are short and intense, but I recognise something of the feel of a family, a solidarity which may be questioning but is dependable. On reflection this is probably the age-old bonding that a theatre company needs it if is to survive. As a writer I am nervy and self-critical, and I find the atmosphere in the group both stimulating and reassuring.

However, the play begins before I enter the scene. This question of what the piece is to be will have been explored intensively in a week or two of work led by one member of the group. This time Danie is leading with Warwick at hand to share the responsibility. During this period, Warwick Dobson, as company director, came to see me at home with a question: "What does oblivion mean to you?" This sparked a monologue which ranged from my distant memories of teenage Keatsian inertia, strongly coloured by a reading of *Oblomov*, a novel about an alienated Russian, to my very recent experience of observing patients in the last stages of senile dementia. It turned out that in the first week of work, madness had been a recurrent theme – again partly inspired by a literary association because everybody had read the novel, *Restoration*. Such parallels and apparent coincidences are not really surprising to me, because my experience of running creative writing workshops – when time and patience and money allow for the luxury of communication – has often thrown up such correspondences. At this stage it simply means that we are inhabiting the same territory and can go forward and see where the path takes us into the forest.

At this first meeting Warwick also filled me in on the practical details. The play was to be fifty minutes long, for 7-9 year-olds, and given this age group there was a tacit understanding that it might well take the form of a fairy story. As a writer I like to work within these precise parameters. To know the size of the piece, the age of the audience, the number and capabilities of the performers and the intention of the group gives me a firm framework. The creative process can be anarchic, even chaotic, but these simple points of reference help to keep things in order. On my first day I become the audience while the group present the images they have invented. Usually I am not present in the first phase of devising and there may be a slight sense of breaking in on a private ritual; it's a little like being given a privileged glimpse into a secret world. In fact, I deliberately try to be receptive rather than active at first because what a writer gains from working in this way is the opportunity to be fed by other people's imagination. At the same time, because in the end I have the ultimate responsibility to provide a play, I always keep that goal in mind and if the process of devising begins to seem self-perpetuating or blocked, I become exasperated. On occasion, I have started to write the play while the devising is still going on. It goes on because it is an extremely absorbing game at one level and like any game it has an addictive quality. Alternatively one might say that it is a process of discovery that is deeply satisfying, often tapping into layers of experience that are hidden in ordinary life. Being given an outlet for one's creative impulses in a safe environment is a rare treat; this can make it difficult for the group to leave the devising in order to go on to the production phase of the work. Invariably it is the running out of time that determines the end rather than a sense of finality; on the day they hand over to me there is often no real acceptance of closure.

However, as I look back at my notes for Day One I recall that there was still a long way to go. The images shown to me that day were surreal, bizarre and violent. The novel, *Restoration*, is a period piece full of contradictions, a black comedy, in which the anti-hero is a sexually exuberant, amiable grotesque, while his ascetic friend runs an asylum, for the mad, the more mad and the maddest of all. At the centre of the novel the restored King Charles rules over the frantic antics, which includes the partial anatomising of a living man, whose exposed and throbbing heart thrills our hero. Such material might seem a far cry from the world of the junior school child. But our discussions quickly revealed that our memories of our childhood reveries and fantasies ranged over this same ground, often with even greater ferocity. In fact, very early in the devising process we recognised the overlap between the novelist's literary obsessions, our childhood recollections, and the realm of the folk and fairy tale. The fears and frustrations of childhood, the half-heard, half-understood facts, the conflict between the individual will of the new human being and its restraining family finds its imaginative correlative in the battle between good and evil that is presented in fictional form.

This being the case at this point, the short route to a play would have been to choose a tale and revamp it as a drama. But to identify the area of experience, which we might call the field of moral consciousness, was still too general, too impersonal to provide the substance of a play. The group works intuitively towards a 'felt' experience. I might intellectualise or verbalise the possibilities even on Day One, but the imagery which is the flesh and blood of the thing had yet to be invented. To 'choose' an extant fairy tale would be arbitrary. This is a difficult area because clearly as the process continues sometimes actions do seem arbitrary. The group is not uniform; it is a bunch of individuals. What "feels" right to one or two might be questioned by others. Such splits are sometimes mended by argument; sometimes by an act of faith – ignored in the hope that they will go away; sometimes allowed to develop so that the work proceeds on two fronts for a while until an umbrella form can be found which encompasses both.

In this case my eager pragmatism – find a play quick and let me write so I can be secure – is suppressed in favour of further exploration. Day Two and Danie creates a space at the centre of which she places a heart. The walls are delineated by quotations and notations from the earlier work. She asks people to place in this space things which are important. This acting space is quickly filled with what looks like litter and is actually bits of paper covered in writing. There are fragments of poetry remembered or copied from books or composed by the performers. There are snippets of Shakespeare, Keats, Tennyson. There are accounts of contemporary events: family, war, rape, death. There are descriptions of states of mind – not only madness but rapture as well as bafflement. There are photostats of paintings as well as art-books. A seventeenth-century *Massacre of the Innocents* appears from somewhere and a Cranach *Adam and Eve*. Near the heart I place my notebook. I am beginning at this point to feel slightly feverish with interpretations. I suppress the desire to babble. For some of those present the space is a room, for others a world. For me it is a person at first because it has a heart, and then it becomes human consciousness burdened by the great rag-bag of human history and human culture. The actual place –

the studio of the theatre is dark, dingy, untidy with painters' dust covers and bits of scaffolding, but in this dim interior the sight of these ten people reverently placing their offerings is strangely moving. Naïve as it may sound at this distance there is a sense of something growing here. There is a reaching towards meaning which is exemplified in all these writings, paintings, political statements, but also in the living people who are trying to add to the sum total of understanding.

At the end of each day emerging from the spell of this shared exploration I struggle to make that arbitrary choice of direction because I am impelled by the commitment to write it in the end. Each evening informally the talk may continue, but each morning the work resumes as a collective effort taking as its starting point the work of the previous day. Each morning the appointed leader takes the work forward unless there is a block and a strong lead comes from someone else. On Day Three Danie creates the figure of a woman by drawing round a company member on white paper. The figure is pinned upright to some of the scaffolding and immediately becomes known as Eve. The parts of Eve are named and then Danie asks the group to attach the items that were placed in the room to the parts of Eve, using a fine almost transparent thread. Gradually a web-like form is created which contains a complex of meanings. The figure of the woman – Eve – is connected to a vast cultural experience, which both creates and confines her in its encompassing meshes. Making this structure and analysing its meaning takes two days. By the end of the week this dominant figure has moved us from folk and fairy tale into myth. I am now nervous. My first week is running out and I do not want to do a rewrite of the creation story. I foresee infinite complications arising from going anywhere near religious issues in school.

And yet we are definitely committed to the problem of the knowledge of good and evil. This problem seems central. Our audience of children will constantly be exhorted to be good as we were. But what does it mean to be good? What is evil? What is it that we need to know in order to survive with honour? On the last day of the third week (which is Day Five for me) Eve is rediscovered in a series of seven scenes or events. For each of these scenes Danie provided the title and the company working as two groups devised an image. One group worked very rapidly, and impulsively, and their scenes fell into a sort of continuous narrative. The other group talked more and were much more analytical; the images came with greater difficulty and were more diverse. Yet in each case, the woman was under duress; she was battered, oppressed, pursued, even raped. To an extent she was perceived as colluding in her own destiny, but only because survival demanded that she use what skills she had in order to keep herself together. Late on the afternoon of that day, out of the blue, Danie produced an exquisite definition of witch-hazel from a book on herbs. The reason for this intervention eludes me. Did it connect with the idea of skills? Or was it a simple echo of the word 'witch' and our talk of fairy-tales that attracted her to the book? In a coffee-break – off-guard – I found myself reading through an index of plants with herbal properties. In fact, at the end of this day we were ostensibly no nearer a play and had the group now offered me the option of writing something I would have been dismayed. The ferment of impressions is probably best illustrated by the notebook. For example my weekend reflections include the following messages to myself and the company:

1. Need to find a fairy tale and its correspondences with our work;
2. Notice recurrent image of woman encaged;
3. Many motifs belong in children's lit. i.e. apple, heart, mirror, water, twigs;
4. Desire to present concurrent events in order to show interconnectedness;
5. Ambiguity – need for both aspects – horror/joy; despair/euphoria;
6. Family and stranger – stranger brings dreams of another life to poor family. When he goes they sicken and die. This last note testifies to my need for narrative, but it goes nowhere.

My second week – Day Six – saw the arrival of the designer, who like me had a strong vested interest in bringing the work to a point. Informally she and I had several talks in which we explored fairy stories like *Sleeping Beauty* again without coming to a conclusion. She brought in sketches of trees, webs, beds, and a strange quilt with velvety bird-like masks sewn into the fabric. But once again we went back to the imagery of the previous session for our starting point. Several of the scenes of Eve had been set in the night. We talked for a long time about our childhood fears of the dark. This was amicable but unprogressive. Such anecdotal spells are very good for building confidence within the group. There is a pooling of memories which reinforces a belief in the commonality of experience. In the long run, therefore, these periods are a vital part of the process, but at the time I can feel a degree of panic. I am depending on them to show me the way. I want them to act, not talk, to move, not merely move me.

Eventually not until the afternoon of that day the images began to come. This time Danie asked for a recapitulation of the earlier work but in terms of the notion of witch-hazel. At this point the company was still working as two groups. The trio that had been spontaneous, set to and moved into their positions, taking earlier images and modifying them to incorporate new ideas; the other group – like me – seemed bemused by the instruction. The work of both groups was lit now and again by glimpses from the earlier reading of *Restoration*. One of the images on this day showed a group of people staring through a window. I should perhaps have made it clear earlier that when the images have been shown everybody has an opportunity to offer an interpretation. During the analysis it was suggested that the people were perhaps watching the Great Fire. This back-tracking is alarming to me. I can easily begin to fear that I shall be left with a proliferation of inchoate forms and no clear direction. Yet this fear is counterbalanced by confidence because so often in the past – like magic – the pathway has suddenly emerged.

Thus that same afternoon an image was formed which became very potent for me. During the analysis it was interpreted as Eve in the clasps of a creature, a Beast of the Forest. Instead of fear her face had registered ecstasy. The tie-up with *Beauty and the Beast* seemed very inviting. Yet at the end of the afternoon the note to myself diverges from the archetype. I wrote: I see a man in quaint attire, leading a chained bear. He plays. The bear dances. The people stare. This was a mental image, related to the dramatic images but different because existing purely in the mind as an abstraction.

That evening I went back to my lodgings and wrote a scene of the play. I had no story, no "dramatic question", no idea of who the characters were or how as they spilled out they were informed by everything that had happened in the preceding days. When this happens to a writer it is like magic – an effortless process that is a delight. I had no doubt that this scene would be the nucleus of the play. Yet on Day Seven, the second day of the second week for me, and the fourth week for the group the exploration continued. Danie, as leader, confessed to a high degree of anxiety about the outcome of the work. Claiming that they were not ready to brief me yet, they also felt blocked. Each member of the group was called on to comment. Again this analytical process is slow and time-consuming but important. In a work of art thought and feeling coalesce through form by an interior process that we call imagination. With one individual at work this is a complex and often painful process. With eight it is bound to be difficult. The thoughts of each member – the doubts, reservations, frustrations – are an important ingredient in the final product. Once I am secretly hugging my seed to myself I am happy to share in this process. If I do not instantly reveal what I have made this is because I want to make it stronger before I let it be seen. It is fed by these thoughts of the others.

My notebook records that each person says something. Sue, the Education Development Officer, comments that the 'knowledge' of what we want is in the group and either they dare not or cannot speak. With hindsight this seems a very perceptive statement. At that point with my little scrap of dialogue I had knowledge which I was deliberately with-holding – for safety's sake. Each person adds something of value. Being certain now that this is all going to work out, I am happy, grateful for every word. Chris reminds us of our question: what is it that is important to say to these children. He speaks of a sense of crisis: what shall I do with myself. He wants to relate this individual problem to the social context and to understand the class content. At length they reach the conclusion that the play continues to be elusive. They need to go on making images in the light of these redefined objectives.

Once again the stock of images is reworked in the afternoon of that day but this time when the images are examined Danie asks us to determine which figure is the keeper. In the evolving language of the play the keeper is the person who holds the power. The analysis of the images reveals that power is partly a matter of perception. Power is complex, diffuse, often covert, almost if not always cruel.

From my point of view it is intriguing that the figure of the keeper has become dominant since he has already taken the form of a character in my rudimentary play. In the play that is rapidly beginning to take shape the keeper is a travelling player, a mountebank, a cruel master, his sensibility blunted by power. He has a performing animal, an abused son, a dead wife, probably his victim. He has a coarse vitality. Against his brute strength is opposed the wit of a weak but wise old woman. To begin with, being natural enemies, they merely exchange insults, but a relationship starts to crystallise. She is his nemesis. He has force, but she has knowledge – a knowledge of herbs as well as an understanding of character and morality. The images that have been worked and reworked, examined and justified, began to fall together into a pattern as if they are magnetised by each other and know where they belong. In this way during the evenings of this second week the play begins to write itself without permission, though I share this emerging drama with Danie and the designer, whose sketches of foliage also inform the work. The forest – a term we have used throughout to mean impenetrable thicket of meanings – becomes the fairy-tale forest, the testing place where the good and the bad will meet their destiny. In the end folk-lore and fairy-tale provide not a narrative but a number of elements – witch, beast, lost children, forest, spell, incantations – which carry the answer to our opening question. My elation at this point makes it clear to the group that I am well on the way. I am keen to get on now with the writing and real events – (to do with their actual survival as a company) – claim their attention. The process of devising does not end therefore with a grand finale; towards the end of the second week it has been a whole month nearly for the rest – they simply let go.

Taken from: 'Writing A Play with *The Dukes' TIE Company*' by Maureen Lawrence, *SCYPT Journal*, No 24, 1992, pages 12–18.

In this section, we have gained some insight into some of the methodologies used in the devising process. The work of the drama in education theorist and practitioner, Dorothy Heathcote, has been enormously influential within the theatre in education movement. In the following extract, she offers some thoughts on working in role and a list of conventions which can be used in work with young people in school contexts (and, of course, beyond).

52: Signs (and Portents?)

Actual living and theatre, which is a depiction of living conditions, both use the same network of signs as their medium of communication; namely the human being signalling across space, in immediate time, to and with others, each reading and signalling simultaneously within the action of each passing moment. We cannot help signing so long as there is another human being who needs to read the signs. Actions become *sign* whenever there is more than one person present to read the action.

Balanced between these two kinds of occasions are drama used in education (i.e. in the classroom mainly) and Theatre in Education teams. I should like to explore the relationship of these four kinds of events in this paper.

When I first began teaching, I had no training in the 'proper' ways to make contact with my classes. Coming from a theatre training I therefore used the thing I knew most about. That was, how to make it interesting and exciting to be present at an occasion marked by *conscious* signing of intent... Coming from the theatre, then, I got to thinking it would be important to suit the word and the gesture; AND the relationship with the furniture AND the book; AND indeed anything which at the moment assisted in the total picture becoming available to be 'read' by the class. I also knew that you don't ask questions to which you already know the answers. This is not how theatre works. You signal across space meaningfully, to get a response which will have been born from your own signal, as the person/s alongside you read the SIGN. So, of course, you listen with all your body for messages. Coming from the theatre also, you don't consider SIGN to be 'bad manners'. I still meet colleagues who somehow manage by *their* signing, to indicate to me that there is something rather ungenteel about behaving like that in classrooms. However, I must say that I am glad that more teachers are braving these critics and trying to employ SIGN more coherently in their teaching. I wonder if we would have fewer 'slow learners' if we used a more meticulously selective and complete signing system as our means of communication to such classes. No, persons. Persons read signs, each one, individually, and therefore decipher the code easily if it is rich, full and HIGHLY SELECTIVE, for its present purpose. This is the interesting variation on life and theatre signing which the classroom and the TIE team can exploit.

In the theatre all actors sign for the benefit of the audience. In life we sign for the other person out of need for response. In teaching we make our signs specially interpretable, so that the children are enabled to read all signals with the least possible confusion. We deliberately sign for the responder to come into *active participation in the event*... The most developed skill which children bring to school is that of making sense for their own ends, of sign in their immediate environment. So we do not need to apologise for 'showing off' which is how working in role in the classroom is often seen. One can understand why people criticise it; because the medium of expression is the human person.

Fortunately, working through role is catching on a bit in classrooms, so it may be timely to start looking at the subtlety of this style of approach, which is one of many. But all these many MUST USE SIGN in order to make communication. From now on forgive me if I seem to state the obvious.

We probably all agree that when we say we work in role we mean that we become part of the action of the 'play' and have a voice in the dramatic encounter. There must, by now, be some emergent theory born of practice, which could be brought together so that we can see what the rules are in order to apply them better. What follows are only the basic common denominators which I have isolated, so they won't be complete, because I don't myself understand it all yet.

1. **Now and imminent time**. The factor which distinguishes a dramatic exploration of ideas, seems to be the way in which time becomes different than the usual classroom time. During discussion *of* ideas (though we ourselves exist in life-time) the circumstances we are planning to try to exist in, are still in another time-state. We talk about, 'they would do this or that', or 'why don't we try this or that', because though we are breeding future action of the event we are still only planning. I am constantly amazed by the miracle of how *thinking* about dramatic ideas, can in an instant become that of carrying it into action. There is a world of difference between someone in a class saying, 'Well, they would take all their belongings with them', and saying, 'Let's pack and leave'. That is the switch I work for, to enable a dramatic exploration of ideas to take place. It stands to reason then, if I want to assist in this switch to imminent time, the most effective way is to very carefully start to use my contribution to the discussion in the NOW time-state. That is role at its simplest. 'I talk like I'm there'. There is a lot more to it than that of course. One does not just become a person in the play, because one is teaching as well as signing...

2. **Role as contract maker**. I have already indicated that social encounters need sign. The sign of the person, in action, using all objects, significant space, pause, silences, and vocal power to make the meaning available to others in the encounter. This total acceptance of signing allows children to bring their profound experience to bear in interpreting the scene... In role, I give myself two kinds of encounter. One is the power to get out of the expected teacher system of relating with the class. The other, is the opportunity to make contracts as myself and encounter the class signing system through the role I artificially and totally consciously take up...

3. **'The other'**. This is a somewhat fanciful name to give to what might be perceived as just something to deflect attention from the class. I spend a lot of time preventing classes to feel stared at. Everything else in the world except oneself is 'an other'. The actor in the theatre, the TIE team and the teacher have all made a

contract to allow people to stare at them, but the children have not made that contract. And teachers of drama who take it for granted that children have given them permission, spend useless time in eroding the embarrassment which happens during drama lessons when children feel stared at. The obvious way to avoid this is to give them something so attractive in the room that they feel they are staring at it. Role is one of the most efficient 'others'. Do not mistake what I am saying; I do not mean something which is merely interesting, or entertaining... What I am discussing here is that, 'the other' be the gateway to all the full depth of exploration which will follow as the class get involved with the issues...

4. **Sharing and giving information**. Teachers are noted for their propensity to share their understanding, by a process of telling in one form or another. This often tends to look like one-way transmission. A teacher in role can undermine this approach because the theatre gets its message over more indirectly as the range of signs which come into play function in synchronic time. Many *kinds* of information are available simultaneously when role is inducted...

5. **Negotiation**. Artists work from two positions of power. The *doing* position, where they are involved in the action of their art, and the *seeing* position from which they perceive what is happening and what might need to be done. By sometimes working in the action of the play, and sometimes from the spectator position I can give this power to the class. Role helps them *do*, and teacher helps them *see*. In the early stages, contracts and decisions are often best taken from the spectator position so that everyone can see there is no con-game going on...

6. **Shifts position of class**. By taking up a role one offers not only a point of view to the others, but places them in a position from where it is assumed that they will also find a point of view... Note that I have said assumed. One cannot endow people with commitment to a point of view, but often by placing them in the response position, they begin to hold a point of view, because they can see it has power. The crudest power to give others is that of disagreeing with the role, spotting the weakness in the role's position, or even opposing the role. If a class really want to oppose a teacher it is often somewhat bitter in tone... but opposition to a role places the class in a very safe position from which to disagree, and it establishes their *right* to oppose the teacher's power. No-one loses face. But the best thing of all, the role, not the teacher, can

respond to the communication, thus holding it in the 'no penalty' zone. In this way good relations can be built, on a very sure basis...

So far I have been mainly looking at role from the point of view of the teacher in the classroom. What of TiE teams? The first advantage they have is, that, under theatre conventions they are accepted as total signifiers. They have given permission to others to stare so they can employ significance from the start. It is accepted as normal for the actor/teachers to employ such aspects of sign such as clothing, properties and setting for action. This is not so easy for the teacher because of different expectations of behaviour. One of the most fundamental decisions which TiE teams have made is that of working with classes from within and from without the action of the play. They have a problem however... if changing their signing system to indicate and accommodate to these *two* positions. This is because of the very strength of their sign position when in the action of the play. A teacher by her *in*ability to strongly sign on clothing, setting and accuracy of properties, can sign mainly in the language and body position areas, and these are more easily shed than the clothing and prop signs of the TiE actor. Thus it is I think, that the TiE teams often find difficulty in their negotiations from outside or when seeking to bring their audience into their action. Children can't help being reminded that they are not quite in the action like the actors are.

So we come to the fascinating area of conventions which can be used to enable children to become involved in drama experiences of many types. The ability of children to achieve truthful behaviour under both TiE and classroom drama, and to become committed to the decisions they are enabled to take during the action of the play, is phenomenal. Conventions, as I shall outline, seem to me to be a most useful additive to both types of work. *Avant Garde* theatre has always used them, and film can wonderfully exploit them. I use them more and more in my classroom work and they are comparatively easy to manage with a little care and practice. They exploit the use of signing and significance in a very special way because most of them shift the way in which contact with Role and 'immediate time' works. Most drama that moves forward at seeming life rate is too swift for classes to become absorbed in and committed to.

The conventions offered here *all slow down time* and enable classes to get a grip on decisions and their own thinking about matters. They all function as 'other', but in relation to people.

1. Role actually present, naturalistic, yet significantly behaving, giving and accepting responses.
2. The same, except framed as a film. That is, people have permission to stare but not intrude. 'Film' can be stopped and restarted, or re-run.
3. The role present as in 'effigy'. Can be talked about, walked around, and even sculptured afresh if so framed.
4. The same, but with the convention that effigy can be brought into life-like response and then returned to effigy.
5. The role as portrait of person. Not three dimensional, but in all other ways the same as effigy.
6. The role as portrait or effigy activated *to hear* what the class is saying. This causes selective language.
7. The role as above, but activated to speak only, and not be capable of movement.
8. The role depicted in picture: removed from actual life, as in a slide of role, a painting, a photograph or drawing. This includes those made by a class, as well as prepared depictions.
9. A drawing seen in the making, of someone important to the action, as on a blackboard.
10. Stylised depiction of someone, *eg* identikit picture made by class in frame, *eg* as detectives.
11. Same, except made beforehand, so it is a *fait accompli*.
12. Life size (cardboard) model with clothing (real) of role *eg* 'framed' as if in a museum or sale rooms. 'This is the dress worn by Florence Nightingale when she met Queen Victoria after Scutari.'
13. Same, except the class is dressing the model so as to see 'how it was' on that day when these events happened.
14. Clothing of persons cast off in disarray, *eg* remains of tramp's presence, or a murder, and escape as in a highwayman situation.
15. Objects to represent person's interests. Works as above, but more closely can indicate concerns rather than appearance, *eg* a ring of a Borgia.
16. An account of a person by another person in naturalistic fashion, *eg* 'Well when last I saw him he seemed alright. I never dreamed anything was wrong."
17. An account of a person written as if from that person, but read by someone else, *eg* a diary or letter.
18. An account written by the person who now reads it to others, *eg* a policeman giving evidence or a confession. The role is present in this case but in contact through their writing as an author might well be.

19. An account written by someone, of someone else and read by yet another.
20. Story told of another, in order to bring that person close to the action, *eg* "I saw him open a safe once. It was an incredible performance. I'm not sure if he would assist us though."
21. A report of an event but formalised by authority or ritual, *eg* an account of bravery in battle on an occasion of the presenting of posthumous medals.
22. A letter read in the voice of the writer. This is an emanation of a specific presence, not just any voice, communicating the words.
23. The same, but the letter is read by another with no attempt to portray the person who wrote it, but still expressing a feeling.
24. Letter read without feeling, *eg* as evidence, or accusation in a formal situation.
25. Voice of person overheard talking to another – informal language, *ie* a naturalistic tone.
26. Same, but in formal language.
27. A conversation overheard. (Person not seen.) Deliberate eavesdropping as in spying.
28. Report of a conversation, written and spoken by another.
29. Reported conversation with two people reading the respective 'parts'.
30. Private reading of conversations, reported as overheard.
31. The finding of a cryptic code message, *eg* 'tramps' or 'spies'.
32. Signature of a person found, *eg* a half-burned paper.
33. Sign of a particular person discovered, *eg* Scarlet Pimpernel, (his special mark).

All the above can be used to make classes feel involved with the immediate time of the action, and in personal touch with the human person, but it will not be achieved if the negotiations do not endow the class with the power to influence, not only watch. This means that the participation needs to be framed. There are many ways of doing this but the most important factor is that the participants have to be framed into *a position of influence*. In TIE then it would seem an advantage to consider the many frames from which audiences may enter the action. If they are asked to use their judgement, as themselves, or share in an endeavour with the actors, as in a spinning-mill situation, the number 1 on the conventions list would seem to be the one which would serve and feel right. But if they were asked to *comment on* the action as if it were in frozen time (as in a museum), then the frame can be different.

For example the actors may become portraits in a gallery and the participants may then be asked to reactivate them and make them 'play it again' in another way. Or, when teaching a Shakespearean play for 'A' level, a TiE team might play a scene of some seminal importance to the study, but then in effigy or portrait convention, each protagonist in the situation might be 'hung' in a gallery and the children in groups invited to take one such painting and activate it to walk the scene again, asking it at each stage to explain itself. If they are framed as mediums then the tension will be different from that of being cleaners, wondering 'what he did with himself to end up like that'.

I take it as a general rule for myself that people have most power to become involved at a caring and urgently involved level if they are placed in a quite specific relationship with the action, because this brings with it inevitable responsibility, and, more particularly, the viewpoint which gets them into an affective involvement. By doing this, the social encounters, either during or after the main action of the play, become more complex and various. It *is* often done, of course, as, for example, when the audience are invited to be a jury or soldiers at a firing squad, or indeed any situation where they may join in the moral or action decisions. However, often the participation functions in action time, the seeming life rate of the theatre. The list mentioned before has only one such convention, number 1: all the other encounters with people, their behaviour and motives are in another kind of time. The roles exist to be rebuilt in one way or another, and in one form or another. The class can be invited to reconstruct, or re-interpret, and this has the remarkable effect of getting them hooked into the power to think about influence and hold a viewpoint, because the action is a process of *rebuilding*, not sharing someone else's materials.

Unlike television with its fast moving action/image, these other conventions function more like stills or slides, causing infinitesimal decisions to be made by the children. 'Theatre' proper, as it were, finds it difficult to cause audiences to reframe themselves, for it is not the mood in which most people come to the theatre. They anticipate the security of the spectator of action. Likewise the teacher who prefers to teach *about* things often uses the consciously cognitive approach. This type of teaching can avoid the immediate decision time of drama. TIE and classroom role work are ideally suited to exploit these types of work and it pays well to explore them further. I said at the beginning of this paper, however, that if you only join the cast of the play, as it were, it adds very little to the meaningful action which takes classes through the layers from mere attraction, to interest, to attention and finally to concern.

The whole negotiation of role involves delicate linguistics in vocal sign, plus the equally selective body and space sign. Both areas of signalling require the power to be passed over to others. Let us take an example to try to make this clear. Suppose the class are working members of the team of the Scarlet Pimpernel, rescuing an aristocrat from the Revolution, and the action has involved a teacher in role as one of the revolutionaries in order to place the class in danger as the 'brave Englishmen'. The first episode may be dealt with in life-like style; but see the difference in thought, and the social demands made, if the second episode has to deal with the aristocrat being brought into an inn where on the wall is the portrait of that aristocrat, and the loyalties of the innkeepers are not known. The convention of *portrait* makes it possible here for a new look at danger, and the complexity of signing (which the class will of course handle without difficulty) creates an entirely new social and linguistic encounter. Whichever convention is selected will always be designed to serve the particular ends of the work...

Finally, having spent a long time wondering why I have for years been irritated by the cry of 'let's have more drama in our schools', I now realise why I always wanted to say, 'Don't lobby for dramatics, lobby for better learning!' It is of course because the heart of communication in social situations is THE SIGN. *All* teachers need to study how to exploit it as the first basis of their work. The theatre is the art form which is *totally* based in SIGN and the drama additive to learning is the urgency possible through using NOW/imminent time. This is why we lobby for better schools when we ask that teachers wake up to the possibilities of the power of resonances in classrooms instead of verbal statements.

Taken from: 'Signs (and Portents?)' by Dorothy Heathcote, *SCYPT Journal, No 9*, 1982, pages 18–28.

Contributors' Biographies

Andre ANTOINE was a French actor, director and theatre manager who founded *Theatre Libre* in Paris in 1887.

ARISTOTLE was a Greek philosopher of the fourth century. BC. His *Poetics* represents the earliest surviving attempt to describe and analyse drama practice.

Antonin ARTAUD was a French poet, writer of essays, actor, theatre theorist and director.

Roland BARTHES is a French post-structuralist critic, and writer on cultural issues.

Edward BRAUN was formerly professor in the Department of Theatre at the Univesity of Bristol. He is a renowned expert on the work of Meyerhold.

Bertolt BRECHT was a playwright, director, poet and theatre theoretician. Forced to flee from his native Germany during the 1930s, some of his best plays were written in the United States. He returned to Germany after the second world war, where he founded the *Berliner Ensemble*.

Peter BROOK is an English director who set up the *International Centre for Theatre Research* and has written extensively on directing and the theatre.

Chris COOPER was an actor/teacher with the *Dukes' TIE Company* and is now director of *Big Brum Theatre in Education Company*.

Edward Gordon CRAIG, son of the great actress Ellen Terry, was responsible for the modern conception of design as an integral part of theatre production. He worked with Stanislavski in Moscow, and found support for his ideas across Europe.

Frantisek DEAK is professor in the Department of Theatre at the University of California in San Diego, USA. He has written extensively on symbolist theatre.

Martin ESSLIN is well known as a director, a dramaturg and a critic. For 14 years he was head of BBC Radio Drama.

Howard GOORNEY was a member of *Theatre Workshop* for over 30 years.

Jerzy GROTOWSKI was a Polish director who founded the Theatre Laboratory and published his ideas in *Towards A Poor Theatre*.

Arnold HAUSER was a Hungarian art historian and critic whose best-known work is the four-volume *Social History of Art*.

Dorothy HEATHCOTE was lecturer in drama in education at the School of Education, Newcastle-upon-Tyne.

Louis JOUVET was director of the *Theatre Athenee* in Paris.

Elia KAZAN was formerly an actor with the *Group Theatre*, and is one of America's leading directors.

Maureen LAWRENCE is a novelist, a writer of short stories and a play-wright.

Joan LITTLEWOOD is an English director who co-founded *Theatre Workshop* whose most famous production was *Oh What A Lovely War*.

Vsevolod MEYERHOLD was an actor in the original Moscow Art Theatre and then became the leading experimental director in Russia.

Sonia MOORE studied with Stanislavski in Moscow and wrote several books on his training methods.

Friedrich NIETZSCHE was a nineteenth century German philosopher, whose major works were written between 1872 and 1889.

Max REINHARDT began his career as an actor, and then became direc-tor of the *Deutsches Theatre* where he staged a number of spectacular productions.

Rob RITCHIE is a dramaturg, a director and a writer.

Duke Georg II of SAXE-MEININGEN was director of the Saxe-Meiningen Company.

Ekkehard SCHALL was a member of the *Berliner Ensemble*.

William SHAKESPEARE was an Elizabethan/Jacobean dramatist, and is generally considered to be the world's greatest ever playwright.

Konstantin STANISLAVSKI was a Russian director who subjected the art of acting to its most rigorous analysis. He co-founded the Moscow

Art Theatre with Vladimir Nemirovich-Danchenko, where his ideas on the realist acting style were put into practice.

Lee STRASBERG, much influenced by Stanislavski, was co-founder of the American *Group Theatre* before he set up the *Actor's Studio*, a training centre in New York.

August STRINDBERG was a Swedish playwright who originally wrote in the naturalistic manner. Subsequently he experimented with symbolism in his 'chamber plays' and opened the *Intima Teatern* ('Intimate Theatre') in Stockholm.

Darko SUVIN is Professor of English at McGill University in Canada.

Arthur SYMONS was a British symbolist poet, playwright and critic and was associated with the Abbey Theatre in Dublin.

Raymond WILLIAMS was Professor of Drama at the University of Cambridge until his retirement in 1983.

Ian YEOMAN was an actor/teacher with the *Dukes TiE Company*, and is now director of *Theatre Powys*.

Emile ZOLA is best known as a novelist, although he also tried his hand at playwriting. He was the first writer to outline a theory of naturalism in literature.

Acknowledgements

The editors and publishers would like to thank the following for permission to reproduce copyright material:

pp1–5 *The Field of Drama,* M. Esslin, Methuen, 1987; pp6–13 'Drama from Ibsen to Brecht' in *The Conventions of Drama Structure and Feeling,* R. Williams, Hogarth, 1968; pp14–21 Reprinted from Aristotle: 'De Poetica', translated by I. Bywater from 'The Oxford Translation of Aristotle' edited by W.D. Ross (Volume II, 1925) by permission of Oxford University Press; pp21–29 'Naturalism on the stage' in *The Experimental Novel and Other Essays* by Emile Zola, trans. B. N. Sherman, Haskell House, 1964; pp29–35 Author's Preface to *Miss Julie* in *Five Plays* by A. Strindberg, trans. H. G. Carlson, University of California Press, 1983; pp36–39 'The Ideas of Richard Wagner' by Arthur Symons in *The Theory of the Modern Stage,* ed. Eric Bentley, Penguin, 1990; pp39–43 *The Birth of Tragedy and the Geneaology of Morals* by Friedrich Nietzsche, translated by Francis Golffing, © 1956 by Doubleday, a division of Random House, Inc. Used by permission of Doubleday, a division of Random House, Inc; pp43–44 'Symbolist Theatre: The Formation of an Avant-Garde' by Frantisek Deak in *The First Manifesto of Theatrical Symbolist Theatre,* John Hopkins University Press, 1993; pp45–46 'The Book: The Ideal Symbolist Theatre' by Mallarmé in *The First Manifesto of Theatrical Symbolist Theatre,* John Hopkins University Press, 1993; pp46–48 *Meyerhold: a Revolution in Theatre* by Edward Braun, Methuen, 1995; pp49–50, pp50–53 *On the Art of Theatre* by Edward Gordon Craig, Heinemann, 1968; pp53–61 'The Theatre of Cruelty: First Manifesto' in *The Theatre and its Double* by Antonin Artaud, Calder Publications, 1958; pp61–63 *The Social History of Art, Vol. I: From Prehistoric Times to the Middle Ages* by Arnold Hauser, Routledge & Kegan Paul, 1962; pp64–70 'Theatre for Pleasure or Theatre for Instruction' by Bertolt Brecht in *Brecht on Theatre,* ed. John Willett, Methuen, 1964; pp70–71 'The Mirror and The Dynamo' by Darko Suvin in *Tulane Drama Review,* No. 37, 1968; p72 *Theatre Poems and Songs* by Edward Bond, Methuen, 1978; pp74–90 extracts from *An Actor Prepares* by Konstantin Stanislavski, trans. Elizabeth Hapgood, Methuen, 1948; pp91–94 *The Stanislavski System* by Sonia Moore, Gollancz, 1966; pp94–95 'Sense Memory' in *An Actor in the Theatre* by L.Stasberg, ed. John Gassner, Holt, Rhinehart and Winston, 1953; pp95–97 'A Dialogue about Acting' by Bertolt Brecht in *Brecht on Theatre,* trans. John Willett, Methuen, 1963; pp97–101 'The *Verfremdungseffekt* in Chinese Acting' by Bertolt Brecht in *Brecht on Theatre,* trans. John Willett, Methuen, 1964; pp101–5 'The Street Scene: A Basic Model for an Epic Theatre Acting' by Bertolt Brecht in *Brecht on Theatre,* trans. John Willett, Methuen 1964; p106 'Short Description of a New Technique in Acting which Produces a *Verfremdungseffekt*' by Bertolt

Brecht in *Brecht on Theatre*, trans. John Willett, Methuen, 1964; pp107–8 'The Silent Scream' from *The Secret Art of the Performer* by Eugenio Barba and Nicola Savarese, Routledge, 1991; p109 'Some of the Things that can be Learnt from Stanislavski' by Bertolt Brecht in *Brecht on Theatre*, trans. John Willett, Methuen, 1964; pp110–11 'Two Myths of the New Theatre' in *The Eiffel Tower and Other Mythologies* by Roland Barthes, translated by Richard Howard. Translation © 1979 by Farrar, Straus & Giroux, Inc. Reprinted by permission of Hill and Wang, a division of Farrar, Straus & Giroux, LLC; pp111–13 'Ancestor Worship' in *True and False: Heresy and Common Sense for the Actor* by David Mamet, Faber and Faber, 1997; pp114–18 'Find Your Mark' in *True and False: Heresy and Common Sense for the Actor* by David Mamet, Faber and Faber, 1997; pp119–22 quoted by Max Grube in *Geschicte der Meininger*, reprinted in *Directors and Directing*, ed. Toby Cole and Helen Krich Chinoy, Bobs Merrill, 1976; pp122–24 'Causerie sur la mise en scene' in *La Revue de Pari*, Vol. X, reprinted in *Directors on Directing*, ed. Toby Cole and Helen Krich Chinoy, Bobs Merrill, 1976; pp124–30 *On the Art of Theatre* by Edward Gordon Craig, Heinemann, 1968; pp130–33 'The Stylized Theatre' by Vsevolod Meyerhold in *Meyerhold on Theatre*, ed. Edward Braun, Methuen, 1991; pp133–38 extract from 'The Theatre's New Testament' reprinted in *Towards a Poor Theatre* by Jerzy Grotowski, Methuen, 1968; pp141–44 'The Profession of the Director' by Louis Jouvet, reprinted in *Directors on Directing*, ed. Tony Cole and Helen Krich Chinoy, Bobs-Merrill, 1976; pp144–50 'Notebook for *A Streetcar Named Desire*' by Elia Kazan, reprinted in *Directors on Directing*, ed. Tony Cole and Helen Krich Chinoy, Bobs-Merrill, 1976; pp151–60 '*Regiebuch* of *The Miracle*' by Max Reinhardt in *Max Reinhardt and His Theatre*, ed. Oliver M. Sayler, Ayer Company Publishers; pp160–62 'Formless Hunch' by Peter Brook in *The Shifting Point*, Methuen, 1987; pp162–65 'An Audience With One' (a speech delivered to the Royal Society of Arts by Tyrone Guthrie) reprinted in *Directors on Directing*, ed. Tony Cole and Helen Krich Chinoy, Bobs-Merrill, 1976; pp165–66 'Working with Joan' in *Encore*, Vol. VII, July-August 1960, reprinted in *Directors on Directing*, ed. Tony Cole and Helen Krich Chinoy, Bobs-Merrill, 1976; pp167–69 Extract from *20ᵗʰ Century Theatre: A Sourcebook*, ed. Richard Drain, Routledge, 1995; pp170–72 *The Theatre Workshop Story* by Howard Goorney, Methuen, 1987; pp172–75 *The Joint Stock Book: The Making of a Theatre Collective*, ed. Rob Ritchie, Methuen, 1987; pp175–83 'In Good Faith: A Creative Process' by Ian Yeoman with Chris Cooper in *SCYPT Journal*, No. 24,1992; pp183–91 'Writing a Play with the Dukes TiE Company' by Maureen Lawrence in *SCYPT Journal*, No. 9, 1982; pp191–99 'Signs (and Portents?)' by Dorothy Heathcote in *SCYPT Journal*, No. 9, 1983.

Every effort has been made to trace copyright holders of material reproduced in this book. Any rights not acknowledged here will be acknowledged in subsequent printings if notice is given to the publisher.